Grant Seeker's Budget Toolkit

Wiley Nonprofit Law, Finance, and Management Series

The Art of Planned Giving: Understanding Donors and the Culture of Giving
    by Douglas E. White
Beyond Fund Raising: New Strategies for Nonprofit Investment and Innovation by Kay Grace
Budgeting for Not-for-Profit Organizations by David Maddox
Charity, Advocacy, and the Law by Bruce R. Hopkins
The Complete Guide to Fund Raising Management by Stanley Weinstein
The Complete Guide to Nonprofit Management by Smith, Bucklin & Associates
Critical Issues in Fund Raising edited by Dwight Burlingame
Developing Affordable Housing: A Practical Guide for Nonprofit Organizations, Second Edition
    by Bennett L. Hecht
Faith-Based Management: Leading Organizations That Are Based on More than Just Mission
    by Peter C. Brinckerhoff
Financial and Accounting Guide for Not-for-Profit Organizations, Sixth Edition
    by Malvern J. Gross Jr., Richard F. Larkin, Roger S. Bruttomesso, John J. McNally,
    PricewaterhouseCoopers LLP
Financial Empowerment: More Money for More Mission by Peter Brinckerhoff
Financial Management for Nonprofit Organizations by Jo Ann Hankin, Alan Seidner,
    and John Zietlow
Financial Planning for Nonprofit Organizations by Jody Blazek
The First Legal Answer Book for Fund-Raisers by Bruce R. Hopkins
The Second Legal Answer Book for Fund-Raisers by Bruce R. Hopins
The Fund Raiser's Guide to the Internet by Michael Johnston
Fund-Raising Cost-Effectiveness: A Self-Assessment Workbook by James M. Greenfield
Fund-Raising: Evaluating and Managing the Fund Development Process, Second Edition
    by James M. Greenfield
Fund-Raising Fundamentals: A Guide to Annual Giving for Professionals and Volunteers
    by James M. Greenfield
*Fund-Raising Regulation: A State-by-State Handbook of Registration Forms, Requirements, and
    Procedures* by Seth Perlman and Betsy Hills Bush
Grant Seeker's Budget Toolkit by James A. Quick and Cheryl S. New
Grant Seeker's Toolkit: A Comprehensive Guide to Finding Funding by Cheryl S. New
    and James A. Quick
Grant Winner's Toolkit: Project Management and Evaluation by James A. Quick and Cheryl S. New
*High Impact Philanthropy: How Donors, Boards, and Nonprofit Organizations Can Transform
    Nonprofit Organizations,* by Kay Sprinkel Grace and Alan L. Wendroff
High Performance Nonprofit Organizations: Managing Upstream for Greater Impact
    by Christine Letts, William Ryan, and Allen Grossman
Intermediate Sanctions: Curbing Nonprofit Abuse by Bruce R. Hopkins and D. Benson Tesdahl
International Fund Raising for Nonprofits by Thomas Harris
International Guide to Nonprofit Law by Lester A. Salamon and Stefan Toepler & Associates
Joint Ventures Involving Tax-Exempt Organizations, Second Edition by Michael I. Sanders
The Law of Fund-Raising, Second Edition by Bruce R. Hopkins
The Law of Tax-Exempt Healthcare Organizations by Thomas K. Hyatt and Bruce R. Hopkins
The Law of Tax-Exempt Organizations, Seventh Edition by Bruce R. Hopkins
The Legal Answer Book for Nonprofit Organizations by Bruce R. Hopkins
A Legal Guide to Starting and Managing a Nonprofit Organization, Second Edition
    by Bruce R. Hopkins
The Legislative Laberynth: A Map for Not-for-Profits, edited by Walter Pidgeon
Managing Affordable Housing: A Practical Guide to Creating Stable Communities
    by Bennett L. Hecht, Local Initiatives Support Corporation, and James Stockard
Managing Upstream: Creating High-Performance Nonprofit Organizations
    by Christine W. Letts, William P. Ryan, and Allan Grossman
Mission-Based Management: Leading Your Not-for-Profit In the 21st Century, Second Edition
    by Peter C. Brinckerhoff
*Mission-Based Management: Leading Your Not-for-Profit In the 21st Century, Second Edition,
    Workbook* by Peter C. Brinckerhoff
Mission-Based Marketing: How Your Not-for-Profit Can Succeed in a More Competitive World
    by Peter C. Brinckerhoff

Grant Seeker's Budget Toolkit

JAMES AARON QUICK
CHERYL CARTER NEW

Burroughs Learning Center • BETHEL COLLEGE
325 Cherry Ave. • McKenzie, TN 38201

John Wiley & Sons, Inc.

New York • Chichester • Weinheim • Brisbane • Singapore • Toronto

This book is printed on acid-free paper. ⊚

Published by John Wiley & Sons, Inc.
Published simultaneously in Canada.

This publication is designed to provide accurate and authoritative information
in regard to the subject matter covered. It is sold with the understanding that
the publisher is not engaged in rendering legal, accounting, or other
professional services. If legal advice or other expert assistance is required, the
services of a competent professional person should be sought.

Library of Congress Cataloging-in-Publication Data:
Quick, James Aaron.
    Grant seeker's budget toolkit / James A. Quick, Cheryl C. New.
      p.   cm. — (Wiley nonprofit law, finance, and management series)
    ISBN 0-471-39140-9 (pbk./disk : alk. paper)
    1. Fund raising. 2. Proposal writing for grants. I. New, Cheryl Carter.
  II. Title. III. Series.
  HG177 .Q53 2001
  658.15'224—dc21   00-061957
Printed in the United States of America.

10 9 8 7 6 5 4 3 2

To my wonderful mom, Elizabeth Carter New, and extraordinarily
talented husband, James Aaron Quick, who love, support, and sustain me
in whatever I do no matter how outlandish, eccentric, or intense.
And always to my dad, Lawrence David New.

—Cheryl Carter New

To Marlin A. Quick.

—James Aaron Quick

Acknowledgments

Considering the subject matter and my general distaste for numbers, I should acknowledge my very best mathematics teacher, Mary Hubbard, who actually managed to "bore a hole and pour it in." And thanks, also, to my dear dad, Lawrence David New, who made me use a slide rule supposedly to help him with his reports.

—Cheryl Carter New

To the person who has forgotten more about grant seeking than I will ever know; to my mentor, my friend, and to my everlasting benefit and appreciation, my wife Cheryl Carter New: Thank you is totally insufficient.

—James Aaron Quick

About the Authors

James Aaron Quick is the Chief Executive Officer for Polaris, a South Carolina Corporation. He has served in this capacity since 1989. As the Senior Instructional Specialist for Polaris, he has spoken before thousands of potential grant seekers from the fields of education, healthcare, and nonprofit management. He has written successful grant proposals for over 10 years, for projects ranging from $10,000 to $7.9 million to grant makers including federal sources, foundations, and corporations. He is coauthor of many Polaris publications as well as the best-selling trade book on grant seeking entitled *Grant Seeker's Toolkit: A Comprehensive Guide to Finding Funding* (New York: John Wiley & Sons, 1998) and *Grant Winner's Toolkit: Management and Evaluation of a Granted Project* (New York: John Wiley & Sons, 1999). Jim also authors nonfiction articles and books, as well as novels and short stories.

Cheryl Carter New is the president of Polaris Corporation. She is the founder of the company, which was incorporated in 1984. Her background includes instruction at kindergarten, primary, and middle school levels; administration at kindergarten and primary school levels; and curriculum, course development, and instruction at college level. She wrote her first successful grant proposal in 1969 and has continued to be active in the field to the present. She has authored numerous articles in the field as well as on negotiation, management issues, and strategic planning. She has spoken on the subject of grants acquisition and negotiating at many national, regional, and state conferences. She is the developer of several college level courses and workshops in the field of grant seeking, offered and presented in 45 states. She is coauthor of many Polaris publications as well as the best-selling trade book on grant seeking entitled *Grant Seeker's Toolkit: A Comprehensive Guide to Finding Funding,* published by John Wiley & Sons, and the upcoming *Grant Winner's Toolkit: Management and Evaluation of a Granted Project,* also to be published by Wiley. Cheryl also authors and illustrates children's books. More information about Polaris and free information for grant seekers can be found at http://www.polarisgrantscentral.net.

Contents

Chapter 1   What Is a Budget: And Where Does One Come From?   1

Define Project Budget   1
Project Budget Creation and Accountants   5
Project Budget as Summary   6
Project Budget and Grant Request   8
Careless Use of Terms   10
Where Does a Budget Come From?   12
Wise Guy and Wise Lady   12
Conclusion   13
   Key Definition   13
   Key Concepts   14

PART I   DEVELOPING YOUR PROJECT

Chapter 2   What Is a Project: And Where Does One Come From?   17

General Concept   18
   Project or Program?   18
   A Rose by Any Other Name   18
   Program or Project?   20
Organization   20
More Terminology   24
Where Does a Project Come From?   24
Wise Guy and Wise Lady   25
Conclusion   26
   Key Definition   26
   Key Concepts   27

Chapter 3   What Is a Problem: And How Does a Project Come from One?   28

Problems   29
   In General   29
   Characteristics of Problems   30
   Alignment between Organization and Problem   32
   Focus on People   32
   Fund-Raising vis-à-vis Grant Seeking   34
   Avoid Circular Logic   35
   Solutions Masquerading as Problems   36
   Keeping the Language Straight   37
   The Two Parts   37
   Putting It All Together   37
Project Design   38
   Step 1: State a Problem   38
   Step 2: List the Causes of the Problem   38
   Broad Problem: Youth Crime and Violence Are Increasing   39
   Step 3: Eliminate, Recast, Group, and Choose Causes   39
   Broad Problem: Youth Crime and Violence Are Increasing   40
   Step 4: Identify a Solution   41
   Broad Problem: Youth Crime and Violence Are Increasing   41
   Step 5: Identify Resources Needed   42
Project Profile   43
Hit List   44
Wise Guy and Wise Lady   45
Conclusion   46
   Key Definition   46
   Key Concepts   47

Chapter 4   Project Development   48

Similarities among Projects   48
   Project Preparation and Logistics   49
   Partnership Activities   49
   Implementation with Target Population   49
   Monitoring and Management of the Project   49
Create the Project Outline   50
   Outlining a Grant Project   50
   Examples Are Just Examples   51
Project Outline to Goals and Objectives   54
   Goals: General Discussion   54
   Goals: The Tool   55
   Goals: The Source   56
Objectives: General Discussion   59

Objectives: Plain Language Definition   61
   Objectives: The Three Characteristics   61
   Objectives: The Five Parts   61
   Objectives: The Tool   61
Activity Analysis Worksheet   62
Wise Guy and Wise Lady   67
Conclusion   68
   Key Definition   69
   Key Concepts   69

PART II   DEVELOPING YOUR BUDGETS

Chapter 5   Fundamentals of Project Budgets: Concepts and Terms   73

The Two Types of Budget Costs   74
   Defining Direct Costs   74
   Defining Indirect Costs   77
   Example of Direct and Indirect Costs   78
   Calculation of Indirect Costs   79
   Indirect Cost Calculation Tool   82
A Variety of Direct Costs   82
   Questions and Answers   84
An Old Standby: SF-424   86
   Thoughts on Budget Totals   87
   Project Revenue   88
Project Partners   88
Looking with "New Eyes"   90
Small Form Does Not Mean Small Money   93
In-Kind   94
   In-Kind: The Concept   95
   In-Kind: A Short Grammatical Discussion   96
   In-Kind Contribution: The Definition   96
Wise Guy and Wise Lady   102
Conclusion   102
   Key Definition   103
   Key Concepts   103
   The Three Rules of Grant Seeking   103

Chapter 6   Direct Costs: Definitions and Explanations   105

Personnel   106
   Project Personnel: Grant Request   107
   Your Organization: In-Kind Contribution   108

Contents

Partner Organizations: In-Kind Contribution   109
Volunteers: In-Kind Contribution   109
Fringe   109
Travel   110
   Air Travel   112
   Ground Travel   114
   Other Travel   116
   Meals   117
   Lodging   117
   Gratuities   117
   Tolls   117
   Parking   118
   Courtesy Expenses   118
   Disallowed Expenses   118
Equipment   118
Capital   120
Supplies   121
Materials   122
Contractual Services   123
   Contractors   124
   Consultants   125
   Contractor or Employee?   125
   In-Kind Contribution: Employee or Contractor?   126
Endowment   127
Other or Miscellaneous   127
Materials and Supplies Revisited   128
Project Development and the Budget   129
Operating Funds   129
Wise Guy and Wise Lady   132
Conclusion   132
   Key Concepts   132

Chapter 7   Personnel Costs: Compute and Capture   134

Exempt or Nonexempt Employee?   135
Salaried Personnel Funded from Grant Request   136
   Calculation Formula   136
   Definitions   137
Salaried Personnel Funded from Other Sources   138
   Calculation Formula   140
   Definitions   140
Hourly Wage Personnel Funded from Grant Request   141
   Calculation Formula   142
   Definitions   142

Hourly Wage Personnel Funded from Other Sources   144
    Calculation Formula   145
Personnel Fringe (One Rate)   145
    Calculation Formula   148
    Definitions   148
Personnel Fringe (More than One Rate)   148
    Calculation Formula   149
    Definitions   151
Combined Personnel Expense Calculation Worksheet   152
    Calculation Formulas   154
    Salaried Positions   154
    Hourly Wage Positions   154
    Personnel Fringe   154
    Definitions   154
Wise Guy and Wise Lady   161
Conclusion   161
    Key Principle   162
    Key Concepts   162

Chapter 8   Travel Costs: Compute and Capture   **164**

Initial Travel Planning   165
    Example Trip   167
    Completing a Travel Planning Worksheet   168
Calculation Worksheet: Ground Travel by Private Vehicle   168
    Formula   170
Calculation Worksheet: Ground Travel by Rental Vehicle   172
    Formula   172
Calculation Worksheet: Ground Travel by Hired Vehicle (Shuttle,
    Taxi, Hired Car, Limousine, Bus, or Rapid Transit)   176
    Formula   176
Calculation Worksheet: Air Travel   179
Calculation Worksheet: Meal Expense   181
Calculation Worksheet: Lodging   184
Compiling Expenses   185
Wise Guy and Wise Lady   185
Conclusion   186
    Key Concepts   186

Chapter 9   Other Direct Costs and Prices   **187**

The Calculation   188
    Unit of Purchase   188
    Formula   189

Equipment	190
Materials and Supplies	191
Contractual Services	192
Other/Miscellaneous	192
Endowment	193
Capital	198
Finding Prices	198
Personnel	199
Fringe	199
Travel	200
Air Travel	200
Ground Travel—Private Vehicle or Car Rental	202
Ground Travel—Train	203
Ground Travel—Bus	204
Ground Travel—Taxi, Shuttle, Limousine, or Hired Car	204
Ground Travel—Mass Transit (Train, Subway, or Bus)	205
Meals	205
Lodging	205
Gratuities	205
Tolls	206
Parking	206
Courtesy Expenses	206
Equipment	206
Capital	207
Land Purchase	207
Building Purchase	208
Land Improvement	208
Building Improvement	209
Supplies and Materials	210
Contractual Services	210
Wise Guy and Wise Lady	211
Conclusion	212
Key Principle	212
Key Concepts	213

PART III   REPORTING YOUR BUDGETS

**Chapter 10 Putting It All Together:
             Developing a Finished Budget**   **217**

Activity Analysis Worksheet	218
Develop All the Data	222
Key Concept	222
A Short but Advanced Discussion of Goals and Objectives	223

From Objective to Activities   226
Using the Calculation Worksheets   228
A Practical Matter   228
Master Budget Development Checklist   229
Preparing to Complete a Budget Form   231
Completing a Budget Form   234
Wise Guy and Wise Lady   235
Conclusion   235
    Key Concepts   236

Chapter 11 The Budget Narrative   237

Personnel and Fringe   238
    The Why   238
    The How   238
Travel   239
    Air Travel   239
    Ground Travel   239
    Meals   240
    Lodging   241
    Gratuities   241
    Tolls   242
    Parking   242
    Courtesy Expenses   243
Equipment   243
Capital   244
    Building and Land Purchase   244
    Building and Land Improvement 245
Supplies   246
Contractual Services   247
Endowment   247
Wise Guy and Wise Lady   248
Conclusion   249
    Key Definition   249
    Key Concepts   249

Index   251

About the CD-ROM   259

Grant Seeker's Budget Toolkit

Chapter 1

What Is a Budget: And Where Does One Come From?

For it is impossible for any one to begin to learn what he thinks that he already knows.

Epictetus, circa A.D. 60

In this chapter we present several simple concepts that are fundamental to grant project budgets. Our goal is to construct a firm foundation on which to build a solid budget structure, as described in the succeeding chapters. To do that, we provide the first draft of several definitions. As the chapters proceed, more specificity and detail are added to these basic, easy-to-understand definitions. Next we deal with the possibly delicate subject of project budgets and accountants. We answer the question: Is your accountant the person to whom you should turn to develop the project budget?

This chapter includes sections that deal with the twin facts that what is submitted on a budget form is not a budget, but rather a summary of the budget, and that a project budget and a grant request are not the same thing. These topics bring us to one of the major problems encountered when communicating about budgets, careless use of terms. Getting clear on the meaning of a few key terms as early as possible simplifies further discussion.

Finally, this chapter highlights the key question, for which everyone wants a clear, simple, and easy answer: Where does a budget come from? While the answer is clear, simple, and easy, its application is not. It takes the rest of the book to explain how to apply the simple answer to this key question.

Define Project Budget

The English word "budget" derives from the Middle French *bougette,* which is the diminutive of *bouge,* a leather bag. At its most basic, therefore, a budget is a small leather bag. During the Middle Ages in England, letters of particulars about taxes and spending were brought before Parliament by putting them in a small leather bag (a bougette), which was placed on a table before the assembly. As centuries passed, the word came to be applied to the contents as well as to the bag itself, though originally only in the sense of a group of things. Such a use is found in the title of August De Morgan's observations on mathematics, mathematicians, and divinity, *A Budget of Paradoxes* (1672).

In current usage, several closely related meanings emerge that approach much closer to our day-to-day understanding. Here are a few examples of usage that are familiar, but do not quite fit our purposes. "The departmental budget was submitted to corporate headquarters" (an itemized summary of estimated or intended expenditures for a given period along with proposals for financing them). "This project has a budget of two million dollars" (the total sum of money allocated for a particular purpose or period of time). And returning to an older usage, "He quickly expended his budget of understanding" (a stock or collection with definite limits). Unless otherwise noted, all standard definitions are from *The American Heritage Dictionary of the English Language,* Third Edition (Boston: Houghton Mifflin, 1992).

The standard (dictionary) definition that approaches closest to what we mean by a project budget is "a statement of the financial position of an administration for a definite period of time based on estimates of expenditures during the period" (*Merriam-Webster's Collegiate Dictionary,* Springfield, MA: Merriam-Webster, 1996).

Several features of this definition make it a useful starting point. The definition points out that a budget is a statement, as in a report of facts or opinions. The definition adds that a budget concerns financial matters: It relates to money. It states that a budget covers a defined period of time. And, perhaps most importantly, the definition introduces the concept that a budget contains estimates of expenditures; the amounts are calculated approximately. Many would go further and classify the amounts in a project budget as guesstimates. Experience has taught us, however, that when a budget is developed using our methodology, the resulting figures will be amazingly close to reality.

The particular type of budget in which we are interested is for a project to be funded by a grant. Therefore an excellent source of guidance will be a grant maker itself. The Public Health Service of the U.S. Department of Health and Human Services defines a budget as

the financial expenditure plan.

A new concept is introduced here, that of the budget as a plan: a program, or method, worked out beforehand for the accomplishment of an objective. In our case, it is a plan for spending money.

In Colorado, educators and librarians will find in *Resources in Grant Writing for Colorado Schools & Libraries* that a budget is

> a plan for anticipated expenditures, activities, and accomplishments stated primarily in fiscal terms.

This is an interesting and useful slant. Activities and accomplishments take center stage. A budget, in this view, explains activities and accomplishments in terms of spending money. We revisit this concept at length in later chapters.

Bringing higher education into the discussion, the Research Administration of University of California at Los Angeles (UCLA) defines a budget as

> the detailed statement outlining estimated project costs to support work under a grant or contract.

By now, we're familiar with several of the elements and can identify them quickly: a statement or plan, costs that are estimated, and costs that relate (support) the work (activities) that will be done. This definition suggests two additional characteristic of a budget. The first characteristic is that a budget is detailed; it is thorough and characterized by abundant use of particulars. Second, this definition suggests, through the use of the plural phrase "project costs," that several distinct amounts be provided, not just a single, total amount.

The characteristics uncovered so far lead to the conclusion that a project budget will:

- Concern project activities.
- Explain activities from the standpoint of spending money.
- Concern a defined length of time.
- Be a plan.
- Be detailed.
- Contain estimated expenditures.
- Contain various amounts calculated for various purposes.
- Include all expenditures from all sources.
- Include project revenue.
- Include appropriate subtotals and totals.

Putting these attributes together yields the following working definition.

Grant Project Budget

A grant project budget is the project plan from a financial view. It contains detailed itemized estimates of all expenditures and contributions from all sources, project revenue, subtotals and totals, and the amount and distribution of funds needed to perform the project activities over their allotted time spans.

Each of the eight characteristics embodied in this definition will prove to be significant and important as we move forward. We may seem to belabor an insignificant point, but as Plato admonished in *The Republic,* in the fifth century B.C., "The beginning is the most important part of the work." It is only now that we can get off on the right foot. As the chapters roll by, the characteristics embedded in the definition will become second nature, but now we need to look with new eyes and listen with new ears. We need to look again at what we think we know and approach our subject with as few preconceptions and assumptions as possible.

Before leaving this section and moving to the next topic, review the following eight characteristics of a project budget. Much of the material in chapters to come flows logically and naturally from the concepts in the definition:

1. Project activities (tasks, jobs, work, accomplishments, etc.) serve as the source material for calculating budget amounts and therefore are the fundamental material on which the budget is based.

2. Project activities are explained from a financial standpoint.

3. Project activities are explained and finances are calculated for defined periods of time.

4. Taken as a whole, a project budget is a restatement of the project plan from the viewpoint of finances.

5. A project budget is developed with sufficient detail to illustrate and explain fully and clearly the calculation and derivation of amounts.

6. Expenditures are estimates, as accurate as practically possible.

7. A project budget contains amounts for a variety of expenses, as many as are necessary to fully document the plan to accomplish the project activities.

8. A project budget contains the appropriate financial totals.

The characteristics are couched in general terms. Purposefully so, this is the beginning, and beginnings are often broad and ambiguous. Certainty and specificity comes with time and experience gained, in our case, over the span of this book's chapters.

Here's a final thought about the definition. Did you notice that somewhere along the way we stopped using the word "budget" and started using the phrase "project budget"? "Budget" all by itself is a slippery word, prone to mean different things to different people. The budget for a project, or project budget, on the other hand, conveys a relatively clear intent. It is also what grant makers mean when they ask for a budget. They want you to provide a budget for your proposed project—a project budget.

Project Budget Creation and Accountants

Just about everybody has some level of discomfort with budgets. Very few of us truly feel at ease putting all those figures down on paper, knowing that any serious mistake will come back to haunt us. Maybe we forget to include funds for insurance or travel or supplies and our organization must dig into its already insufficient funds to pay for items that should have been covered by the grant. To lighten the burden, we look for someone familiar with money and budgets.

This leads us inexorably to our accountant. It makes good sense. Our accountant messes about with figures, money, and budgets all the time. After all, it is what they do. As a result, accountants everywhere inherit the task of developing grant project budgets.

The process usually goes something like this. First, the accountant attends a meeting with the people who are developing the project and writing the proposal. At the meeting, they explain the project to the accountant, who then is given the budget forms for the application and asked to develop the budget. The accountant goes away now, labors mightily for a time, bringing forth finally a budget that is delivered back to the people putting together the application package. What happens next is easily predicted. The project budget doesn't align with the expectations of the people developing the proposal. It's not the accountant's fault. It is the fault of the people who asked the accountant to take the task off their hands. Two important concepts are at work here.

First, the training accountants receive does not necessarily equip them to develop a project budget any better than most of the rest of us. Their familiarity with financial terms and concepts gives them certain advantages, but they are slight in the long run. An accountant's main purpose is to take the myriad figures generated by financial transactions and produce coherent reports that accurately reflect the financial condition of an organization. This highly specialized and technical work is essential to the operation of every organization.

This is not to say that accountants cannot develop budgets. Many accountants can do a better job than most of the rest of us. But, when they do a good job, it is because they have learned how to do so, not because their accountant's training prepared them for the task.

Second, the project budget cannot be developed effectively at a distance or apart from the project itself. The project and its budget are inextricably intertwined and cannot be separated. The best people to develop the project budget are the same people who initially put together the project.

Special training in finance is not needed to develop a project budget. What is needed is common sense, a willingness to work, the ability to follow directions, and the consistent application of a logical process that captures all the necessary information. Accountants automatically meet all the criteria. Unless, however, your accountant is an integral part of your project development team throughout the process, he or she is not the best choice for budget development. The project development team is the proper choice. We are going to show you how. That is the purpose of this book.

Project Budget as Summary

Visualizing a budget generally brings to mind the image of a form, perhaps one required by a grant maker or used by your organization. Such a form usually has various labels naming rows and columns of blocks or cells into which numbers are placed. The form can be large or small, simple or complex. It can occupy several pages or only part of a single page. It may be on paper or exist as a computer file.

All such forms possess several characteristics in common. They are laid out in horizontal rows and vertical columns. Empty spaces are provided to enter amounts. Rows and columns are labeled to identify the values entered onto the empty spaces.

Exhibit 1.1 illustrates a budget form, probably similar to what most of us visualize when we think of a budget. This form looks relatively simple and might easily imply that the grant program using it is a small one. That impression would be wrong. This budget form was used for several years by a federal agency in its application package for a multiyear program in which awards averaged $1.25 million a year.

The budget form illustrated in Exhibit 1.1 serves as an excellent example of the main point of this section; what is commonly identified as the "budget" (what we now know is actually the project budget) is only a

EXHIBIT 1.1

Example Budget Form

	Project Year One		
A. Direct Costs	**Requested**	**Support from Other Sources**	**Total**
1. Salaries (professional and clerical)			
2. Employee Benefits			
3. Employee Travel			
4. Equipment (purchase)			
5. Materials and Supplies			
6. Consultants and Contracts			
7. Other (equip. rental, printing, etc.)			
8. Total Direct Costs			
B. Indirect Costs			
C. TOTALS			

summary of that budget. When the form shown in Exhibit 1.1 is completed, it will *not* be the project budget, but will be a summary of it.

With the expected exceptions of line items A2, A8, B, and C, the amounts on the budget form represent the sum of the expenses of an unknown number of items. Descriptions of the items are also unknown, except that they fit into a general category. To illustrate the point, line item A3, Employee Travel, is shown, completed, in Exhibit 1.2. The grant request for Employee Travel is $20,740. The support from other sources for Employee Travel is $14,875. Total project cost for Employee travel is then $35,615.

EXHIBIT 1.2

Example Completed Employee Travel Cost Line Item

	Project Year One		
A. Direct Costs	**Requested**	**Support from Other Sources**	**Total**
3. Employee Travel	$20,740	$14,875	$35,615

The pertinent questions are easy to formulate. How did the applicant know to use those particular amounts? On what are the amounts based? How are the amounts calculated? Because, if the applicant cannot explain the basis, the sources, and the methods, then the amounts are not calculations, they are guesses. Using guesses as the basis for budget requests is a sure formula for fiscal problems during project implementation.

A collection of amounts such as those shown in Exhibit 1.2 are not a budget. They are the summary of a budget. The amounts shown for Employee Travel were calculated after computing the cost of the travel as illustrated in Exhibit 1.3.

Exhibit 1.3 does not show a complete itemization, only subtotals. Each of the travel cost subtotals shown in Exhibit 1.3 is itself the sum of individual costs of travel, a few of which are airline tickets, ground transportation, lodging, and meals. These are not all the costs that can be incurred during travel. A full discussion of the complex subject of travel and computing its cost is found in Chapter 8.

A completed grant application budget form does not contain the project budget. It contains the summary of the project budget. Grasp firmly this simple concept. It, together with the definition of a project budget, is the starting point from which everything else in the book flows.

Project Budget and Grant Request

The explanation for another helpful fundamental concept begins like this. The grant request is not the same as the project budget. Using a more

EXHIBIT 1.3

Total Employee Travel Costs Partial Itemization

National Project Leadership Conference 3 staff attend 1 meeting (three-night stay)	$ 5,440.00
Regional Project Leadership Conferences 3 staff attend 2 meetings (two-night stays)	8,920.00
Project Director local travel 12,000 miles @ 27¢ per mile	3,240.00
NAASP National Conference 2 staff attend (two-night stay)	3,140.00
Total Employee Travel	$20,740.00

precise but less interesting wording, the amount of the grant being requested is not the same amount as the project budget total.

The amount expended on a grant project cannot possibly be less than the amount of the grant, unless a bit of the grant disappears before getting to the project. This is commonly called theft or fraud, depending on how it's done, and is frowned on by everyone from the grant maker to the judicial system.

To start this topic, we hypothesized that the grant request and the project budget total are never the same. The only remaining alternative, therefore, is that the project budget total is always larger than the grant request. We are cautioned to beware of absolutes such as always and never. An anonymous wit put it this way. "Always be careful to never use always and never." In this case, however, never and always are exactly appropriate.

Phrased differently, the project budget is always larger than the grant request. Or, the grant request is always less than the project budget total. The simplest way to illustrate this concept is to imagine how the grant request could possibly be exactly the same as the grant request. For this to be true, your organization would not spend a single penny in any fashion on the project.

No staff time could be used, none of your facilities could be used, not a sheet of paper from your supplies, no pencils or pens, no heat or air conditioning, no volunteer time, no partner time. Nothing of any kind could be used toward the project without payment from the grant. A moment's thought makes it clear that no such thing is possible. For example, what happens when your organization first receives the check from the grant maker? Someone deposits it in a bank account, right? How much salary and overhead did your organization expend for staff to accomplish that task? Not much, it's true, but it is something and it's just the start.

Are you going to purchase things with the grant, such as equipment, supplies, and materials? How much time of how many staff members will it take to accomplish the activities involved in the purchases? How much is that staff time worth? You might not know exactly, but you know it's worth something. And it goes on and on.

As a result, a project budget total is always larger than a grant request. This is not to say that a grant maker always cares enough to ask you to show what share of the project budget is absorbed by you and your project partners. Many grant makers do not require such information. Many others do. A look at Exhibit 1.1 shows that this grant maker does care and does want to know the amount of support from sources other than itself.

Careless Use of Terms

Almost every field or area of interest one can imagine has its own language. Sailors have decks and galleys. Printers have galleys and slugs. Physicists have quarks and strings. Violinists have strings and bows. Archers have bows and quivers. The specialized or technical language of a group—jargon—enables group members to communicate clearly, easily, and without confusion. An outsider, on the other hand, can find it difficult to penetrate specialized jargon.

Grant seeking does not have a universal jargon for all members of the "group." While jargon abounds, asking what a term or phrase means will garner different answers based on whom you ask. The range of backgrounds of the people seeking grants makes agreement on a common set of terms highly unlikely. It hasn't happened yet.

Educators at the college and university level (higher education) and educators at the elementary and secondary level (K-12) use different terms for similar concepts. Municipal and county governments use terms differently than educators. The field of healthcare has a language all its own. Museums talk differently than police departments. Small social service nonprofits speak a language unlike that of national or international service organizations. To round out the problem, jargon can differ depending on what part of the country you happen to choose. Throw into the mix that different grant makers also use different language and the problem goes from bad to worse.

We make no attempt here to provide a unified language or jargon for grant seeking. We attempt only to be understood in this book. For that purpose, we set up specific meanings for terms, and then make every effort to use those terms consistently. The following terms and their definitions are not necessarily universal, though some of them are. They apply in the context of this book and its topic:

- A *grant* is money. One simply cannot be a grant writer, just as one cannot "write a grant," because a grant is the money. The U.S. Department of the Treasury takes a dim view of people who "write money." Also, one cannot apply to a grant. A grant cannot read the proposal. One can apply for a grant, but not to a grant.

- A *grant maker,* also known as a *grantor,* is the organization that makes or awards grants. Grant makers can be categorized into four types: federal agencies, foundations, corporations, and state and local governments. The different types of grant makers require different approaches and use different jargon.

- For our purposes, a grant is awarded as a result of a competition. Grants are made in other ways, but this book is concerned with *competitive* grant programs. Specifically, the book is about how to put together an effective budget for entry into the competition for a grant.

- A grant maker creates and funds a *grant program* for specific purposes, such as reducing domestic violence, increasing literacy, or eliminating cancer. A grant program follows a time line of announcement of a competition and publication of the application guidelines, deadline for application submission, evaluation of submitted applications, award of grants, administration of projects, preparation of application guidelines for the next granting cycle, and then coming full circle, announcement of another competition.

- The *grant request* is the amount of money solicited from the grant maker. This amount, combined with expenditures by the applicant, volunteers, and partners will be sufficient to accomplish all the planned activities of the project.

- The *project budget total* is the sum of the expenditures from all sources necessary to accomplish the project. The grant request is a part of the project budget total.

- The *budget summary* is what one usually finds on the budget form that is either supplied by the grant maker or created by the applicant. The budget summary usually condenses the project budget into a line item format.

- The *project budget* is the project plan from the financial viewpoint. A project budget is time limited, detailed, itemized, and includes all expenditures from all sources. In this book, you will seldom find the word "budget" standing alone, because the word has too many meanings to too many different people. When it is used alone, budget means project budget.

We do not suggest that you necessarily adopt these terms for your organization. What we do highly recommend is that your grant-seeking team recognize that communicating clearly saves time, frustration, and money, leading ultimately to more successful grant proposals. The best way to communicate clearly is to agree on a set of labels for the items with which you will be working. As artificial as it may seem at first, using consistent language contributes greatly to communication. It will decrease the amount of time spent straightening out misunderstandings, and increase the amount of time spent getting grants to solve real problems for your target population.

Where Does a Budget Come From?

By now, the answer to this question has become obvious. The budget comes from the project. One of the most common questions we get asked is, "How much money should I ask for?" Our answer is always the same, "As much as you need to run the project." Though it is correct, this answer does not satisfy people very well. The reason, we suspect, is that the motivation behind the question is a search for the magic shortcut, that mythical secret way to get the project budget figures down on paper without work. We have no shortcuts. We know of no way to develop a project budget without work. What we have is a step-by-step process. The rest of the book explains the process.

Saying that the project budget comes from the project has the ring to it of circular reasoning, as many simple but true concepts do. To explain the concept, focus on one simple task or action instead of thinking about the project as a whole. Ask yourself what resources will be needed to accomplish that task. Next, ask yourself how much these resources will cost. Once you have done this for every task and activity in the project, you will have gathered the raw data for developing a project budget.

The amount of money you need is driven directly by the activities you plan to accomplish. It is easy to see that some activities are expensive while others are cheap. Choices made during project development determine budget figures.

A common occurrence is to settle beforehand on the size of the grant request and then develop a project budget that fits the preordained figure. Perhaps there are times when this strategy is necessary, but in general, it is a poor substitute for letting the project drive the budget.

Wise Guy and Wise Lady

Wise Guy

Hey, I'm not a financial manager—so how can I do the budget? Don't I need a CPA or some financial guru? This is going to be too complicated for me. I have trouble balancing my own checkbook. I hate numbers. And besides, can't we just put down some good guesstimates and let it go? After all, all I want is $25,000. I am going to be the project manager and I'll spend the money the way I see fit.

> ### Wise Lady
>
> Oh my. We're starting where we left off in the *Grant Winner's Toolkit!* Let's put it this way. What if you were investing, say $25,000 of your money with a brokerage firm. When you ask what the firm is doing with your money, the broker says, "Just trust me. I am putting some here and some there. Just give me your money and trust me." Would you buy that? I know you well enough now to know you most certainly would not. Neither will the grant maker. You have to specifically tell them what you are going to do with the money. If you receive the grant, your proposal, including the budget, is a legal and binding contract. And if you are a good project manager, you have to know what resources are needed to run your project. Right? Well all those resources cost something. Nothing is for free. As a project manager, you are the person who should determine resources and put together the budget. It's a natural.

Conclusion

In this chapter, we introduce a number or terms and concepts for the purpose of setting the stage or preparing the way for the remainder of the book. We go into detail to define what we mean by "project budget." We determine that a complete definition contains a number of characteristics. The result is shown in the following Key Definition.

Key Definition

> ### Grant Project Budget
>
> A grant project budget is the project plan from a financial view. It contains detailed itemized estimates of all expenditures and contributions from all sources, project revenue, subtotals and totals, and the amount and distribution of funds needed to perform the project activities over their allotted time spans.

We introduce several key concepts. One important idea not in the following list is that the people in the best position to develop a project budget

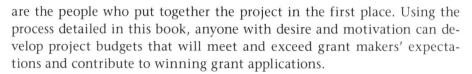

are the people who put together the project in the first place. Using the process detailed in this book, anyone with desire and motivation can develop project budgets that will meet and exceed grant makers' expectations and contribute to winning grant applications.

Key Concepts

- A grant project budget is the project plan from a financial view.
- Special training in finances is not necessary to develop project budgets.
- A completed grant application budget form is not the project budget; it is the summary of the budget.
- The project budget is always larger than the grant request.
- Defining terms and using them consistently contributes to success.
- The budget comes from the project.

The last key concept is that the budget comes from the project. The logic of this is fairly obvious. If we serve steak, the bill will be one amount. If we serve hot dogs, the bill will be a different amount. The next logical question becomes then, what is this thing we call a project and where does it come from? This is the topic of Chapter 2.

Developing Your Project

Chapter 2

What Is a Project: And Where Does One Come From?

He had been eight years upon a project for
extracting sunbeams out of cucumbers, which were
to be put in vials hermetically sealed, and let out
to warm the air in raw inclement summers.

Jonathan Swift, *Gulliver's Travels*

Chapter 1 ends with the question, "What is this thing we call a project and where does it come from?" The purpose of Chapter 2 is to answer that question as completely as possible. We start, as these things almost always do, with generalities and work our way toward specifics. The first generality, put as simply as possible, is that a project is a set of activities, a group of things to do, or that are done.

Does everyone label or name a set of activities with the term project? Of course not—projects are known by different terms by different organizations and people. How some of these terms fit together in the overall scheme of grant seeking is a topic in this chapter.

How is a project organized? Are there similarities and commonalities among different projects? Do different projects have predictable parts or attributes? What about the language of project organization: What is it and is it consistent among grant makers? The answers to these questions occupy a major portion of this chapter.

Finally, we answer the question in the subtitle of this chapter, where does a project come from, anyway? The answer to this question brings us to the heart of grant seeking, to the core of the entire process—indeed to the very purpose of grant making itself.

General Concept

In concrete, action-oriented terms, a project is a set of activities. By activity, we mean something that is done, a piece of work, a job, a task. The sense here is of action and work; of things happening; of people accomplishing things, getting things done, expending effort.

An example of a project could be teaching youngsters, say of kindergarten age, to fish. The process of instruction would involve several activities; for example, gather the materials needed (poles, line, hooks, and bait), transport the children to the fishing hole, demonstrate baiting the hook, oversee each child baiting the hook, oversee the children fishing, and help with the fish that get caught. You can think of other activities, no doubt.

The point of the general concept is that a project consists of stringing together appropriate activities in some order. When the activities have all been accomplished, the project will also have been accomplished, or at least it will have a good chance to have been accomplished. Other factors enter into the relative success of projects, but the central concept is completing a number of appropriate activities in the correct order. If the activities are the correct ones and if the order of their accomplishment is correct, or mostly so, then success of the project is relatively assured.

Project or Program?

This thing that we are calling a project, a number of people and organizations call a program. Therein lies a hurdle difficult for some grant seekers to overcome. Now is a good a time to pause and present our diatribe on terminology, which we call "New-Quick Homily One: Terminology." As might be surmised from the number in the title, more New-Quick homilies lurk in the background waiting to appear at an appropriate time.

A Rose by Any Other Name

> "When *I* use a word," Humpty Dumpty said, in rather a scornful tone, "it means just what I choose it to mean—neither more nor less."
>
> "The question is," said Alice, "whether you *can* make words mean so many different things."
>
> "The question is," said Humpty Dumpty, "which is to be master—that's all."
>
> —*Lewis Carroll*, Through the Looking Glass

Every discipline or field has its own language. The term for this specialized or technical language of a trade, profession, or similar group is jargon. We do not use "jargon" in a pejorative sense at all. Jargon is a valuable tool when used by people in the same discipline, trade, profession, or field. Volumes of information and knowledge, depths of expertise and experience, are all brought into a conversation with a single word or phrase of jargon. Among people with similar experience, training, or education, jargon speeds communication and makes conversation or reading simpler and faster. Jargon is a powerful communication tool when used properly.

In communication among people from different backgrounds, however, jargon fails to convey enhanced meaning. More likely, it does just the opposite. The jargon phrase confuses meaning and makes communication less clear, not more so. A writer or speaker who uses jargon with people from different backgrounds fails at the most fundamental purpose of speaking or writing—precise communication. How does this apply to our subject of projects? More specifically, how does this apply to the project versus program situation?

If every discipline or field has its own language, a further observation is that most people consider the language of their field or discipline to be the proper and correct use of terminology. This belief can border on the pathological, not only denying the validity of other terminology, but placing any use but one's own into the category of ignorance and darkness.

This is the way of it. A word or a phrase is a label for a concept. We assign words and phrases to complex concepts to make our lives easier and simpler. Rather than explain a cooking method, steps of preparation, and a sauce recipe, we say simply that we are having barbecue for dinner. In one part of the country, however, your listener will expect the barbecue to be pork; while in another location, your listener will look for beef. Such is the problem of communicating exactly through our inexact medium of language.

Just about every discipline and field has its own language to describe what we are discussing in this book. Some will say project. Some will say program. Is there a difference? Yes—in the language of a specific field. However, what one person calls a program is exactly the same thing that another person calls a project. Which person is "right" or "correct?" Neither and both, is the answer. From the viewpoint inside each field, each person is correct. From a larger, overall viewpoint, however, neither is correct. Each is simply using a different label for the same thing or concept.

As much as it may seem otherwise, the field of grant seeking does not have its own language. Grant seeking borrows from other fields. Grant makers and grant seekers with similar interests use a language suitable to the interest. A few examples are the many areas of healthcare, K–12 education, research and development of a product or service, a scientific research field, literacy, advocacy, and so on for a very long list. Trouble arises when a grant seeker in one field pursues a grant from a grant maker that uses the language of a different field. A typical example is a public school pursuing a grant from a healthcare grant maker.

The upshot of all this is that while it is important to understand concepts, it is even more important to be flexible about what the concepts are named. Keep firmly in mind that the name you put on a concept may not be the same name that some others put on the same concept. This one little fact is the cause of a great deal of trouble in grant seeking. Insisting on placing one's own meaning onto grantor's terms probably causes more heartache than any other single mistake.

The solution is to understand concepts and let the labels fall where they may. As Shakespeare told us, "What's in a name? That which we call a rose/By any other name would smell as sweet." The Bard is saying the same thing we have been. Concepts are important. Names are not.

We simply must not get hung up on names and labels. Within our own specialties, labels, titles, and names have specific and exact meanings and to use them otherwise is to prove ourselves less than adept in our area of expertise. When it comes to grant seeking, however, think outside the box. Do not get hung up on words. See them for what they are, labels on concepts.

Program or Project?

In grant seeking, generally but by no means universally, a program is an overall effort, for example, "our program to aid the homeless." When the generalities of a program are broken into manageable parts, these often become sets of activities called projects. Continuing with the example of aiding the homeless, one project might be to provide temporary shelter. Another project might be to provide permanent housing. The separate activities are both part of the overall program but probably would take widely different approaches. The two efforts could be called projects. Does it make any real difference what we call these efforts? No, it does not, as long as everyone involved understands what is being described.

Some people call the thing we are describing in this chapter a program. That is just fine with us. We are not trying to establish a rigid nomenclature for grant seeking. For simplicity and consistency, we use the term project. Just keep in mind that the important thing is the concept, not what the concept is called.

Organization

So far, we have explained a project as a set of activities. Graphically, this conceptualization might look similar to the illustration in Exhibit 2.1. The overall project, Project A, is represented by the large, outside rectangle.

Exhibit 2.1

Project Organization as a Set of Activities

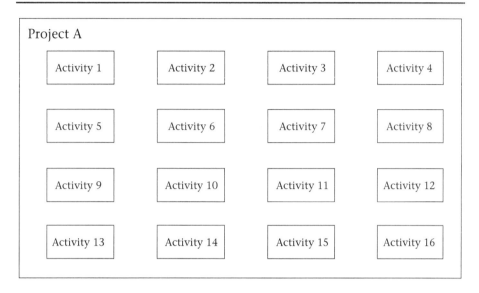

Inside this rectangle are 16 activities. The result or sum of all 16 activities produces or accomplishes Project A.

While technically accurate, the representation of a project in Exhibit 2.1 leaves a lot to be desired. Fortunately, all projects follow a predictable organizational scheme, so we can improve on our illustration without knowing the first thing about the content or subject of the project. First comes a reason or purpose for the project. Next come the major steps it will take to accomplish the purpose. This simple concept is illustrated in Exhibit 2.2.

One of the basic truths about a project is that it serves a purpose. Each project has a reason for its existence, a purpose for its activities. The name or title or label applied to this highest level of project organization depends on who is doing the naming. A common, but by no means universal, label for this highest level of project organization is "mission." We use mission and purpose interchangeably. Another closely allied term is outcome. Discussing the mission or purpose of a project in terms of the outcome expected is common.

The next basic truth is that the completion of a series of major steps is necessary to accomplish the mission. Another way to say this is that the project activities can be grouped into several large categories. These categories become major steps to accomplish the purpose of the project. Some people and organizations call these major steps goals. Others call them

EXHIBIT 2.2

Project Organization, Top Two Levels

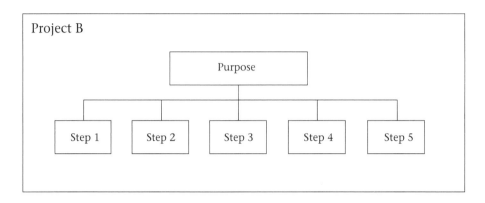

outcomes or objectives. Again, what we call these major steps is not important. What is important is that we realize that each and every project will have a set of major steps.

A major step will itself consist of smaller steps. By its very nature, a major step is made up of substeps. After all of these substeps have been done, the major step that they constitute should be accomplished. Once all the major steps are completed, the purpose of the project should also be accomplished. This concept of starting at the top and breaking a project into progressively smaller and smaller parts is the basic and fundamental and universal way that all projects are organized. What these levels are called is debatable, but that they exist is indisputable. Exhibit 2.3 illustrates dividing a major step into its constituent substeps.

Three labels commonly used for the first three levels of project organization are mission, goals, and objectives. This set of terms is by no means universally used, however. Exhibit 2.4 is reproduced from page 76 of *Grant Winner's Toolkit*. Twelve sets of terms are shown. This list is not complete. There are others. You may find yourself looking at some of terms in Exhibit 2.4 and saying something like, "Oh, they don't understand about that word. It has a definite meaning, and it's not how it's being used here." Our answer to you would be to take it up with the grant maker. Do not get hung up on words. Everyone does not use your definitions.

In this book, we use "mission," "goal," and "objective" as the labels for the top three levels of project organization. While not universally used, this set of terms seems to be used more often than any other set. If our word choice causes you distress, then simply insert the word you prefer whenever you run across the offending term. From a combined 40

EXHIBIT 2.3

Project Organization, Substeps

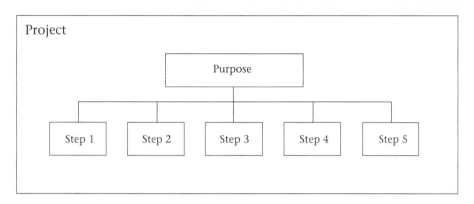

years of experience in grant proposal writing, one thing we have learned is that we do not get to name things. The grantor names things. Today, we use mission. Last week, we used purpose. The week before that, we used outcome. One week earlier, we used goal. And a month ago, we used vision. How did we know what word to use? At some place in the grant maker's guidelines for application (variously called request for proposal,

EXHIBIT 2.4

Various Sets of Terms Used by Grantors for the First Three Levels of Project Organization

Possible Labels for Organization Levels

1	Mission	Vision	Purpose	Outcome
2	Goals	Strategies	Objectives	Goals
3	Objectives	Tactics	Activities	Tasks
1	Mission	Objective	Mission	Purpose
2	Objectives	Action Plan	Objectives	Outcomes
3	Methods	Steps	Action Plans	Activities
1	Outcome	Goal	Goal	Vision
2	Objectives	Outcomes	Objectives	Objectives
3	Action Plans	Methods	Activities	Tasks

request for application, application guidelines, application solicitation, or others), an applicant is asked to explain, in general, the overall purpose of the project. The word the grant maker uses when asking the question is the one a wise applicant uses. Another hint: It is the term without an "s." It is singular. Suppose a grant maker asks for project outcomes (note the "s"). Outcomes cannot be our highest level, since there is only one of the highest level. On the other hand, a request for the project goal (note the absence of an "s"), means the grantor wants one "something." We have called this one "something" a mission, but for this grantor, we will call it the project goal. And so it goes.

More Terminology

For the amount of detail needed in a grant proposal, usually, three levels of organization are sufficient (mission, goals, and objectives). They are all a grantor normally asks to see. However, the narrative of the project description obviously provides more detail than found in the goals and objectives. So, the fact is, you will need more detail than just goals and objectives, even though that detail will not go into the proposal in a formal tabular way, only selected segments of it and that in narrative form.

Our purpose is to develop a project budget. For that we need more detail than goals and objectives provide. We need to break the objectives into constituent parts. The two most common terms used for this level of complexity are task or activity. Either one is a good choice. We will use activity, because we started this discussion with the concept that a project is a set of activities. Therefore, in our project organizational scheme, we have finally worked our way down to those activities that make up the individual units or pieces of actions that in their totality make up a project. In Chapter 4, we introduce a tool called the Activity Analysis Worksheet, and discuss activities in detail. For now, it's sufficient to add to our organizational model that the objectives will be made up of small individual actions, and those bits of work will be called activities.

Where Does a Project Come From?

The question asked in the subtitle of this chapter is "Where does a project come from?" This question deals with the theoretical aspect of a project. The simple truth is that a project is a solution to a problem. Therefore, projects come from, or originate with, the desire to solve a problem. When a solution to a problem is planned and the activities needed are identified, the outcome of the planning is a project.

Chapter 3 deals in depth with exactly what a problem is. For now, we will let a problem be a cause of worry or concern, something that is wrong. A project then is a set of activities the purpose of which is to solve a problem. This is the complete definition of a project. It combines the concrete action-oriented aspect and the theoretical aspect into a coherent definition:

Project: Real Aspect

A project is a set of activities.

Project: Theoretical Aspect

A project is a solution to a problem.

Project: Plain Language Definition

A project is an organized set of activities the accomplishment of which solves a problem.

Admittedly, saying in the definition that the accomplishment of the activities "solves a problem" is bold and perhaps even unrealistic. Living in the real world probably should create caution, causing us to include "weasel" words; instead of the definition ending with "solves a problem" it might say something like "works toward solving a problem" or "contributes to the solution of a problem." If it pleases you to think that way, be our guest. Despite "reality," the reality is that if a project is researched, planned, and developed properly, thoroughly, and completely, it will indeed solve the problem. And if it doesn't, through the evaluation component, we should come to know why it didn't and be able to incorporate the changes necessary to make it work.

Wise Guy and Wise Lady

Wise Guy

Hey, why are we talking about projects? I just wanted to know about budgets. That's all. I want to know where to put the numbers.

> **Wise Lady**
>
> Think what the budget stands for—purchases. Purchases of people's time, of supplies, of services—purchases of the things you need to run the project. The budget can't be developed in a vacuum. No one can tell you where to put the numbers. The numbers flow from the needs of the project. If you don't have a project, then there's no need for a budget. Actually, a budget comes very naturally from your project. Numbers. We tell you where to put them in this book (no offense intended). But you have to first define what they are.

Conclusion

In Chapter 1, we said that a budget comes from a project. In this chapter, we add that a project comes from a problem, or more precisely, from the desire to solve a problem. Along the way, we decided that a project, from an action-oriented viewpoint, is a set of activities, a bunch of things to do. Putting the two concepts together yields our plain language definition.

Key Definition

> ## **Project**
>
> A project is an organized set of activities the accomplishment of which solves a problem.

A key concept worth repeating concerns terminology and the labels we apply to concepts. To be successful as a seeker of grants, flexibility must be your byword. The definitions and jargon that you know so well from your own discipline may not be the definitions and terms used by the grantor receiving your proposal. Some people also find it disturbing that terms will change from one proposal to the next. It is important to realize that all projects are organized the same. Different grantors using different terms does not change the basics of project organization. It only changes what you call things. Practically speaking, all grantors want to know the same things. They just ask for them in such different ways that unless you stay mentally agile and flexible it can get confusing.

Key Concepts

- A project is a set of activities.
- Concepts are important; labels are not.
- Concepts are fixed; labels change ("a rose by any other name").
- All projects have a predictable organizational scheme.
- A project has an ultimate purpose, which we label as the mission.
- The major steps necessary to accomplish the mission we call goals.
- The smaller steps necessary to accomplish a goal we call objectives.
- The even smaller steps necessary to accomplish an objective we call activities.
- A project is a solution to a problem.

In Chapter 3, we discuss problems in detail and in depth. We explain what they are and their characteristics. We describe a few problems that can crop up when working with problems. Then we outline a four-step process to design a project, leading to a project profile. By the end of Chapter 3, we will be ready to move into the more detailed process of project development. This is the topic of Chapter 4.

What Is a Problem: And How Does a Project Come from One?

> "Then you should say what you mean," the March Hare went on.
> "I do," Alice hastily replied; "at least—at least I mean what I say—that's the same thing, you know."
> "Not the same thing a bit!" said the Hatter. "Why, you might just as well say that 'I see what I eat' is the same thing as 'I eat what I see!'"
>
> Lewis Carroll, *Alice's Adventures in Wonderland*

When we come finally to consider problems, we arrive at the core of grant seeking. After peeling away the layers of grant seeking to the ultimate center, we find there a problem. The hub around which all grant seeking revolves, as the planets of our solar system revolve around the sun, is a problem. The core, the essence, of all project grant seeking is a problem.

This fundamental concept demands careful and thorough explanation. Many basic flaws in projects, and also therefore in project grant proposals, stem from misunderstanding or mishandling of the problem on which the project is based. The principle is simple. It is much easier to finish correctly and well if one starts correctly and well.

This chapter has two main purposes. First, we explain and define problems fully, and point out pitfalls to avoid when defining problems. Second, we demonstrate how to create a project from a problem, a process we call "Project Design." The Project Design leads to the creation of what we call a "Project Profile." And finally, we discuss briefly how creating a "Project Hit List" materially aids a grant-seeking effort.

Problems

Understanding the general concept of a problem is easy enough, but defining "problem" exactly is not so simple. The situation is analogous to the famous position taken on pornography by U.S. Supreme Court Justice (1958–1981) Potter Stewart when he wrote that while he found it difficult to define, "I know it when I see it." Just so, we may have difficulty defining precisely what a problem is, but we certainly know one when we see one.

In General

Grant makers use the term "need" interchangeably with problem. In plain language, the two words mean different things, but in grant seeking, need and problem are normally synonymous. This gives us an avenue of approach to a definition because need is clearly defined as "a lack of something required or desirable" while problem is rather murkily defined as "a situation, matter, or person that presents perplexity or difficulty." By combining the two definitions, we arrive at a useful working statement that conveys the fundamental character of the term as used in grant seeking:

Problem: Plain Language Definition

A situation that presents difficulty because of a lack of something desirable.

To repeat and clarify, we intend this definition to apply to grant seeking only. While it may apply elsewhere, our only purpose here is to define and understand concepts currently in use in grant seeking. Understanding might be furthered now with a few examples.

Example Problems

Teen pregnancy	Test scores	SIDS
Illiteracy	Handguns	Racism
Homelessness	Voter turnout	Hunger
AIDS	Poverty	Violence

A few thoughts may occur to you about these problems. First, to you, some of the items in the list may not be problems at all. Or, stated another way, not everyone will consider all the items in the list to be problems. This leads to a truth about problems. One person's problem is another person's shrug of the shoulder. This has consequences that we deal with later in this chapter (see "Alignment between Organization and Problem").

Next, the items in the list of examples seem somehow incomplete; that is, they lack sufficient information. Or, at the least, we would like to know more. This is correct. The information normally included in the statement of a problem is the subject of the next topic.

Characteristics of Problems

Our discussion applies only to projects for which grant funding is being sought. While much of this material has wider application, our subject is narrow and focused on obtaining grants. With that in mind, almost every usefully stated problem has several characteristics in common. We would say "all" except for the ubiquitous exception that "always" lurks just around the corner waiting for careless use of absolute modifiers.

It may seem to be picking nits, but we actually are discussing the statement of problems, not the problem itself. A problem exists in and of itself. It naturally possesses all the characteristics of a problem. After all, it is one, and it does not need us to define it. What we are doing is putting the problem into the form of a statement. The characteristics that we are discussing are not, therefore, of the problem itself, but rather of our statement of the problem. With that in mind, we will be discussing the statement of a problem, rather than the problem itself. Again, the problem exists in a fullness all its own. What we must do is describe the problem well and thoroughly. An aside here is that moving to discussion of statements of problems rather than problems themselves relieves us of being in the uncomfortable position of discussing "good" problems. Problems are not good, but the way a problem is stated can be good or bad, useful or not.

Another important point is that a single problem statement comes in two basic formats, the short and the long. The short form is a single broad-brush sentence that states the problem with little or no details or statistics. This format allows a reader to gather the essence of what is to come. The long form can occupy several pages providing great detail and specificity with attendant statistics and impact. The long form is a staple of grant proposals asked for under many different names. The two most commonly used names are statement of need and problem statement.

An applicant receives instructions on how to put together the problem statement in its long form. A grantor does not, however, give directions or instructions on how to design and develop a project, which is what we are about in this chapter and the next. An applicant is expected to know about projects and have the project fully developed before beginning the proposal. Most grant seekers do not have a project fully developed before they start to write the grant proposal. This causes the one universal problem about which all grant seekers complain—lack of time. The time crunch is not because there is not enough time to write the proposal, because usually the grantor allows sufficient time. The time crunch happens because applicants are not just writing a proposal, they are also making up the project as they go along.

Writing the proposal and developing the project are two different things. When they occur simultaneously, nerves frazzle, corners are cut, all the bases are not covered, and the normal result is a noncompetitive proposal. Project development should be done in the relatively calm and unhurried atmosphere of a grant seeker's normal work time. When a fully developed project exists, the proposal writing process becomes one of simply answering questions.

A proposal, at its most basic, consists simply of the answers to several questions put to you by the grantor. The questions divide neatly into only three categories: (1) There will be questions about your organization and your community; (2) there will be questions about your problem; (3) there will be questions about your solution (your project). Questions about your organization and community should not pose any difficulty at all. Questions about the problem should not pose difficulties either. Perhaps right now that is not obvious, but by the end of this chapter, we hope you agree. The only category with difficulty is the project, your solution to the problem. If, however, you have the project fully developed and know everything there is to know about it ahead of time, then answering even these questions will be simple.

And that is the truth of the matter. Good grant seekers see proposal writing as simply answering a grantor's questions with answers they already know. The answers already exist in three places: your organization and community, your problem, and your project. What is needed is a process for developing projects independent of a grant maker's request for proposal. That process begins with the problem statement. The following list contains the characteristics of a good problem statement of the short form, single-sentence variety:

Characteristics of a Problem Statement

- The problem aligns with your organization.
- The problem focuses on people.
- Problem statements cannot be circular.
- Problem statements cannot be solutions masquerading as problems.
- Problem statements contain at least two parts: (1) the circumstance or situation and (2) who it affects.
- With regard to positives, problem statements are expressed in negative terms (lack, dearth, sparseness, deficiency, not enough).
- With regard to negatives, problem statements are expressed in positive terms (many, often, large, high, too much).

Alignment between Organization and Problem

Every organization, agency, department, or division—hospital, school, museum, library, arts council, rape crisis center, veteran's outreach, parks and recreation, waste management, rescue squad, volunteer fire department, police department, county council, research facility, consortium, or partnership—has (or certainly should have) a statement of vision, purpose, or mission. Such a statement is often part of the articles of incorporation or the bylaws and usually is found as well in a decorative frame hanging on the wall of either the entrance area or the conference room, or both. The statement establishes the thing or things in which an organization involves itself and on which it expends resources. Such statements tend to be general and lofty as well as purposefully indefinite on ways and means.

Under the general umbrella of the statement of vision, purpose, or mission, an organization normally crafts several specific aims, strategies, or goals. The efforts, events, programs, and projects of an organization flow forth as the logical results of these specific guidelines. When the time comes to look for a problem to form the basis of a new project or program, it is essential that the problem align with and flow from those established aims, strategies, or goals.

It is sad and regrettable to watch a nonprofit chase and catch a large grant, big money, perhaps hundreds of thousands of dollars, not because the grantor's interests align and fit but because the money is available, because it's there for the taking. A year later, maybe two, the realization comes that the organization has pulled itself off its laid course in the pursuit of big bucks. The master compass swings to the magnet of money. The compass no longer points true. The people who came to the organization out of personal conviction and commitment find themselves working at "just another job."

The first characteristic of a good problem statement is that it aligns naturally and fully with the principles of the organization. Choosing that particular problem fulfills a portion of the purpose of the organization. No parsing of words or twisting of meanings is necessary. The fit and alignment are real and clear, not only to concerned and involved staff but also to unbiased knowledgeable observers.

Focus on People

Somewhere, somehow, every project must focus on a group of people. Animals, plants, rocks, water, buildings, research, technology, administrative policy, stars, planets, comets, or asteroids may be an important part of a project. Ultimately, however, the project must have a human focus.

The work with animals to asteroids is done for the benefit of a group of people. It must always come back to people.

The term for this group of people is target population. A target population is a group of people who will benefit when the project succeeds. The target population is the group of people with the problem. This is not always obvious at first glance. The following list has five example problems. Possible target populations are placed beneath each problem. Note how changing the target population changes how you think about the problem:

1. The opera is losing money.
  - People who attend the opera.
  - People who do not attend the opera.
  - Both.

2. Youth crime between hours of 3:00 P.M. and 6:00 P.M. is rising fast.
  - Children in elementary school.
  - Children in middle school.
  - Both.

3. Elderly people in the community are not living as many years as the national average.
  - Elderly people in the community.
  - Young people in the community.
  - Both.

4. The local river is polluted.
  - People living in the community.
  - People living outside the community.
  - Both.

5. Fewer students than the national average are seeking postsecondary education.
  - Students.
  - The general population.
  - Both.

Before moving to the next characteristic of a problem statement, it needs to be said emphatically that grants are not always the answer to your need for money. For many problems and solutions, a funding method other than a grant must be found. Fund-raising is often much more appropriate for a particular problem and solution than seeking a grant. This brings us to New-Quick Homily Two: Grant Seeking Is Not Fund-Raising. Not understanding that there is a difference between fund-raising and grant seeking leads to many mistakes and failures by grant seekers.

Fund-Raising vis-à-vis Grant Seeking

Fund-raising has several facets.

1. It seeks to identify organizations that give to charity. It sends mailings that solicit funds. The mailings describe the "cause" and ask for money because it's "the right thing to do."

2. It seeks to identify people who give to charity. It sends mailings that solicit funds. The mailings describe the "cause" and ask for money because it's "the right thing to do."

3. It purchases mailing lists of people with "correct" demographics. It sends mailings that solicit funds.

4. It seeks benefactors that will give money to the organization.

5. It seeks benefactors that will commit to donating money on a regular basis for the "cause."

6. It holds fund-raising events such as charity balls, dinners, raffles, and the like.

7. It sells things such as candy, candles, cookies, popcorn, magazines, and Christmas paper.

8. It holds "drives" and ". . . thons" during which, through publicity and advertising, it seeks funds from the public at large.

9. There's more, lots more. These are just a few of the basic strategies. You know many more yourself. After all, you are on the receiving end on a regular basis.

Grant makers aren't really "into" charity.

In fact, grants are not charity. Though it is true that grantor's activities are classified as charitable or philanthropic, in this case it's more of a tax issue than anything else (an IRS thing). Grant makers are interested in solving problems. They're focused on one or more issues such as stopping drug abuse or illiteracy. They're looking for a targeted *investment*. They want to fund a *project* that offers a potential solution to the problem they're interested in. They're not specifically interested in your community or group, per se. They are interested in you testing a solution that might be applied in other communities to solve the problem they're interested in. Grant makers want to see a project. They want a proposal that specifically addresses the issues they've identified. They want you to persuade them that your project is the best investment they can make. You don't approach a grant maker by tugging at heartstrings, but rather by making a professional, businesslike case that your project has a reasonable chance of solving the problem.

Local grant makers are interested in your community or group. Almost always, however, they also want a proposal that describes a project specifically tailored to the problem(s) they want to solve. They are still looking for a good investment, this time not as a model program but as a step toward improving the quality of life in their (and your) community.

Some grant makers (foundations) do "straight" charitable giving. They become benefactors rather than grantors, and though the funds are often called grants, they do not fit the definition of a competitive project grant.

In *fund-raising*, it is quite common to hire a consultant to write one letter and then mail it to hundreds, thousands, or even millions of potential donors and contributors.

In *grant seeking*, however, each grantor is unique and requires its own proprosal. You might write several proposals about one project, but each grantor gets its own, custom-written, individual proposal.

Avoid Circular Logic

If we were in one of our workshops now, we would say, "Write this down word for word, because it sounds complicated." Here, it is written down, so we must suggest instead, "Read this carefully, because it seems complicated."

The absence of the solution cannot be the problem.

Circular logic, in this case, sounds like this imaginary interchange between an applicant for a grant and a grant maker.

Grant applicant: "We need to build a swimming pool."
Grant maker: "Please tell me why you need to build a swimming pool."
Grant applicant: "Because we do not have a swimming pool."
Grant maker: "And because you do not have a swimming pool?"
Grant Applicant: "We need to build a swimming pool."

When the absence of the solution ("we do not have a swimming pool") becomes the problem ("We need to build a swimming pool"), a circle of reasoning is produced. This must be avoided at all times. The solution for eliminating circular logic is simple. Notice the item that is omitted from the entire preceding interchange. Any reference to people is missing. The only reference is to a thing, the swimming pool. To avoid circular reasoning, focus on people not things.

In the situation just described, perhaps the real problem is that there are no facilities for supervised youth recreation in the summer when school is out, at least none that are attractive to youth. In this case, a swimming pool could be a solution, and the building and operation of one could be a project.

Solutions Masquerading as Problems

Over the past 16 years, in hundreds of workshops in all parts of the country we have asked participants to give us problems. A solution masquerading as a problem is, by far, the thing that most often needs straightening out. Examples look like this:

- "We need more staff."
- "Our staff needs more training."
- "Our material is old and outdated."
- "We do not have computers."
- "Our computers are old and slow."
- "We need a Web site."

In each of these examples we are given a solution, not a problem. We know clearly from each of these statements what is wanted, what is seen as a solution. Starting at the top, the solutions that are wanted are more staff, staff training, new material, computers, computers, and a Web site. What we do not know from these statements, however, is the problem. None of these "problems" have any content. They do not discuss people and what is happening or lacking or needed.

The solution is to focus on people. A good rule of thumb is that resources such as staff and equipment should never be mentioned in the short-form problem statement. Stay on target, and the target is your target population and its situation.

Another way to look at this is to say that an organization's problems are never the problems on which to base a grant project. You do not have problems. You provide solutions. Only your target population has problems. If your project is to improve administrative functions, the purpose is to help your target population and the problem is stated in terms of the target population. If your project is to provide additional professional development for your staff, it is because your target population needs what the training can provide.

Yes, we know your organization has problems. Every organization has needs and problems. To be successful seeking grants, however, it is necessary

to focus problems on a target population, not on service providers. This simple problem of focus on the organization rather than the target population accounts for much failure in grant seeking.

Keeping the Language Straight

One of the oddities of problem statements is that good is bad and bad is good. Many times the worse your statistics look to your constituents, the better they look to a grant maker. Fifty-seven percent poverty is *awful* but if you're seeking money to establish community gardens, it's good.

The Two Parts

The short-form, one-sentence problem statement needs only two parts. More information can be included, but it is not necessary and will probably only confuse the issue. Keep it lean, mean, and simple. There is plenty of time to explain and paint the complete picture with all the details. Everything does not need to be put into one sentence. Keep this one short and simple. The two parts that must be in every one-sentence problem statement are the identity of the target population and the target population's problem. That is it. Say it simply and say it short.

Putting It All Together

Putting it all together is a simple process, as shown in the following examples. First, in a short phrase, identify the target population; three to five words is sufficient. Use a phrase, not a sentence. When the description of the target population grows to more than five words, stop and simplify. Next, state the problem or need of the target population, in a short phrase. A sentence is not needed, in fact, it is not helpful now.

Target Population	Elderly citizens
Problem	High incidence of heart disease
Target Population	Youth
Problem	Rate of crime and violence growing fast
Target Population	Middle-aged workers
Problem	High incidence of alcoholism and drug abuse

Once the two parts are stated clearly, a problem statement is drafted by simply joining the two parts into a coherent sentence:

- Elderly citizens in the community have a very high rate of heart disease.

- The rate of youth crime and violence is growing fast.
- Workers, thirty to forty-five, have a high incidence of alcoholism and drug abuse.

Project Design

We now are ready to move from a problem to a project. We call the first phase of this process Project Design. In this book we only outline the process to illustrate the progression from problem to budget. If, however, you want or need a full discussion of the subject, including worksheets and checklists, then see *Grant Seeker's Toolkit: A Comprehensive Guide to Finding Funding,* also by the authors, a volume in the Wiley Nonprofit Law, Finance, and Management Series.

Project Design is a five-step process: (1) State a large problem, (2) list the causes of the problem, (3) sort and choose causes, (4) identify a solution, and (5) identify resources needed.

Step 1: State a Problem

The first step is to state a problem that affects a target population served by your organization. Note carefully the final clause in the preceding sentence, "that affects a target population served by your organization." This is the key. Think in terms of people. Focus on the people you serve. We will get to your organization and its needs later. For now, think only of people you serve. Here are several examples:

- Youth crime and violence are increasing.
- The incidence of babies born prematurely or at very low birth weight is high.
- More families are moving out of the area than into it.
- Healthcare professionals are treating more people for drug and alcohol abuse.
- Graduates of our college are not able to get good jobs.
- Pollution levels in our creeks and the river are increasing.
- Physically disabled people cannot get jobs.

Step 2: List the Causes of the Problem

In this step, list the causes of the problem in Step 1, as many as possible. Questions like the following ones often help the mental effort of identifying causes. Why does the problem exist? What are the barriers to the removal of the problem? What makes this problem continue? What causes this problem? What are the sources of the problem? What makes this problem thrive and get worse?

Broad Problem: Youth Crime and Violence Are Increasing

Causes of the Problem or Barriers to Solving It

- In our community, there are few constructive and attractive activities for young people.
- Some people are very trusting and don't lock doors or protect their property.
- Some people do not trust youth at all and have given up on them.
- Young people have too much unsupervised time on their hands (especially between the time school is out and working parents get home).
- Alcohol and drugs are easy for children to get.
- Churches, schools, and neighborhood groups are not reaching beyond their normal hours and activities.
- Churches, schools, and neighborhood groups are not working together.
- Children roam in gangs.
- There is a high rate of dropouts and unemployment among young people.

Step 3: Eliminate, Recast, Group, and Choose Causes

Several actions are taken in this step. First, eliminate all those causes over which you can exert no control. There is a simple way to visualize this first step concretely. Imagine that you have the money and you are running the project. Are there any causes listed in Step 2 that you cannot change or affect? If so, mark them off your list. They may be valid causes of the problem, but if you have no control over them—cannot change or affect them—they have no part in your project planning. This one small step, by the way, will help you avoid the sense of hopelessness that often overcomes planners. When faced with so many intractable causes, we often throw up our hands in defeat. Rather, you should mark off all the causes over which you can exert no control and focus on the ones you can control. It is the "light a candle rather than curse the darkness" concept.

We choose to eliminate the second and third causes in the preceding list. We base the decision on the probability that our project will not be able to change the attitudes of either those who trust too much or those who do not trust at all.

The next thing to do is to recast those causes that are stated in such a way that the project cannot affect them. For example, "Alcohol and drugs are easy for children to get" is a true statement. The direct solution is to make alcohol and drugs harder to get—an effort certainly worth undertaking, but beyond the scope of the project that we have in mind. We do want to address the drug and alcohol problem, however, therefore, the cause needs to be recast to focus on the target population, not the availability of alcohol and drugs. Restating the cause in terms of the target population could go like this: "Children are using drugs and alcohol." Recast in terms of a behavior of the target population (or more correctly some portion of the target population), the cause now becomes something over which we can exert influence.

Third, group causes that fit together. Perhaps several of your listed causes could be called education; then group them together as a training component. Perhaps several of your listed causes are outreach or publicity oriented; then group them as a public relation component.

Once you have eliminated those causes over which you can exert no control, once you have recast those causes that need it, and once you have organized the causes into their natural groupings, look carefully and thoughtfully at what you have. Choose one or more groups of causes. This is your real problem and will be the focus of the activities of your project.

Broad Problem: Youth Crime and Violence Are Increasing

Group One

- There is a high rate of dropouts.
- There is a high rate of unemployment among youth.
- Children are using drugs and alcohol.

Group Two

- Young people have too much unsupervised time on their hands (especially between the time school is out and working parents get home).
- Children roam in gangs.

Group Three

- In our community, there are few constructive and attractive activities for young people.
- Churches, schools, and neighborhood groups are not reaching beyond their normal hours and activities.
- Churches, schools, and neighborhood groups are not working together.

After eliminating two causes, recasting one, and grouping as shown in the preceding list, our overall problem begins to come into focus. The three groupings lead to the next step of Project Design in which we identify the solution (the project).

Step 4: Identify a Solution

At this stage of putting together a project, all that is necessary is to accept the obvious. For example, if we agree that one cause of the increase in youth crime and violence is that young people have too much unsupervised time on their hands, then the solution is to arrange for supervision of the youth. If we agree that another cause is the use of drugs and alcohol, then we want to decrease the use of drugs and alcohol. Accept the obvious, state it, and the methods and means will come along later.

Applying the principle of "Accept the Obvious" results in the following project parts or strategies. We do not know exactly what they are now. We just know that they will be some part of the project.

Broad Problem: Youth Crime and Violence Are Increasing

Project Strategies

Group One

- Decrease dropouts.
- Give youth knowledge and skills to be more employable.
- Decrease use of drugs and alcohol.

Group Two

- Provide supervision especially between the time school is out and working parents get home.
- Decrease number of youths roaming in gangs.

Group Three

- Provide constructive and attractive activities for youth.
- Organize churches, schools, and neighborhood groups to reach beyond their normal hours and activities.
- Organize churches, schools, and neighborhood groups to work together.

Observe how simply changing the causes into their opposites, their solutions, begins to show the outline of the project. This simple step usually occurs automatically in one's mind, but the exercise of putting the information on paper is well worth the small time it takes. The project starts to form right before your eyes. The next step is to take the parts and fit them together into a project concept. Craft one or two sentences that broadly summarize the project. It is best not to repeat the items from the list, rather generalize in broad summary. This is not a project summary yet. It probably will not be complete enough for a project summary. A better label for it is project concept.

Example Project Concept

A communitywide partnership, led in tandem by city and county government, will establish an after-school program. The program will address the personal, social, emotional, and educational needs of participating youth. Academic, vocational, recreational, social, and personal skills development activities will be provided.

Several comments (perhaps criticisms) can be made about the preceding three-sentence project concept. It does not include a description of the target population. It mentions a partnership but does not give the composition of the partnership. It lists several types of activity but does not go into any detail about them. It does not give times or days or any scheduling information.

All this is true. It is also irrelevant. All the details will come in time. In fact, digging too quickly into detail often derails project design and development by bogging down discussion in minutia when for now the main effort needs to stay at higher levels of organization.

Step 5: Identify Resources Needed

The next and final step in project design is to make a preliminary list of the resources that will be needed to implement the project just envisioned. Again, at this point in the process, the list does not need to be complete or exhaustive:

Example: Resources Needed

- Facility (inside and outside space for participants; adequate rest rooms and water fountains).
- Equipment (computers, printers, network, minor athletic equipment, copy machine, fire extinguishers, lighted exit signs).
- Furniture (desks and chairs, shelves, storage cabinets).
- Materials (CD-ROM learning materials, books, games, reference publications, paper, office supplies, and desk accessories).
- Contractual (phone lines or cable for Internet connections; food service for beverages, snacks, and food for special events; computer networking company for installations; school district and city bus system for transportation; community health program for on-call nurse; local printer for brochures, publicity pieces, and manuals; training organizations for professional development activities; paving contractor for small ball court; community recreation center for swimming lessons).

- Personnel (instructors, facilitators, tutors, group assistants, coordinators, counselor).
- Travel (for home visits by instructors and coordinators; to attend two national and one state conference).

Project Profile

The next step in our process is to develop a Project Profile. This is a handy summary of everything we have figured out about our project so far. It will provide the reference to guide us through the further development of the project and the project budget. The Project Profile has seven parts as indicated in the following example list based on the project we have been discussing in this chapter.

1. *What is the problem?* Youth crime is increasing. The major increase is in young people ages 11 to 16. Other related issues include a high dropout rate, high unemployment, gang-related activity, and increasing use of alcohol and drugs.

2. *What are the causes of the problem?* The problem is caused by many factors including the lack of supervision especially after school hours, the lack of constructive and attractive activities for youth, and lack of community coordination to combat the problem.

3. *What is the synopsis of the project?* A communitywide partnership, led in tandem by city and county government, will establish an after-school program. The program will address the personal, social, emotional, and educational needs of participating youth. Academic, vocational, recreational, social, and personal skills development activities will be provided. The project should eventually accommodate up to 300 youth, ages 11 to 16.

4. *How long will it take to get the project up and running?* It will take 9 to 10 months to get set up after coordinators are hired and funding is acquired. This includes the implementation of a community public relations campaign and the recruitment phase. The project should be ready to accept participants in the eleventh month after funding.

5. *How much money will it take?* The facility is being donated by the city as are several of the key personnel positions. The county is supporting some of the equipment and a few more personnel positions. Community businesses have volunteered to do the paving if we pay for materials, and some of the equipment is being donated. The total startup budget for the first year is $1.3 million. Of this, a little more than $800,000 is being donated by city and county governments and

business either in cash or in kind. This leaves a funding gap of $500,000 for Year One. After the acquisition of the equipment and the initial project setup costs, funding needs should be reduced to about $150,000 a year for two more years, giving us time for project establishment and to acquire local funding to cover this amount.

6. *What partners will we involve?* City and county governments, local school district, library, five area churches, the city business association and the county development league, the health department, individual businesses such as Joe's Paving Contractors and Sue's Network Services, the State Wildlife Commission, the Greenleaf Community Club (for the swimming pool for lessons), the doctor's association (for classes), the police and sheriff's departments, and two area private schools.

7. *Resources?*

- Facility (inside and outside space for participants; adequate rest rooms and water fountains).
- Equipment (computers, printers, network, minor athletic equipment, copy machine, fire extinguishers, lighted exit signs).
- Furniture (desks and chairs, shelves, storage cabinets).
- Materials (CD-ROM learning materials, books, games, reference publications, paper, office supplies and desk accessories).
- Contractual (phone lines or cable for Internet connections; food service for beverages, snacks, and food for special events; computer networking company for installations; school district and city bus system for transportation; community health program for on-call nurse; local printer for brochures, publicity pieces, and manuals; training organizations for professional development activities; paving contractor for small ball court; community recreation center for swimming lessons).
- Personnel (instructors, facilitators, tutors, group assistants, coordinators, counselor).
- Travel (for home visits by instructors and coordinators; to attend two national and one state conference).

Hit List

The origin of the Hit List concept is the alignment of grant seeking with an organization's mission and goals. The point is simply made. Identify all the problems about which your organization cares and to which your organization wishes to commit resources, and then design a project as a solution to each problem. Quickly now, before thoughts of thousands of problems and projects run through your mind; 16 years' experience shows that most organizations will finish a thorough problem- and priority-setting session with 3 to 15 problems, certainly a manageable number.

Certainly you know what problems need to be solved in your area of expertise. It is not necessary to have a funding source in hand to create the project. While a novice grant seeker may not see the similarities, the vast majority of grant proposals ask for the same things. They may call them by different names and ask for them in different order and give them different emphasis, but nevertheless, once a project is designed and developed, it is ready for any grant maker.

Once a project is designed for each problem, create a Project Profile and file them in a binder. This is your Hit List. You now have clear purposes for funding source research, the projects. Also, when that grant proposal application guideline drops on your desk with no warning, you have something on which to fall back. Pick through the Project Profiles in the Hit List and find the one that most closely matches the grant program, and you are well ahead of the game.

The prime reason for creating a Hit List is that it keeps your grant seeking focused on the mission and goals of your organization. It also allows you to get a head start on the work necessary for application. A project and a grant proposal are two different things. You can create a project long before it is time to write about it in a grant proposal. Two truths make this possible. First, all projects, by their very nature, have many similarities of organization. Second, all grant proposals are very similar. It might not seem so, if your experience is now with less than 10 or 20 proposals. Wait till you have experience with hundreds of proposals and you will begin to see obvious similarities despite all the apparent differences.

Wise Guy and Wise Lady

 Wise Guy

More project development. My problem is that I don't have money. I need money. That's my problem. Why can't I just ask for money?

Wise Lady

Well, in a way, you can "just ask for money." But what if you got a letter saying, "I'm a good guy. I have a very good idea. I need you to give me money for it." Would you send money? I think not. You have to prove to the potential funder that your project is worthy of their investment. You do this through a proposal. This proposal is your way of communicating information about your project idea to the funder. It's frequently your *only* communication; therefore, you have to do a good job the first time. You may not get a second chance. To do a good job and "ask for the money" properly, you have to go through the process we outline in this book and discuss in more depth in our other two books, *Grant Seeker's Toolkit* and *Grant Winner's Toolkit*.

Conclusion

The material in this chapter is a condensed form of the information contained in several days of workshops plus approximately a hundred pages from two previous books. We have necessarily hit only the high points for a complex and important part of successful grant seeking. However, it is beyond the scope of this book to dig deeply into the complexities of Project Design and Development. We must move along to get to the budget subjects.

It is important though to be sure that the project gets off to a good start, and a good start begins with a good problem statement. Once the problem is clearly stated, it is much easier to design and develop a project that has not only a chance to get funded, but has a chance to succeed as well, to accomplish something beneficial.

Key Definition

Problem Statement

A problem statement identifies a target population and defines the situation that presents difficulty.

If the idea of thinking and working in terms of problems strikes you as overly negative, there is another way to get at exactly the same thing from a positive standpoint. Set before you a mission or goal to attain or accomplish. Keep in mind that you still need the target population who actually will attain or accomplish the mission or goal. Missions and goals are stated positively, so we do away with those horribly negative problems, though the mission or goal you set derives from a problem, a need, or a lack. A moment's thought shows that the reason for setting any mission or goal is that there is a need for it. If there were no need, there would be no mission or goal. At any rate, once the positive mission or goal is set, you can define the barriers that exist to achieving it. The project consists of activities designed to overcome the barriers. This methodology is helpful for some people, but it amounts to the same thing as the process described earlier. It simply uses different terminology to arrive at the same end.

Key Concepts

- Grant seeking is not fund-raising.
- A project and a proposal are two different things.
- Projects can be developed on their own, independent of any funding source.
- Problems must align with your organization's mission and goals.
- Problems must focus on people.
- The absence of your solution cannot be your problem.
- Watch for solutions masquerading as problems.
- The Project Design process takes you from problem to project concept.
- The Hit List concept keeps you focused on your organization's mission and goals.
- The Hit List concept, coupled with Project Development, allows you to split project development from proposal writing.

We are far from having a complete description of a project yet. Chapter 4 takes us from a Project Profile up to a fully developed project. With a fully developed project, we are ready to write a proposal and we are ready to develop a project budget.

Chapter 4

Project Development

Failing to plan is planning to fail.
Anonymous

**You got to be careful if you don't know where
you're going, because you might not get there.**
Yogi Berra

In Chapter 3, we illustrated how to move from a problem to a project concept, a process we call Project Design. The end point of Project Design is the Project Profile (called by some people and organizations a concept paper). The information compiled in a Project Profile is not sufficiently detailed to serve as the basis for either a complete project description or a project budget. The purpose of this chapter is to illustrate how to move from the general Project Profile to a fully detailed project description, a process we call Project Development.

We divide Project Development into three main steps: (1) Create a project outline, (2) craft goals and objectives, and (3) complete the activity analysis. Again, for a full treatment of Project Design and Project Development including tools and checklists for all aspects, see *Grant Seeker's Toolkit: A Comprehensive Guide to Finding Funding,* by the authors, and also in the Wiley Nonprofit series.

Similarities among Projects

All projects follow a predictable progression in process, but not in content. The subject matter of projects varies as widely as the mind can imagine, but the path, or process, that projects take is predictable. The predictable progression can be described, as can most things, in more than one way.

We choose to divide the process into four major steps or parts. Exhibit 4.1 lists these steps.

Project Preparation and Logistics

This is the setup component of a project. It includes such activities as hiring staff, purchasing and installing equipment, curriculum development, staff training, planning, facility preparation or renovation, material evaluation and selection, purchasing supplies and materials, and any other activities that must be accomplished before implementing the project with the target population.

Partnership Activities

This component reasonably could be split between Project Preparation and Logistics and Implementation with Target Population. We choose to make it a separate component because of the present great emphasis placed on partnerships by most grant makers. For several years, it has been rare to find a project grant program that does not require the applicant to integrate partners into the activities of the project. Examples of partnership activities could include recruiting partners, training partners, scheduling partner activities, meeting and communicating with partners, and accepting input and feedback from partners.

Implementation with Target Population

These are the activities that are performed after the preparations are concluded and the project begins to function. Listing possible activities under this topic is somewhat fruitless, since the list is, for all practical purposes, infinite. The activities that occur will be determined by the content of the project and the approach or methodology that is used.

Monitoring and Management of the Project

In this component are all the various oversight and administrative activities necessary to the operation of the project. The following list includes

EXHIBIT 4.1

The Four Components Common to All Projects

Common Project Components

1. Project Preparation and Logistics.
2. Partnership Activities.
3. Implementation with Target Population.
4. Monitoring and Management of the Project.

most of these activities. You may run across additional items, but this list is relatively complete:

- Management of personnel.
- Management of funds.
- Coordination of partnership.
- Evaluation.
- Communication.
- Documentation.
- Dissemination.
- Continuation.
- Advisory boards or committees.

One item, evaluation, requires special comment. It often is appropriate to elevate evaluation to the highest possible level of project organization. In other words, instead of four components, you may want to use five, with project evaluation being one of them. This demonstrates to the grant maker that you give high priority to evaluation. When a grantor attaches great importance to evaluation, it is a good strategy to show a corresponding emphasis on your part.

Create the Project Outline

An outline is simply an organizational tool or plan to help organize ideas and activities. An outline presents the project material in a logical format and shows the relations among activities through the construction of an ordered overview.

In an outline, related activities are grouped together. Material is arranged in sections and subsections moving from general to specific. The higher the level, the more general the material. The lower the level, the more specific the material.

Outlining a Grant Project

For the inexperienced, creating the project outline often goes faster and easier when a team does this task. A person working alone often omits important project activities and easily develops brain-lock getting totally stuck. A group of people, on the other hand, usually can work through difficult spots as long as they maintain an open brainstorming atmosphere. Also, it is less likely that several people working together will overlook necessary project activities. What one forgets, another remembers. What one does not see, another notices.

Start with a Project Profile. Also have before you the four major components of projects discussed earlier. Using a brainstorming approach, think through the actions that will take place if you run the project. As actions are identified, place them under the most appropriate of the four headings. There are several techniques for this exercise. Large sheets of paper, such as flip chart pages, butcher's paper, or plain wrapping paper, can be attached to the walls and team members can write the actions on them. Or they can write necessary actions on index cards and simply place them in appropriate piles. We do not suggest using a computer for this exercise. Keep the suggestions out in the open so members of the team can see them and physically manipulate them with lots of walking around and waving of arms.

You may find, as in the following example, that you need one or more additional project components or parts to accommodate some of your actions. That is not unusual. Simply make a new heading and keep going. Once it appears that most of the actions have been recorded—when the brainstorming slows to brain "chance-of-occasional-showers"—it is time to organize the actions into some semblance of order. From this organization comes your project outline. As with any plan, the outline probably will be altered over time, perhaps drastically altered. Do not expect it to be exactly right on the first try. The point is to get a plan (the outline) down on paper, even if it is flawed. Adding to, subtracting from, or changing a plan that already exists is amazingly easy compared with creating it. Exhibit 4.2 is an example outline developed from the Project Profile in Chapter 3.

Before moving forward, a short discussion about examples is needed. Over the years—in the process of creating more than 100 presentations, 6 formal workshops, over 30 magazine articles, our site on America Online (AOL), our Web site, several books, and a number of miscellanies—we have dreamed up literally hundreds of example projects. Interaction with thousands of grant seekers over the past 16 years has taught us a few hard lessons about examples. Thus we come to New-Quick Homily Three.

Examples Are Just Examples

To paraphrase a current celebrity, we do not mean to get off on a rant here, but examples are just examples. Here are just a few of the things that are true about this example and all the other examples in this book or for that matter in any book:

- Yes, necessary actions have been left out.
- Yes, unnecessary actions have been included.
- Yes, things could be done differently.
- Yes, things could be done better.

EXHIBIT 4.2

Example Project Outline

Example Project Outline

Communitywide After-School Program

I. Project Preparation and Logistics Management

   A. Set up oversight council.

   B. Prepare facilities.

   C. Purchase and install equipment.

   D. Select and purchase materials.

   E. Hire and train staff.

   F. Design and plan student orientation.

   G. Develop transportation plan.

   H. Develop a parent involvement plan.

   I. Develop continuing professional development plan for staff.

   J. Design and plan tutor and session assistant program and orientation.

II. Partnership Coordination, Monitoring, and Recruitment

   A. Implement partnership liaison committee.

   B. Hire partnership coordinator.

   C. Plan and write partnership manual.

   D. Plan and implement partnership orientation.

   E. Develop guidelines for recruitment of new partnerships.

III. Community Orientation and Recruitment

   A. Establish media committee.

   B. Create brochure and flyers.

   C. Hold town hall meetings.

   D. Write and publish articles.

   E. Design and record radio and television public service announcements.

   F. Plan and schedule presentations.

   G. Plan opening day ceremony.

   H. Implement publicity campaign according to plan.

IV. Project Implementation

   A. Recruit, enroll, and orient tutors and session assistants.

   B. Recruit, enroll, assign, and orient participants and parents.

EXHIBIT 4.2 *(Continued)*

    C. Hold opening day ceremony.

    D. Provide transportation.

    E. Begin sessions.

    F. Begin parent involvement activities.

    G. Provide ongoing staff development activities.

 V. Project Monitoring and Management

    A. Evaluate project effectiveness.

    B. Provide adequate fiscal oversight.

    C. Maintain facilities and equipment.

    D. Catalog and administer materials.

    E. Coordinate with partnership liaison and oversight council.

    F. Report progress.

    G. Communicate with funding agencies.

    H. Maintain and secure pertinent records.

    I. Ensure project continuation.

    J. Provide for project information and dissemination activities.

    K. Attend required conferences and meetings with funders.

- Yes, the project could be organized differently.
- Yes, the project could be organized better.
- Yes, some items are too simplistic.
- Yes, some items are too complicated.
- Yes, some items are overly vague.
- Yes, some items are overly specific.
- Yes, the quantities seem at times to be too small.
- Yes, the quantities seem at times to be too large.

We could continue, but these few items make the point. Our purpose here is not to explain how to plan and implement an after-school project or any other project. Our purpose is to illustrate the project development process. The process is independent of subject matter content. While the process remains the same, the project can be about anything. The project could be to build a fire and roast marshmallows. It could be to provide medical screenings in rural communities that lack healthcare providers. It could be to combat family violence. It could be to find a cure for the common cold. The subject of the project depends on the mission and goals of your organization.

Project Outline to Goals and Objectives

Goals: General Discussion

Project organization methodology and the names of the various levels within an organizational scheme cause no end of confusion. Rereading New-Quick Homily One in Chapter 2 is appropriate here, because the statements we are calling goals may be called something else by your organization as well as by a grantor. A grantor may ask for outcomes or objectives rather than goals. The key is to realize, as mentioned in Chapter 2, that, perforce, all projects are organized the same. Terminology and definitions differ, but underlying organization remains constant. Exhibit 4.3 illustrates this basic constancy. In Exhibit 4.3, those boxes labeled as steps correspond to our goals.

Every project has an ultimate outcome, which is the result or benefit that is expected after or during the accomplishment of the planned activities. In this book, we call this ultimate outcome a mission, though it can be called many things including goal, objective, outcome, vision, or purpose.

Immediately under the mission fall a number of steps the accomplishment of which will lead to the accomplishment of the mission. These steps we call goals, though others may call them by many other names. This leads us to our definition of a goal, or more correctly, of the second level of project organization.

EXHIBIT 4.3

Project Organization, Two Levels

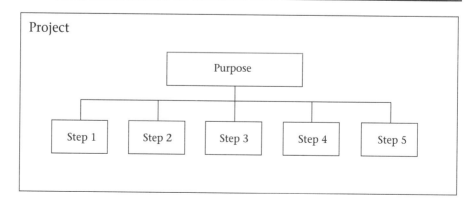

Before we give our plain language definition, however, an additional item is worth discussion. At times, practitioners of project planning point out that there is a difference between an expected outcome and the actions that lead to its accomplishment. Often these practitioners use the word goal to signify the expected outcome thereby leaving out action (activities). They are correct that cause and effect (action and outcome) are two different things and can be discussed separately. In our methodology, however, we combine the two aspects into one coherent statement. For us, a goal contains both action and outcome. With that in mind, here is our plain language definition of a goal.

Goals: Plain Language Definition

Goals are statements of the major steps to accomplish the mission of the project.

Three characteristics are fundamental to the project goals used in grant seeking. Goals must be realistic, measurable, and clear. Realistic means that there is a reasonable chance for success, that the goal can be accomplished, that it is "doable." Measurable means that the extent or degree of success can be assessed quantitatively, with numbers. Clear means that goals are written in plain English without acronyms, jargon, and "bureaucratese" (or as Cheri says, bureaucrap). Clear means that your average peer with average comparable knowledge and experience can read your goals and understand your intentions. Keeping firmly in mind the characteristics of realism, measurability, and clarity, we find in our methodology that goals have five parts:

1. Do what? (action).
2. Using what approach? (methodology or "the how").
3. By when? (time delimited).
4. For how many or by how much? (quantitative measurability).
5. With what result? (outcome or benefits).

Goals: The Tool

To help make the job of creating goals as easy as possible, we use a worksheet similar to the illustration in Exhibit 4.4. A Goal Creation Worksheet for your use is included on the CD-ROM that accompanies this book. The worksheet is labeled as CH0401.

This worksheet, and all the other tools in this book, can be used in two ways. One method is to print the worksheet and write in the spaces provided. The other method is to use your word processing software and data-enter information into the space provided. Both methods have in

EXHIBIT 4.4

 CHO401.DOC

Goal Creation Worksheet

Do What?	Using What Approach (How?)	When?	How Many or How Much?	With What Outcome?

common that you enter information directly into the space provided—one uses pen or pencil, the other a keyboard (or voice recognition software).

To create goals, simply answer each of the questions. Do not use sentences. Phrases and clauses are just fine. Use as few words as possible, but be absolutely sure to include all the information that a reader needs to understand your meaning fully and easily. If more words are necessary, use them. Clarity always has priority over short, though keep in mind that the piling up of many words is not being kind to your reader: the person who is grading your proposal. William Strunk, Jr., in the classic *Elements of Style* gives the ultimate advice on the subject. He tells us, "Omit needless words. . . . Vigorous writing is concise." In no place should one's writing be more concise than when writing goals (and objectives). Finally, eliminate jargon and use acronyms rarely if at all.

Goals: The Source

The source materials for goals are found in your project outline at the Roman numeral level (if you use a numbering methodology that uses Roman numerals). A more general expression of the same thought would be that the source materials for goals are at the highest level in your project outline. Normally, the information in the project outline is insufficient to answer all the questions on the Goal Creation Worksheet. Often, the only item of information you have is the answer to the "Do What?" question. This means that a great deal more creative and careful work (thought and research) is necessary at this stage of the project development process. It probably will pay dividends to involve the team again in an application of the old saw that "two brains are better than one."

To illustrate how a set of completed Goal Creation Worksheets might look, we created the goals for our example project, the Communitywide After-School Program. The goals are shown in Exhibit 4.5. You will notice

EXHIBIT 4.5

Example Project Goals Communitywide After-School Program, Using Tool 0401, Goal Creation Worksheet

Goal I

Do What?	Using What Approach?	When?	How Many or How Much?	With What Outcome?
Establish project organization and logistical foundation.	By fully developing a workable plan of action using accepted management techniques.	During Project Month One.	To accommodate XX participants, XX administrators, XX staff, and XX volunteers.	Project plans are complete and adequate to ensure successful project implementation.

Goal II

Do What?	Using What Approach?	When?	How Many or How Much?	With What Outcome?
Establish partnership organization, coordination, monitoring, and recruitment plan.	By first implementing a partnership liaison committee and then working in concert with the committee, developing a workable plan of action and set of guidelines.	During Project Months One and Two.	To provide a variety of intellectual, academic, physical, and creative activities for XX participants.	Using the skills of partners, significantly enriching the lives of participants and preparing them to realize their potentials to be fully functional, happy, and productive citizens.

(continued)

Exhibit 4.5 *(Continued)*

Goal III

Do What?	Using What Approach?	When?	How Many or How Much?	With What Outcome?
Create print, audio, and video presentation pieces; plan and implement project publicity campaign.	Committee of media partners uses their expertise, materials, and equipment on a volunteer basis.	During Project Months One, Two, and Three.	To recruit XX participants and XX new partners.	Full community backing for the project, and adequate recruitment and partners to successfully carry out the project mission.

Goal IV

Do What?	Using What Approach?	When?	How Many or How Much?	With What Outcome?
Implement project.	Initiate, coordinate, and manage work according to developed action plans.	Project Month Four.	For XX participants.	Youth violence statistics reduce in all areas, gang-related activity decreases, the number of high school graduates increases, the number of dropouts decreases, the number of youth continuing education or training beyond high school increases.

EXHIBIT 4.5 *(Continued)*

Goal V

Do What?	Using What Approach?	When?	How Many or How Much?	With What Outcome?
Manage, administer, track, and evaluate project operation and outcomes.	Perform tasks according to developed action plans and evaluate using best practices XXX.	On-going starting Project Month One.	To accommodate XX participants, XX administrators, XX staff, and XX volunteers in coordination with XX partners.	The project is managed effectively and efficiently, within budget and to accepted management and fiscal standards.

five goals, one more than the four common project components listed in Exhibit 4.1. We have included Goal III, Community Orientation and Recruitment. Because of the vital importance of the communitywide aspects of the proposed project, we have elevated to goal level those activities that focus on informing the community and recruiting community members as project partners.

Objectives: General Discussion

In *The American Heritage Dictionary,* Third Edition, the definition of goal is "the purpose toward which an endeavor is directed, an objective." The definition of objective, in the same dictionary, is "something worked toward or striven for; a goal." The synonym cross-referencing is the crux of the terminology problem. When we take two synonyms and assign specific and different meanings to each one, unless we have the stature and authority to impose our arbitrary definitions on all users of the words, confusion is certain to follow. This is why we go out of our way to reiterate the importance of understanding underlying concepts rather than focusing on the words used as identifying labels.

In our model, objectives are the third level of project organization. Objectives are the actions that are necessary to meet a goal. Exhibit 4.6 illustrates this concept graphically. In Exhibit 4.6 the boxes labeled as substeps correspond to our objectives. This level of organization, directly beneath goals, is often called an action plan. When grantors use this term, it usually looks something like this: "Describe in detail an action plan for the accomplishment of each goal." Too many grant applicants disregard their existing objectives and start creating something new—an action plan—when, in fact, they already have the action plan for accomplishing the goals. An action plan for a goal comprises all the objectives under that goal, perhaps labeled as Action Plan Step One, Two, Three, and so on.

The definition of an objective is abundantly clear. Objectives are statements of the major steps to accomplish goals. Objectives must, like goals, possess three characteristics. Objectives must be realistic, measurable, and clear. Objectives have five parts, four of which are the same as goals:

- *Part One* "Do what?" which is a short statement of the action to be taken.
- *Part Two* "Using what approach?" which is a short description of the methodology, application, or "how to" of the action.
- *Part Three* "By whom?" which is the allocation of responsibility for the completion of the action.

EXHIBIT 4.6

Project Organization, Three Levels

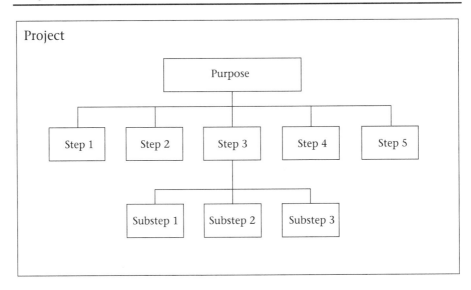

- *Part Four* "By how many or how much?" which is the measurability that must be built into all goals and objectives.
- *Part Five* "With what result?" which is a statement of the expected outcome or benefit.

Objectives: Plain Language Definition

Objectives are statements of the major steps to accomplish goals.

Objectives: The Three Characteristics

- Realistic.
- Measurable.
- Clear.

Objectives: The Five Parts

- Do What?
- Using what approach?
- By whom?
- By how many or how much?
- With what result?

Objectives: The Tool

As with goals, we have included on the CD-ROM an Objective Creation Worksheet, labeled as CH0402. A partial example of CH0402 is illustrated in Exhibit 4.7.

EXHIBIT 4.7

 CH0402.DOC

Objective Creation Worksheet

Do What?	Using What Approach?	By Whom?	By How Many or How Much?	With What Result?

Activity Analysis Worksheet

To get to the details necessary for an effective budget analysis, we use an Activity Analysis Worksheet. You have the goals and objectives in measurable form already developed. Look at your charts and make statements—string the phrases together into a cohesive statement.

For example, Exhibit 4.8 shows Goal I and several objectives, as previously stated in the project outline, along with succinct phrases about them. The following examples are appropriate sentences for Goal I and Objective B:

- *Goal I* During PM 1, establish project organization and logistical foundation through a plan of action to accommodate XX participants so that the plan is complete and adequate to ensure successful project implementation.
- *Objective B* Prepare indoor and outdoor facilities to accommodate project activities, ensuring all regulations and codes are met, by the end of PM 4 so that all sites are ready to fully, adequately, and safely accommodate XX participants.

After you have formed sentences from your charted phrases, then enter them in the appropriate place in the Activity Analysis Worksheet (see Exhibit 4.9, included on CD-ROM as CH0403). The project can be broken down into even smaller steps that we call "activities." They may be called "tasks" or "duties." They are the discrete actions that must be taken to accomplish the objective under the listed goal. List the activities necessary to accomplish the specified objective.

For example, look at Objective B; what activities might be necessary to accomplish that objective?

- Run conduits in three rooms to accommodate computer hookups.
- Pave three basketball half-courts.
- Install appropriate three-prong outlets.
- Resurface the old gym floor.
- Fence the wood playground area.
- Repair light fixtures in two rooms.
- Install more light fixtures in two rooms.
- Install window air conditioner in smallest room.
- Loosen stuck windows in two rooms.
- Clean all rooms.
- Paint all rooms.

EXHIBIT 4.8

Selected Example Objectives for Example Project Goal One

Goal I

Activity	Using What Approach?	When?	How Many or How Much?	With What Outcome?
Establish project organization and logistical foundation.	By fully developing a workable plan of action using accepted management techniques.	During Project Month One.	To accommodate XX participants, XX administrators, XX staff, and XX volunteers.	Project plans are complete and adequate to ensure successful project implementation.

Objective B—Prepare Facilities

Do What?	Using What Approach?	Who Will Do It?	By When?	With What Result?
Prepare indoor and outdoor facilities to accommodate all planned activities.	Ensure all pertinent electrical, building, safety, and locally established regulations and codes are met.	Project coordinator in conjunction with volunteer construction industry professionals and paving contractors.	End of Project Month Four.	All sites are ready to fully, adequately, and safely accommodate XXX students.

(continued)

EXHIBIT 4.8 *(Continued)*

Objective C—Purchase and Install Equipment

Do What?	Using What Approach?	Who Will Do It?	By When?	With What Result?
Purchase and install computer equipment and outdoor recreation equipment where needed.	Ensure all pertinent electrical, building, safety, and locally established regulations and codes are met.	Project coordinator in conjunction with city and county purchasing managers using volunteers for labor.	End of Project Month Six.	There are computers and printers sufficient to accommodate every three students, and at each site, a basketball court, a tennis court, and a volleyball court.

Objective D—Select and Purchase Materials

Do What?	Using What Approach?	Who Will Do It?	By When?	With What Result?
Select and purchase effective and adequate materials to accommodate project activities.	Project coordinator with the head session leader and a representative of each partner organization form a committee to make choices.	Project fiscal officer makes purchases.	End of Project Month Five.	All sites have materials to accommodate project activities and students' individual needs.

EXHIBIT 4.8   (Continued)

Objective E—Hire and Train Staff

Do What?	Using What Approach?	Who Will Do It?	By When?	With What Result?
Hire three head session leaders, nine session assistants, one physical education assistant, one assistant coordinator, one administrative assistant, and one special activities coordinator.	Follow city/county personnel procedures for hiring.	Project coordinator with school superintendent, city and county managers or assistant managers form a review and hiring committee.	Head session leaders, assistant coordinator and administrative assistant by middle of Project Month One—balance of staff by the end of Project Month Six.	Project is adequately staffed to manage XXX participants and administer all planned activities.

Objective H—Develop a Parent Involvement Plan

Do What?	Using What Approach?	Who Will Do It?	By When?	With What Result?
Develop a plan to ensure a wide variety of opportunities for parents to be involved with their children in the project.	Elicit parent input along with professional guidance in developing a working action plan.	Assistant project coordinator, head session leaders, five volunteer parent representatives, and a community facilitator develop the plan.	End of Project Month Three.	A feasible plan is developed to accommodate XXX families.

EXHIBIT 4.9

Activity Analysis Worksheet

Goal I During PM 1, establish project organization and logistical foundation through a plan of action using to accommodate XX participants so that the plan is complete and adequate to ensure successful project implementation.

Objective B Prepare indoor and outdoor facilities to accommodate project activities, ensuring all regulations and codes are met, by the end of PM 4 so that all sites are ready to fully, adequately, and safely accommodate XX participants.

Activity Description	Time Line		Personnel Needed		Facilities Needed		Other Resources Needed	
	Start	End	Describe	Cost	Describe	Cost	Describe	Cost
Run conduits 3 rooms for computers	3/1	3/10	Tech Services, Inc.	$1,250				
Pave 3 basketball half-courts	3/1	4/12	Jones Construct.	3,640				
Install three-prong outlets (22 each)	3/7	3/8	In-house	220				
Resurface gym floor	3/1	4/1	Tom's Paint Co.	4,350				
Fence playground area	3/7	3/14	In-house	750			Posts, Concrete, Wire	$1,400
Repair light fixtures (2 each)	3/14	3/14	In-house	20			Light Units	70
Install light fixtures (5 each)	3/18	3/19	In-house	200			Fixtures, drills	520
Install window air conditioner (1 each)	3/20	3/20	In-house	50			Air conditioner	350
Loosen stuck windows (18 each)	3/21	3/21	In-house	90				
Clean 4 rooms	3/22	3/22	In-house	320			Cleaning products	80
Paint 4 rooms	3/25	4/10	In-house	740			Paint, brush, etc.	424

We enter these activities one by one into the Activity Analysis Worksheet under the "Activity Description" column heading (see Exhibit 4.9). After completing the activity list, then we specify the rest of the details as directed by the other column headings:

- *Time Line, Start and End* This can be days, weeks, months depending on your time line and the task at hand.
- *Personnel Needed, Describe and Cost* Who will perform the activities? This could be in-house personnel or personnel you hire. How much will it cost for the personnel to do the job—in man-hours times cost per hour or a flat cost per job for labor? You need to specify the cost even if full-time in-house personnel will perform the task. Your full-time in-house personnel cost something every time they do an activity. That cost has to be plugged into the project budget somewhere, so the cost for the action must be captured.
- *Facilities Needed, Describe and Cost* The activity must be performed somewhere. If there is a cost for the facility where the activity is being performed, then you must note it. This is especially important if you have to rent a facility or if the activity involves use of electricity, water, and other resources.
- *Other Resources Needed, Describe and Cost* Here is where you list individual items of equipment or materials needed for the activity if itemization is necessary to cost the job.

Round off costs to the nearest dollar. Depending on where you are in your project development process, the costs can be specific and based on actual bids by work groups or they can be good, educated guesstimates. If you are working on your final budget for the proposal, then get exact costs to plug into the worksheet (see Exhibit 4.9).

Wise Guy and Wise Lady

Wise Guy

Okay, okay—now I'm beginning to like this. You've started to give me some concrete way to get the numbers down. I can use the Activity Worksheet—I can see that. But this is sure a lot of work! Too much work.

Wise Lady

Well, there's hope for you yet! Yes, you're right, it's a lot of work. But after you've done it, you have your proposal information for sure, but you also have your Management Plan. Do you see that? If you have done a good job on the project development for your proposal, you also wind up with a comprehensive Management Plan. You're going to have to have one anyway to run the project. Your people are going to have to have guidance to do their jobs. It's work that you will wind up having to do anyway. You're just doing it up-front and using it for two purposes: First, you are crafting the *successful* proposal to acquire project funding, and second, after the contract, the grant award, you can hit the road running with a well-thought-out management plan.

Conclusion

At least 95 percent of the Requests for Proposal we read include the request, "write measurable goals," or "write measurable objectives." This translates to "provide us with the necessary detail to judge whether this project has a chance of success." So writing measurable, detailed goals and objectives is not optional. It is a requirement. But beyond that, measurable goals and objectives are the framework, the foundation, on which the budget figures are determined. If you do not have a solid goal and a detailed objective, you do not know what activities, what tasks, are necessary to accomplish your mission. If you do not know what activities are necessary to accomplish your mission, then how do you know what resources will you need? The answer is that you don't. You as a manager, make decisions about activities all the time. You may not work through a process as described in this and our other books, but the methodology is there in your thought process. When someone comes to you and says, "We need to develop and publish a brochure," you as manager may think, "well, that will cost around $5,000." Where did that figure come from? It came from your experience with brochures. Behind that thought process was knowledge of the cost of design, printing, and distribution. All are activities that must take place to develop and publish a brochure. All activities have costs attached to them. Activities and related costs are what the potential funder focuses on to determine whether to invest in your project. The process we have described here will enable you to provide the funder with correct and adequate information leading to a positive decision about your proposed project.

Key Definition

Measurable

In terms of proposal detail, measurable goals or objectives or strategies—whatever term is used—means something specific. It means who, what, when, how, where, by how much, and for what cost. It is both as simple and as complex as that.

Key Concepts

- The overwhelming majority of projects possess the following four parts or components:
  1. Project preparation and logistics.
  2. Partnership activities.
  3. Implementation with target population.
  4. Monitoring and management.
- Examples are just examples.
- Goals and objectives possess three characteristics:
  1. Realistic
  2. Measurable
  3. Clear
- Goals have five parts:
  1. Do what?
  2. Using what approach?
  3. By when?
  4. For how many or how much?
  5. With what result?

PART II

Developing Your Budgets

Chapter 5

Fundamentals of Project Budgets: Concepts and Terms

"The time has come," the Walrus said
"To talk of many things:
Of shoes—and ships—and sealing wax—
Of cabbages—and kings—
And why the sea is boiling hot—
And whether pigs have wings."

Lewis Carroll, *Through the Looking Glass*

The information in Chapters 2 through 4 amounts to a short course in projects—what they are, where they come from, how they are organized, and how to develop them fully. Because the needs of project activities ultimately drive budget development, getting the project right is the first, but all too often overlooked, step to getting the budget right. The Activity Analysis Worksheet (Exhibit 4.10) provides the vast majority of the information needed to develop the project budget; it is the tool for capturing the raw data needed for the budget.

Project development provides only the beginnings—the basics—for completing a grant project budget. To augment and complete our project development, we need the following additional information: (1) an understanding of budget terms and concepts, and (2) methodologies and tools for capturing and computing the costs of project activities. Chapters 5 and 6 focus on the first requirement, an understanding of budget terms and concepts.

We determine the terms and concepts to define and explain by using a "show and tell" strategy. First we display a budget form or budget instructions from a grant maker, and then we discuss one or more terms and concepts illustrated in the example. Grant makers can be categorized into four groups: federal, foundation, corporate, and state and local. There are examples from each grant source, beginning with federal agencies.

The first example, (Exhibit 5.1) is the Summary Proposal Budget form used by the National Science Foundation. The form is labeled "NSF Form 1030." This is the standard budget form that the National Science Foundation uses in all their grant program application packages. If you apply for an NSF grant, you will have to complete this form.

The Two Types of Budget Costs

The final, bottom-line total of a project budget comprises only two categories of costs: direct and indirect. Starting at the bottom and working up, the budget form in Exhibit 5.1 illustrates the principle. Budget Line L is "Amount of this Request (J)," meaning the amount of the grant request. This amount is equal to the amount on Line J (disregarding the possible subtraction of the Residual Funds of Line K). The amount on Line J is the sum of two items: direct costs (Line H) and indirect costs (Line I).

Defining Direct Costs

Exhibit 5.1 shows that the "Total Direct Costs" of Line H is the sum of specific direct costs (Lines A through G). The costs on Lines A through G include a long list of items such as personnel, equipment, materials, and supplies. The temptation is to define direct costs by the sort of things that are purchased. This approach, as obvious as it may seem, is not sufficient.

In the budget process, the phrase "direct cost" is an accounting term with a precise meaning. Safely and fairly, the term can be called jargon, in the positive sense of a specialized or technical language of a trade or profession, in this case, accounting. Since the language of budgets originates in accounting, it is there that we begin our search for meaning.

Direct Cost: Accountant's Definition

Expenses that can be directly identified with the costing object such as a product and department.[1]

This definition involves three concepts: (1) "expenses," (2) "costing object," and (3) "directly identified."

Expense: Accountant's Definition

Results from or measures the using up of an asset.

---

[1] All Accountant's Definitions are quoted from *Barron's Accounting Handbook*, Joel G. Siegel and Jae K. Shim, Hauppauge, NY: Barron's Educational Series, 1990.

EXHIBIT 5.1

National Science Foundation, Summary Proposal Budget, Form 1030

SUMMARY PROPOSAL BUDGET							FOR NSF USE ONLY		
ORGANIZATION						PROPOSAL NO.		DURATION (MONTHS)	
								Proposed	Granted
PRINCIPAL INVESTIGATOR/PROJECT DIRECTOR						AWARD NO.			
A. SENIOR PERSONNEL: PI/PD, Co-PI's, Faculty and Other Senior Associates (List each separately with title, A.7. show number in brackets)			NSF-Funded Person-months			Funds Requested By Proposer		Funds Granted By NSF (If Different)	
			CAL	ACAD	SUMR				
1.						$		$	
2.									
3.									
4.									
5.									
6. ( ) OTHERS (LIST INDIVIDUALLY ON BUDGET EXPLANATION PAGE)									
7. ( ) TOTAL SENIOR PERSONNEL (1-6)									
B. OTHER PERSONNEL (SHOW NUMBERS IN BRACKETS)									
1. ( ) POST DOCTORAL ASSOCIATES									
2. ( ) OTHER PROFESSIONALS (TECHNICIAN, PROGRAMMER, ETC.)									
3. ( ) GRADUATE STUDENTS									
4. ( ) UNDERGRADUATE STUDENTS									
5. ( ) SECRETARIAL - CLERICAL (IF CHARGED DIRECTLY)									
6. ( ) OTHER									
TOTAL SALARIES AND WAGES (A+B)									
C. FRINGE BENEFITS (IF CHARGED AS DIRECT COSTS)									
TOTAL SALARIES, WAGES AND FRINGE BENEFITS (A+B+C)									
D. EQUIPMENT (LIST ITEM AND DOLLAR AMOUNT FOR EACH ITEM EXCEEDING $5,000.)									
TOTAL EQUIPMENT									
E. TRAVEL 1. DOMESTIC (INCL. CANADA, MEXICO AND U.S. POSSESSIONS)									
2. FOREIGN									
F. PARTICIPANT SUPPORT COSTS									
1. STIPENDS $									
2. TRAVEL									
3. SUBSISTENCE									
4. OTHER									
( ) TOTAL PARTICIPANT COSTS									
G. OTHER DIRECT COSTS									
1. MATERIALS AND SUPPLIES									
2. PUBLICATION COSTS/DOCUMENTATION/DISSEMINATION									
3. CONSULTANT SERVICES									
4. COMPUTER SERVICES									
5. SUBAWARDS									
6. OTHER									
TOTAL OTHER DIRECT COSTS									
H. TOTAL DIRECT COSTS (A THROUGH G)									
I. INDIRECT COSTS (SPECIFY RATE AND BASE)									
TOTAL INDIRECT COSTS									
J. TOTAL DIRECT AND INDIRECT COSTS (H + I)									
K. RESIDUAL FUNDS (IF FOR FURTHER SUPPORT OF CURRENT PROJECT SEE GPG II.D.7.j.)									
L. AMOUNT OF THIS REQUEST (J) OR (J MINUS K)						$		$	
M. COST-SHARING: PROPOSED LEVEL $			AGREED LEVEL IF DIFFERENT $						

PI/PD TYPED NAME & SIGNATURE*	DATE	FOR NSF USE ONLY		
		INDIRECT COST RATE VERIFICATION		
ORG. REP. TYPED NAME & SIGNATURE*	DATE	Date Checked	Date of Rate Sheet	Initials-ORG

NSF Form 1030 (7/95) *Supersedes All Previous Editions*   *SIGNATURES REQUIRED ONLY FOR REVISED BUDGET (GPG III.B)

So, "using up an asset" results in expense. Also, the using up of an asset can be measured, yielding the size of the expense. Now, if we could know for sure what an asset is, we might have a complete concept.

Asset: Accountant's Definition

Economic resource that is expected to provide benefits . . . assets are expressed in money or are convertible into money.

So, an asset or "economic resource" can be many things, but whatever form the asset takes, it can be expressed in or convertible into money. For now, we will use the simplest definition—money, cash, currency, legal tender, filthy lucre, moolah. Translated into plain language, therefore, the expenses in accountant's definition of direct cost become "spending money" or "money spent."

The second accountant's concept is "costing object." The most direct path may be through the accounting term "cost allocation." Cost allocation, or more inclusively, cost accounting, is the accountant's term for the process explored in this book, creation of a project budget.

Cost Allocation: Accountant's Definition

Identification of costs with cost objectives . . . There are basically three aspects of cost allocation: (1) choosing the object of costing. Examples are products, processes, jobs, or departments; (2) choosing and accumulating the costs that relate to the object of costing . . . and (3) choosing a method of identifying (2) with (1).

Add "project" and "project activity" to the examples of costing objects in item (1) in the preceding definition, and the second concept needed for a plain language definition of direct costs is complete.

What remains is to clarify "directly identified." The meaning of this phrase coincides with the meanings of the words. "Directly" (in a direct line or manner; straight; without anyone or anything intervening) "identified" (determine identity by ascertaining various characteristics) are linked to mean "define the (financial) characteristics that come straight from the costing object."

Putting all our plain language parts together, we arrive at the following definition of direct cost:

Direct Cost: Plain Language Definition

Money spent (or to be spent) that can be tracked straight to a project activity.

Using money in the place of expenses simplifies the definition, but it also introduces a lack of inclusiveness. As discussed later, resources (assets) other than money can be expended in the accomplishment of project activities. This simplified, plain language definition provides a starting point from which the more precise accountant's definition can be understood fully.

Defining Indirect Costs

On NSF Form 1030 (Exhibit 5.1), indirect costs are shown on Line I. This line item directs us to "specify rate and base." The mathematical concepts and formulas are explained later. For now, the principle is being stressed, not the computation of an amount.

Indirect Costs: Accountant's Definition

Expense that is difficult to trace directly to a specific costing object.

The previous discussion about direct costs now pays off. We understand a costing object. It is our project or one of our project activities. We understand that an expense is (incompletely) spending money. All that remains is to understand the specific meaning of "difficult to trace directly." This is easy, since the phrase means exactly what it says. Paraphrasing, it means hard to follow in a straight line.

Understanding direct costs is relatively simple since the concept itself is "direct." However, understanding indirect costs is more difficult since the concept is by its very nature "indirect." An additional official definition, this time from the federal government, offers greater detail.

Indirect Costs: Federal Government's Definition

Those costs that are incurred for common or joint objectives and therefore cannot be identified readily and specifically with a particular sponsored project, program, or activity but are nevertheless necessary to the operations of the organization. For example, the costs of operating and maintaining facilities, depreciation, and administrative salaries are generally treated as indirect costs.[2]

A problem often occurs when comparing an accountant's definition with the definition of the same term provided by the federal government. The root of the difficulty is that the federal government does not use standard accounting practices: Its financial practices are unique to itself. An example is the inclusion of depreciation as an indirect cost in the preceding definition. The depreciation on an item used exclusively by or for

---

[2] All Federal Government's Definitions are quoted from *Grants Policy Directive System, Grants Policy Directive 1.02, HHS Transmittal 94.01 (3/30/94)*, U.S. Department of Health and Human Services.

a particular costing object can be directly traced and, therefore, by our accountant's definition—and correctly so—is a direct cost.

It will be necessary to overlook such inconsistencies as we move along. However, it will be just as necessary to be aware of them because they can make a difference in our budget when we apply to a federal agency for a grant. Just keep in mind that the federal government operates in a financial world all its own. When applying for a grant from the federal government, play by their rules. When applying for a grant from the private sector, play by its rules. Or, as Country Boy might say, "Them's that's got's the money makes the rules." And as Coach might say, "To play the game to win, know the rules."

Returning to the discussion of indirect costs—when you hire a person to manage a grant project (project director), her salary is a direct cost because the salary "can be directly identified with the costing object," the project.

After you welcome the project director aboard, you provide her, we certainly hope, with a desk and chair and lights that come on when a switch is flipped. You provide her with bathroom facilities, the use of a telephone and fax, and perhaps even one of those "magic" wastebaskets that is empty every morning though it has trash in it every evening when she goes home. Perhaps she has a place to park her car. Someone generates a paycheck for her every so often. Perhaps your organization provides healthcare insurance. If so, the paperwork is handled somehow.

The big question is, how much does it cost to do these things? The honest answer is, you do not know. You know it costs something. A simple mental experiment will prove that it costs something. To start the experiment, assume that your organization provides the preceding items to five employees. Next, hire five more employees and provide them with the same items. Finally, will the amount it costs your organization to provide the items remain the same or increase with the addition of the five new employees? It does not take an accountant to know that the cost will increase. The exact increase might be difficult to calculate, but that an increase occurs is certain.

The costs are spread out among staff members working on a variety of tasks. The amount contributed to the whole varies from staff member to staff member. One may seldom use the fax, while another sends and receives many faxes. These are indirect costs—"expense that is difficult to trace directly to a specific costing object."

Example of Direct and Indirect Costs

Turning to practical aspects of direct and indirect costs, we begin with an example summary budget, shown in Exhibit 5.2. Remember, this is not a budget but rather the summary of a budget.

EXHIBIT 5.2

Example Summary Budget

Project Budget Summary

A. Direct Costs	Requested	Support from Other Sources	Total
1. Salaries (professional and clerical)	$21,000.00	$15,000.00	$36,000.00
2. Employee Benefits	4,200.00	3,000.00	7,200.00
3. Employee Travel	3,000.00	0.00	3,000.00
4. Equipment (purchase)	15,500.00	4,300.00	19,800.00
5. Materials and Supplies	0.00	1,600.00	1,600.00
6. Consultants and Contracts	5,500.00	0.00	5,500.00
7. Other (equip. rental, printing, etc.)	1,400.00	8,500.00	9,900.00
8. Total Direct Costs	50,600.00	32,400.00	83,000.00
B. Indirect Costs	4,352.40	3,484.40	7,836.80
C. TOTALS	$54,952.40	$35,884.40	$90,836.80

Lines A1 through A7 show the individual totals of the various direct costs. Line A8 shows the total for all direct costs. Line B shows the indirect costs. Line C shows the project totals, the sum of direct and indirect costs.

Most of the summary budget of Exhibit 5.2 is easy to understand. The amounts on Line A8 are the sum of the amounts on Lines A1 through A7. The amounts on Line C are the sum of the amounts on Lines A8 and B. So far so good, but, what calculation provided the amounts shown on Line B, Indirect Costs?

Calculation of Indirect Costs

Look back at Line I on NSF Form 1030 in Exhibit 5.1. In that line item, we are directed to "specify rate and base." These two items—rate and base—are the basis for the calculation of indirect costs. Once we understand them, we can apply the formula to develop our budget.

Indirect Cost Rate. The official definition of indirect cost rate is "the ratio, expressed as a percentage, of an organization's total indirect costs to its direct cost base."[3] This definition gives a great deal more than we need to know. The single part of the definition that is important to us is that the indirect cost rate is a percentage. The source of the percentage is your organization's financial people or accountant.

Indirect Cost Base. The official definition of indirect cost base is "the accumulated direct costs (normally either total direct salaries and wages or total direct costs exclusive of any extraordinary or distorting expenditures) that are used to distribute indirect costs to individual Federal grant awards and programs."[4] This definition states that an indirect cost base normally is one of two amounts. The first is "total direct salaries and wages." No doubt this definition is technically correct; however, several decades of experience in grant seeking have taught us that an indirect cost base is seldom (if ever) composed solely of salaries and wages.

The second definition of indirect cost base is "total direct costs exclusive of any extraordinary or distorting expenditures." Most definitely, this is normal. Except for the notable exception discussed, this is the way an indirect cost base is always calculated. Now, all we need to know is what constitutes "extraordinary or distorting expenditures." That has a mysterious and obscure sound, but, in the vast majority of cases, it is quite simple. It means the costs of equipment. We now have sufficient information to compute an indirect cost base, as shown in Formula 5.1.

Formula 5.1: Indirect Cost Base

Indirect Cost Base = Total Direct Costs − Equipment Costs

Formula 5.1 is used when a grant maker requires that you show your indirect cost base, as the National Science Foundation does on Line I of NSF Form 1030 in (Exhibit 5.1). However, many grant makers do not require equipment costs to be subtracted from total direct costs to arrive at the indirect cost base. For these grant makers, the total direct costs is the indirect cost base.

Before going one step further, we must introduce the Grant Seeker's Prime Directive—the one unalterable, axiomatic maxim (purposefully redundant for maximum emphasis) that takes precedence over all else:

Grant Seeker's Prime Directive

Follow directions.

---

[3] Ibid.

[4] Ibid.

It does not matter what you read in this book. It does not matter what a world-famous and highly paid consultant tells you. It does not matter what your successful colleague tells you. It does not even matter what your boss tells you (at least concerning the correct way to present information in a grant proposal). The *only* absolutely positively correct source of information for how to "get it right" is the grant maker. Therefore, regardless of the question, find out how the grant maker wants it done, and do it that way, exactly that way—follow directions.

With the Grant Seeker's Prime Directive firmly in mind, we will say that rule of thumb is to apply Formula 5.1 in all grant applications to federal sources, but not for nonfederal grant sources that allow indirect costs. Generally, when a nonfederal grant source allows indirect costs (many, if not most, do not), the indirect cost base will be simply the total direct costs.

We now know where to obtain the indirect cost rate—from our financial office or accountant. We also now know how to compute the indirect cost base by subtracting the cost of equipment from total direct costs or, if appropriate, using the total direct costs amount itself. We are now prepared to compute indirect costs. That calculation is done with Formula 5.2.

Formula 5.2: Indirect Cost

Indirect Cost = Indirect Rate × Indirect Cost Base

Example Calculation: Indirect Costs.

For the example calculation of indirect cost, we use the amounts from the "Requested" column of the example summary budget (Exhibit 5.2).

Formulas

Indirect Cost Base = Total Direct Costs − Equipment Costs
Indirect Cost = Indirect Rate × Indirect Cost Base

Amounts

Total Direct Costs $50,600.00
Equipment Costs $15,500.00
Indirect Rate 12.4%

Substitute and Calculate

Indirect Cost Base = Total Direct Costs − Equipment Costs
Indirect Cost Base = ($50,600.00) − ($15,500.00)
Indirect Cost Base = $35,100.00

Substitute and Calculate

Indirect Cost = Indirect Rate × Indirect Cost Base
Indirect Cost = (12.4%) × ($35,100.00)
Indirect Cost = $4,352.40

Indirect Cost Calculation Tool

On the CD-ROM that accompanies this book, CH0501 is a small spreadsheet that will computer-calculate indirect cost. The calculation of indirect costs is one of many functions integrated into the larger budget tool spreadsheets discussed and illustrated in later chapters. CH0501, however, has the single purpose of calculating indirect costs. Exhibit 5.3 illustrates the five-step process. You must complete Steps 1, 2, and 4 by entering the appropriate amounts, and then CH0501 completes Steps 3 and 5 for you.

Computing indirect costs is the first calculation to be explained and illustrated in this book. However, that is not when the calculation will occur during actual budget development. This will be one of the final calculations made. After all, the amount to be entered in Step 1 of the calculation is Total Direct Costs, a figure at which one arrives only after totaling the vast majority, (in most cases all), of the amounts that make up a project budget.

A Variety of Direct Costs

Continuing with our show-and-tell strategy, Exhibit 5.4 shows page 4 of PHS-398, Application for a Public Health Service Grant. As stated at the top of the form, this page is the "detailed budget for initial budget period" and contains "direct costs only." Chapter 6 is dedicated to identifying and

EXHIBIT 5.3

 CH0501.XLS

Indirect Cost Calculator

Step 1	
Enter Total Direct Costs	$50,600.00
Step 2	
Enter Total Equipment Costs	$15,500.00
Step 3	
Tool will compute Indirect Base	$35,100.00
Step 4	
Enter Indirect Cost Rate	12.4
Step 5	
Tool will compute Indirect Costs	$ 4,352.40

EXHIBIT 5.4

Public Health Service Grant Budget Form PHS-398, Page 4

DD   Principal Investigator/Program Director (Last, first, middle): _____

DETAILED BUDGET FOR INITIAL BUDGET PERIOD DIRECT COSTS ONLY					FROM		THROUGH

PERSONNEL (Applicant organization only)		TYPE APPT. (months)	% EFFORT ON PROJ.	INST. BASE SALARY	DOLLAR AMOUNT REQUESTED (omit cents)		
NAME	ROLE ON PROJECT				SALARY REQUESTED	FRINGE BENEFITS	TOTALS
	Principal Investigator						
	SUBTOTALS ——————————→						

CONSULTANT COSTS	
EQUIPMENT (Itemize)	
SUPPLIES (Itemize by category)	
TRAVEL	
PATIENT CARE COSTS	INPATIENT
	OUTPATIENT
ALTERATIONS AND RENOVATIONS (Itemize by category)	
OTHER EXPENSES (Itemize by category)	

SUBTOTAL DIRECT COSTS FOR INITIAL BUDGET PERIOD	$
CONSORTIUM/CONTRACTUAL COSTS	DIRECT COSTS
	INDIRECT COSTS
TOTAL DIRECT COSTS FOR INITIAL BUDGET PERIOD (Item 7a, Face Page) ————→	$

PHS 398 (Rev. 5/95)   (Form Page 4) Page _____   DD
Number pages consecutively at the bottom throughout the application. Do not use suffixes such as 3a, 3b..

defining all possible direct costs, so the goal here is not completeness, but rather to introduce a few varieties of direct costs.

Scanning down the left side of Exhibit 5.4 yields the following varieties of direct costs:

Personnel	Alterations and renovations
Consultant costs	Other expenses
Equipment	Consortium direct costs
Supplies	Consortium indirect costs
Travel	Contractual direct costs
Inpatient care	Contractual indirect costs
Outpatient care	

On this budget form, the indirect costs incurred by consortium members and contractors are considered to be direct costs for the purposes of the grant request. "But wait," someone smart and thoughtful might suggest, "The bottom line total on this form might be the total project budget, not the grant request; we learned in Chapter 1 that they are not necessarily the same amount." Yes, we did learn that, and yes it could be, except we have a way of knowing positively. The direction in the bottom line is to place this total in Item 7a on the Face Page, which is Page 1 of form PHS-398. If we inspect Item 7a of the Face Page, illustrated in Exhibit 5.5, we find that Item 7a is indeed "Direct Costs."

Item 7b in Exhibit 5.5 is labeled "Total Costs." Remember the principle learned earlier in this chapter that a final budget total contains only two types of costs, direct and indirect. Therefore, if the amount of 7b (Total Costs) is greater than that of 7a (Direct Costs), the difference can be only one thing—indirect costs.

Questions and Answers

1. Q: What would be the conclusion to draw if Item 7b is the same as (equal to) Item 7a?

A: The applicant is not requesting grant funds to cover indirect costs.

2. Q: Going back to those indirect costs from consortium members and contractors, how can a grant maker get away with calling them direct costs?

A: A corollary of the Prime Directive—Follow Directions—is, "A grant maker can do what ever it wants."

3. Q: What is the difference between "alterations" and "renovations"?

A: To alter a thing is to change it, make it different. To renovate a thing is to revive it, in this case, probably by repairing or remodeling.

EXHIBIT 5.5

Face Page (Page 1) of Public Health Service Form PHS-398

AA

Form Approved Through 9/30/97
OMB No. 0925-0001

Department of Health and Human Services
Public Health Service

Grant Application

Follow instructions carefully.
Do not exceed character length restrictions indicated on sample.

LEAVE BLANK—FOR PHS USE ONLY.		
Type	Activity	Number
Review Group		Formerly
Council/Board *(Month, Year)*		Date Received

1. TITLE OF PROJECT

2. RESPONSE TO SPECIFIC REQUEST FOR APPLICATIONS OR PROGRAM ANNOUNCEMENT ☐ NO ☐ YES *(If "Yes," state number and title)*
Number: Title:

3. PRINCIPAL INVESTIGATOR/PROGRAM DIRECTOR

3a. NAME *(Last, first, middle)*	3b. DEGREE(S)	3c. SOCIAL SECURITY NO.

3d. POSITION TITLE   **3e. MAILING ADDRESS** *(Street, city, state, zip code)*

3f. DEPARTMENT, SERVICE, LABORATORY, OR EQUIVALENT

3g. MAJOR SUBDIVISION

3h. TELEPHONE AND FAX *(Area code, number and extension)*
TEL:
FAX: **E-MAIL ADDRESS:**

4. HUMAN SUBJECTS	4a. If "Yes," Exemption no. or		5. VERTEBRATE ANIMALS	5a. If "Yes," IACUC approval date	5b. Animal welfare assurance no.
☐ No ☐ Yes	IRB approval date	4b. Assurance of compliance no. { Full IRB or Expedited Review	☐ No ☐ Yes		

6. DATES OF PROPOSED PERIOD OF SUPPORT *(month, day, year—MM/DD/YY)*		7. COSTS REQUESTED FOR INITIAL BUDGET PERIOD		8. COSTS REQUESTED FOR PROPOSED PERIOD OF SUPPORT	
From	Through	7a. Direct Costs ($)	7b. Total Costs ($)	8a. Direct Costs ($)	8b. Total Costs ($)

9. APPLICANT ORGANIZATION
Name
Address

10. TYPE OF ORGANIZATION
Public: → ☐ Federal ☐ State ☐ Local
Private: → ☐ Private Nonprofit
Forprofit: → ☐ General ☐ Small Business

11. ORGANIZATIONAL COMPONENT CODE

12. ENTITY IDENTIFICATION NUMBER	Congressional District

13. ADMINISTRATIVE OFFICIAL TO BE NOTIFIED IF AWARD IS MADE	14. OFFICIAL SIGNING FOR APPLICANT ORGANIZATION
Name	Name
Title	Title
Address	Address
Telephone	Telephone
FAX	FAX
E-Mail Address	E-Mail Address

15. PRINCIPAL INVESTIGATOR/PROGRAM DIRECTOR ASSURANCE: I certify that the statements herein are true, complete and accurate to the best of my knowledge. I am aware that any false, fictitious, or fraudulent statements or claims may subject me to criminal, civil, or administrative penalties. I agree to accept responsibility for the scientific conduct of the project and to provide the required progress reports if a grant is awarded as a result of this application.	SIGNATURE OF PI / PD NAMED IN 3a. *(In ink. "Per" signature not acceptable.)*	DATE
16. APPLICANT ORGANIZATION CERTIFICATION AND ACCEPTANCE: I certify that the statements herein are true, complete and accurate to the best of my knowledge, and accept the obligation to comply with Public Health Service terms and conditions if a grant is awarded as a result of this application. I am aware that any false, fictitious, or fraudulent statements or claims may subject me to criminal, civil, or administrative penalties.	SIGNATURE OF OFFICIAL NAMED IN 14. *(In ink. "Per" signature not acceptable.)*	DATE

PHS 398 (Rev. 5/95)   Face Page   AA

Because they are bundled together in the same line item, however, any differences cannot matter much. If it did matter, however, and if a clear and unequivocal answer cannot be found, there is one and only one valid source of information—the grant maker. Query the grant maker when questions arise.

An Old Standby: SF-424

Standard Form 424 (a double-sided form), pictured in Exhibits 5.6 and 5.7, is a remnant of the effort begun in the 1970s during President Carter's administration to reduce the amount of paperwork generated by the federal government. The idea behind SF-424 was to create a single budget form to be used by all applicants to any federal agency. The deeply

EXHIBIT 5.6

U.S. Office of Management and Budget, Standard Form 424A, Page 1

BUDGET INFORMATION — Non-Construction Programs

OMB Approval No. 0348-0044

SECTION A - Budget Summary

Grant Program Function or Activity (a)	Catalog of Federal Domestic Assistance Number (b)	Estimated Unobligated Funds		New or Revised Budget		
		Federal (c)	Non-Federal (d)	Federal (e)	Non-Federal (f)	Total (g)
1 NTIA/TIIAP	11.552	$	$	$	$	$
2						
3						
4						
5 Totals		$	$	$	$	$

SECTION B - BUDGET CATEGORIES

6. Object Class Categories	GRANT PROGRAM, FUNCTION, ACTIVITY				Total (5)
	(1) FEDERAL	(2) NON-FEDERAL	(3)	(4)	
a. Personnel	$	$	$	$	$
b. Fringe Benefits					
c. Travel					
d. Equipment					
e. Supplies					
f. Contractual					
g. Construction					
h. Other					
i. Total Direct Charges (sum of 6a-6h)					
j. Indirect Charges					
k. TOTALS (sum of 6I and 6j)	$	$	$	$	$
7 Program income	$	$	$	$	$

Previous Edition Usable

Authorized for Local Reproduction

Standard Form 424A (4-92)
Prescribed by OMB Circular A-102

EXHIBIT 5.7

U.S. Office of Management and Budget, Standard Form 424A, Page 2

SECTION C - NON-FEDERAL SOURCES				
(a) Grant Program	(b) Applicant	(c) State	(d) Other Sources	(e) Totals
8. NTIA/TIIAP	$	$	$	$
9.				
10.				
11.				
12. TOTALS (sum of lines 8 - 11)	$	$	$	$

SECTION D - FORECASTED CASH NEEDS					
13. Federal	Total First Year	1st Quarter	2nd Quarter	3rd Quarter	4th Quarter
	$	$	$	$	$
14. Non-Federal					
15. TOTAL (sum of lines 13 and 14)	$	$	$	$	$

SECTION E - BUDGET ESTIMATES OF FEDERAL FUNDS NEEDED FOR BALANCE OF THE PROJECT				
(a) Grant Program	FUTURE FUNDING PERIODS (Years)			
	(b) First	(c) Second	(d) Third	(e) Fourth
16. NTIA/TIIAP	$	$	$	$
17.				
18.				
19.				
20. TOTALS (sum of lines 16 - 19)	$	$	$	$

SECTION F - OTHER BUDGET INFORMATION	
21. Direct Charges:	22. Indirect Charges:
23. Remarks	

Authorized for Local Reproduction   Standard Form 424A (4-92) Page

---

ingrained (almost genetic) belief that one's own organization is unique, totally different from others and badly misunderstood by all outsiders, doomed the effort to ultimate failure. After peaking in the late 1980s, the number of federal grant programs that use SF-424 has slowly declined.

Thoughts on Budget Totals

In five areas of SF-424, shown in Exhibits 5.6 and 5.7, information is requested about both federal and nonfederal expenditures:

1. Section A—Budget Summary: Estimated Unobligated Funds (see columns (c) and (d)).

2. Section A—Budget Summary: New or Revised Budget (see columns (e) and (f)).

3. Section B—Budget Categories (see columns (1) and (2)).

4. Section C—Nonfederal Sources.

5. Section D—Forecasted Cash Needs (see lines (13) and (14)).

Through the design of SF-424, the Office of Management and Budget, creator of the form, demonstrates that the budget total for a project or program is, or should be, composed of more than just the amount of a grant. This fundamental concept was introduced in Chapter 1.

Project Revenue

A most interesting project budget concept is introduced in Line 7 of SF-424. (see Exhibit 5.6). This line item provides a place to put the amount of revenue that operation of the project is anticipated to generate. A grant project can generate revenue, produce income, earn money. As strange as the concept may seem, especially to educators in the public school system, many grant programs do generate income, at times substantial income.

A common revenue generator for healthcare projects is performance of procedures covered by Medicare or Medicaid. Other examples of revenue generation are event ticket sales, sales of products or services, sliding scale fees for services charged on an "ability to pay" basis (often with a lowest fee of zero), and regular fund-raising events or campaigns built in as project activities.

Including activities to generate revenue in a project can provide important help with the often troublesome (for applicants) but always very important (to grant makers) project continuation, also called sustainment and institutionalization. For a complete discussion of continuation issues and approaches, see Chapter 17 of *Grant Winner's Toolkit: Project Management and Evaluation.*

Project revenue creates certain problems in budget development. Budget thinking is almost totally oriented toward expenses and costs, funds flowing out, being spent. Anticipating that funds will flow into the project can cause confusion about how to handle their entry into the budget. Chapter 11 of this book contains a more detailed discussion of project revenue and its place in a project budget.

Project Partners

Section C of Standard Form 424 (shown in Exhibit 5.7) provides a grant-making agency a place to ask applicants to show the amounts of nonfederal funding for a proposed project that are to come from the applicant, from state sources, and from other sources. "Other" sources are usually project partners. Column (e) totals the contribution of the nonfederal sources.

Several grant programs of the National Science Foundation use a modified NSF Form 1030 to obtain similar information. The modified form utilizes the same line items as the original NSF Form 1030, but includes new columns for the applicant's contributions to the project budget along with the contributions from two project partners. Two additional columns provide space to show the partner totals and the overall project totals. Exhibit 5.8 illustrates this concept by modifying the Example Summary Budget we used throughout this book. The addition of a new top row with column identifiers (lower-case letters (a) through (f) enables us to generate simple formulas to explain the derivation of the totals.

The figures in column (e), Partner Totals, are the sum of the amounts in columns (b), (c), and (d). The figures in column (f), Project Totals, are the sum of the amounts in columns (a) and (e). Expressing these relations as formulas yields the following for the Summary Budget Form of Exhibit 5.8:

$$(e) = (b) + (c) + (d)$$

and

$$(f) = (a) + (e)$$

EXHIBIT 5.8

Example Summary Budget

Project Budget Summary

	(a) Grant Request	(b) Applicant Share	(c) Partner One	(d) Partner Two	(e) Partner Totals	(f) Project Totals
A. Direct Costs						
1. Salaries						
2. Employee Benefits						
3. Employee Travel						
4. Equipment						
5. Materials and Supplies						
6. Consultants/Contracts						
7. Other						
8. Total Direct Costs						
B. Indirect Costs						
C. TOTALS						

The number of competitive project grant programs that require some form of partnership is so close to 100 percent that finding a program without a partnering component is practically impossible. Such programs are the unicorns of the grant field. Despite the ubiquity of partnering, many grant seekers are unclear about the concept.

For the purposes of grant projects, a partner is an individual or organization that provides concrete assistance with project activities. People and organizations that rave about the great job you do are not partners. They are cheerleaders. People and organizations that appreciate what you do are not partners. They are supporters. People and organizations that use your services are not partners. They are members of your target population.

Partners do things; they perform. Partners contribute; they give time, money, resources, and expertise. Partners participate; they work. Partners are active; they get things done. And, here is a big one. Partners are not paid. If an individual or organization is paid for its participation, it is a vendor or a contractor, not a partner.

Many organizations like to talk about establishing partnership with the people who are beneficiaries of grant project services. Establishing such relations is an exemplary idea. The abysmal lack of success of many social programs can be traced to the failure to include the target population when planning the program. In the language of grants, however, working closely with your target population does not make them a project partner. They remain the target population.

Many companies (vendors) like to talk about establishing partnership with grant projects. What the companies actually want to do is use grant funding to purchase their goods or services. While there is absolutely nothing wrong with that, to reiterate, if a company is paid, it is not a partner. It is a vendor or a contractor. Discounted goods and services do not constitute partnering. Donated goods or services constitute partnership.

Talking is not working. In fact, mistaking talking about work with actual work is one reason so little sometimes seems to get done. An individual or organization that is willing to talk to you is probably a time waster, not a partner. The only instance in which talk (advice) has worth and in which its provider is considered a partner is when the talk has a true, marketplace value. Such talk (advice or consultation) comes from individuals or organizations with knowledge, skills, and experience related to some aspect of the project you are implementing.

Looking with "New Eyes"

The Department of Education recently received approval from Office of Management and Budget (OMB) to begin using its newly created ED Form

524 as its own unique grant application budget form. The form is shown in Exhibits 5.9 and 5.10. Comparison of Section A of the new ED-524 (Exhibit 5.9) with Section B of the old SF-424 (Exhibit 5.6) shows remarkable similarities. The budget category Training Stipends (Line 11) has been added to the ED-524, which seems completely appropriate for a federal agency with education in its title.

An interesting aspect of its addition merits further comment. To begin, the note in Line 9 (see Exhibit 5.9) informs that Total Direct Costs is the sum of line items 1 through 8, thus excluding Training Stipends (Line 11). When applying the process described earlier in this chapter to calculate indirect costs, Training Stipends will not be included in the indirect cost base. The Department of Education has decided that they are "extraordinary or distorting expenditures" and, therefore, should be excluded from the indirect cost base.

The rationale for excluding Training Stipends from the indirect cost base has not been explained by the Department of Education. The most reasonable purpose for the exclusion is to reduce the amount expended by

EXHIBIT 5.9

Department of Education Budget Information Form 524, Page 1

U.S. DEPARTMENT OF EDUCATION BUDGET INFORMATION NONCONSTRUCTION PROGRAMS	OMB Control No. 1880—0538 **Expiration Date: 10/31/99**

Name of Institution/Organization	Applicants requesting funding for only one year should complete the column under "Project Year 1." Applicants requesting funding for multi-year grants should complete all applicable columns. Please read all instructions before completing form.

SECTION A - BUDGET SUMMARY
U.S. DEPARTMENT OF EDUCATION FUNDS

Budget Categories	Project Year 1 (a)	Project Year 2 (b)	Project Year 3 (c)	Project Year 4 (d)	Project Year 5 (e)	Total (f)
1. Personnel						
2. Fringe Benefits						
3. Travel						
4. Equipment						
5. Supplies						
6. Contractual						
7. Construction						
8. Other						
9. Total Direct Costs (lines 1-8)						
10. Indirect Costs						
11. Training Stipends						
12. Total Costs (lines 9-11)						

ED FORM NO. 524

EXHIBIT 5.10

Department of Education Budget Information Form 524, Page 2

Name of Institution/Organization			Applicants requesting funding for only one year should complete the column under "Project Year 1." Applicants requesting funding for multi-year grants should complete all applicable columns. Please read all instructions before completing form.			
SECTION B - BUDGET SUMMARY **NON-FEDERAL FUNDS**						
Budget Categories	Project Year 1 (a)	Project Year 2 (b)	Project Year 3 (c)	Project Year 4 (d)	Project Year 5 (e)	Total (f)
1. Personnel						
2. Fringe Benefits						
3. Travel						
4. Equipment						
5. Supplies						
6. Contractual						
7. Construction						
8. Other						
9. Total Direct Costs (lines 1-8)						
10. Indirect Costs						
11. Training Stipends						
12. Total Costs (lines 9-11)						
SECTION C - OTHER BUDGET INFORMATION (see instructions)						

ED FORM NO. 524

the Department for indirect cost reimbursement. The recent heavy emphasis placed on professional development in Department of Education grant programs has substantially increased spending on Training Stipends by grant programs. Excluding this cost from the indirect cost calculation would, therefore, create significant savings for the Department.

The accuracy of the preceding supposition is not of much importance. Of great importance, however, is learning to look at budget forms with new eyes, learning to interpret and understand the financial consequences of a particular arrangement, such as excluding Training Stipends from Total Direct Costs.

One reason for including so many example budget forms in this chapter is to provide the simple, but useful and powerful experience of seeing them, looking at them—seeing the wide variety of formats in which the same information can be requested.

Small Form Does Not Mean Small Money

So far, all the budget forms have been from federal grant programs, and they all have been fairly complicated. So as not to leave you with the impression that all federal budget forms are horribly complex, we include the example in Exhibit 5.11. This is the budget form used by the Technology Innovation Challenge Grant Program out of the U.S. Department of Education. Exhibit 5.11 might appear familiar to you. It should. The example budget forms in Exhibits 5.2 and 5.8 derive from this original.

The budget form shown in Exhibit 5.11 seems so simple and straightforward that it might be tempting to think that a program that uses such

EXHIBIT 5.11

U.S. Budget Form, Department of Education, Technology Challenge Grant Program, Page 1

5 Year Budget Summary
(YEARS 4 AND 5 ARE ON THE BACK OF THIS FORM)

Budget Item	YEAR 1				YEAR 2		
	Requested	Support by LEA or other sources	Total		Requested	Support by LEA or other sources	Total
A. Direct Costs							
1. Salaries (professional & clerical)							
2. Employee Benefits							
3. Employee Travel							
4. Equipment (purchase)							
5. Materials & Supplies							
6. Consultants & Contracts							
7. Other (equip. rental, printing, etc)							
8. Total Direct Costs							
B. Indirect Costs							
TOTALS							

Budget Item	YEAR 3		
	Requested	Support by LEA or other sources	Total
A. Direct Costs			
1. Salaries (professional & clerical)			
2. Employee Benefits			
3. Employee Travel			
4. Equipment (purchase)			
5. Materials & Supplies			
6. Consultants & Contracts			
7. Other (equip. rental, printing, etc)			
8. Total Direct Costs			
B. Indirect Costs			
TOTALS			

Note: Items 1 through 7 are budget line subtotals that are to be described in the Detailed Budget.

a basic, uncomplicated form must make small grants. After all, getting large amounts of money requires completing complicated budget forms. Everyone knows that. Like much that "everyone knows," however, this is wrong. The Technology Innovation Challenge Grant Program makes grants of up to $1,500,000 a year. The form illustrated in Exhibit 5.11, because it includes budget forms for three project years, could be used to request up to $4.5 million—not small by any standard.

It will take the same amount of hard work and extended effort to generate the totals that go on the budget summary form shown in Exhibit 5.11 as it will to complete the forms illustrated previously. Simplicity of form or format must not be confused with ease of use. To complete this form requires the same basic information as the previous ones that have been examined; therefore, it will be just as difficult to complete as all the rest. It just looks simple. It is not simple at all.

In-Kind

Illustrated in Exhibit 5.12 is the budget form from a state grant program. The program is the Governor's Community Youth Councils Incentive

EXHIBIT 5.12

Budget Form, South Carolina Governor's Youth Councils Grant Incentive Program

BUDGET CATEGORY	AMOUNT REQUESTED FROM DJJ	AMOUNT FROM OTHER SOURCES		TOTAL
		CASH	IN-KIND	
Staff				
Fringe Benefits				
Rental (Space/Equipment)				
Equipment Purchase				
Training & Educational Materials				
Office Supplies				
Travel				
Food				
Contractual/Consultants				
Other (Please List)				
TOTALS				

Grant Program. The "Governor" in question is that of South Carolina. The purpose of the program is to intervene with youth headed toward trouble in the juvenile justice system.

The leftmost column lists many of the same costs shown on earlier budgets. One cost included here but not seen before is food. In fact, food is seldom seen as a grant project budget item. Looking with new eyes, it is only natural to ask, "Why is food a budget line item?" The answer lies— as such answers always do—with the program, its purpose, its methods, and its target population.

To reach, instruct, or educate a target population, you must first make it stand still long enough to listen. This program's target population is young people. Considering the appetite of young people, food may just serve as sufficient motivation to get them to sit still long enough for a message to get through. That is, if you don't serve asparagus and watercress sandwiches.

More important than food as a budget item, however, is the column labeled "Amount from Other Sources." This concept we have seen before. What we have not seen is a grant maker breaking the amount contributed to the project budget from other sources into two types: cash and in-kind. Cash is easy to understand as long as we realize that funds held in accounts with financial institutions are cash.

In-kind, however, to many people is often a hazy and ill-understood concept. This is most unfortunate since most contributions to project budgets other than the grant will be in the form of in-kind. When a grant maker requires "matching funds," the match usually is made with in-kind. Rule of thumb is matching funds can be in-kind unless a grant maker uses the restrictive term "cash match."

Normally when a grant maker requires "matching funds," the match can be made in cash or in-kind, or in a combination of both. When grant makers require a match to be made with cash, the term they use is "cash match." When the phrase "cash match" is absent from the grant makers' discussion of matching funds, it means the match can be made with in-kind contributions. If, however, there is ever the slightest doubt in your mind about exactly what a grant maker means, the only valid solution is to query the grant maker directly.

In-Kind: The Concept

Our trusty CD-ROM Version 3.6a of *The American Heritage Dictionary* defines in-kind as "goods, commodities, or services rather than money." Barter is an excellent example of the use of in-kind. As an example of barter, suppose that a family needs its house roofed. The family, however, has no money either to pay a roofer or to purchase the shingles. What the family does have, however, is a large garden and a 1963 Chevy on blocks.

Negotiations with the owner of the local building supply store results in the appearance of a pile of shingles and the disappearance of the Chevy. A roofer is paid with homegrown vegetables. The owner of the building supply store and the roofer both have been paid with "goods, commodities, or services rather than money." Their payment was in-kind.

In-Kind: A Short Grammatical Discussion

Using the term in-kind while talking or writing gives a lot of people real problems. One simple reason is that in-kind is an adjective, not a noun. Except when discussing the term itself, it is not correct for the term to stand on its own as a noun can. Putting this point into a grant budget context, one might hear a question such as, "Where will we get the in-kind?" Grammatically, this is much like asking, "Where will we get the soft?" With the second question, most of us would ask quickly and probably with some asperity and added emphasis on the final word, "The soft *what?*" Just as quickly and emphatically, we should ask about the first question, "The in-kind what?" The answer, by the way, is "contribution."

In-Kind Contribution: The Definition

From now on, we will use the phrase in-kind contribution, rather than the term in-kind. This solves the grammatical problem and guides us straight to the meaning of the term in the context of a project budget. We are guided by the phrase because when we say in-kind contribution, the immediate question is "Contribution to what? The answer is "The project." We now are ready for the definition of in-kind:

In-Kind: Plain Language Definition

"In-kind" is the fair market value of personnel, goods, and services contributed to the operation of a project.

To completely understand the definition, we need to analyze each of its three constituent parts: (1) "fair market value," (2) "personnel, goods, and services," and (3) "contributed to the operation of a project." For an understanding of "fair market value" we consult the language of accounting:

Fair Market Value: Accountant's Definition

Amount that could be received on the sale of an asset when willing and financially capable buyers and sellers exist and there are no unusual circumstances such as liquidation, shortages, and emergencies.

Fair market value is the amount that something is worth when circumstances in the marketplace are normal. This principle acts as a guide later when we discuss assigning monetary value to in-kind contributions.

The phrase "personnel, goods, and services" is intended to encompass anything and everything, because anything and everything is exactly what can be included as in-kind contribution. An item or service, tangible or intangible—in short, anything and everything—that has value in the marketplace, can be an in-kind contribution.

The import of the phrase "contributed to the operation of a project" is that, to be legitimate, an in-kind contribution must directly aid project activities. For example, a local business allows employees to perform tasks for your agency during normal business hours, time for which the employees are paid by the business. The company therefore contributes the value of those employees' donated time (salary and wages) to your organization. If the employees contributed time on their own for which they were not being paid by their employer, the donation would come directly from the individual, but because they are being paid as employees while they contribute time, the donation comes from the company.

Now, as you prepare the grant application for a new project, you cast about for sources of matching funds. Can you use the contributed employee time? Yes, but only if the work the employees perform directly contributes to the performance of project activities. If the work the employees perform does not involve the activities of this particular project, the donation cannot legitimately be claimed as an in-kind contribution.

For those grant programs that require large matches, such as 100 percent or even more, in-kind contributions become critical to the success of an application. Discussion of methods of calculating in-kind contributions is found in Chapter 11. The same chapter contains process and directions for using the in-kind contribution tools and checklist on the CD-ROM that accompanies this book.

The budget form of another state grant program is shown in Exhibit 5.13. The program is Illinois State Library, Library Services and Technology Act (LSTA).

Continuing with Illinois grant programs, the next example budget form, Exhibit 5.14, is from the Illinois State Board of Education, Goals 2000 Professional Development Grants Program. This budget form is an example of needlessly complicating a process that is complicated enough to start with and does not need additional help to make it more so. The form shown in Exhibit 5.14 is also an example of what happens when the financial department gets involved.

Recall the use of the term "costing object" in the accountant's definition of direct cost. Now note on the budget form of Exhibit 5.14 these items: (Obj. 100s), (Obj. 200s), and on to (Obj. 700s). These are costing objects to which the user of this form is directly applying expenses, direct costs.

EXHIBIT 5.13

Budget Form, Illinois State Library, Library Services and Technology Act Grant

LSTA GRANT BUDGET SHEET

BUDGET CATEGORY	EXPLANATION	AMOUNT (in dollars only)
Library Materials	Books, non-print, software	$
Capital Outlay *	Equipment valued over $500	$
Professional Contracts *	Hiring an individual on contract	$
Contractual Services *	Hiring an agency on contract	$
Personnel	Salaries and benefits for additional agency staff	$
Travel and CE for Staff	Agency staff travel and meeting registrations	$
CE and Meetings for Others	Travel, registrations and honorariums for others	$
Public Relations	Advertising done by outside firm	$
Supplies, Postage and Printing	Equipment/supplies valued under $500	$
Telephones and Telecommunications	Phone charges and rental	$
Equipment Rental, Repair, and Maintenance	Rental, repair, insurance and maintenance of equipment	$
	TOTAL	$

* Please attach on a separate sheet a list of equipment and/or description of all contracts.

EXHIBIT 5.14

Budget Form, Illinois State Board of Education, Goals 2000 Professional Development Grant

B ☐ Initial Budget ☐ Multidistrict Application

ILLINOIS STATE BOARD OF EDUCATION
Grants Management and Evaluation Division, N-253
100 North First Street
Springfield, Illinois 62777-0001
217/782-3810

ATTACHMENT 5

ISBE USE ONLY

PROJECT NUMBER			LEA SUBMISSION DATE
FISCAL YEAR 96	SOURCE OF FUNDS CODE	REGION, COUNTY, DISTRICT, TYPE CODE	
	4946-00		

DISTRICT NAME AND NUMBER

CONTACT PERSON | TELEPHONE NUMBER / FAX NUMBER

FY96
GOALS 2000 PROFESSIONAL DEVELOPMENT GRANT

TOTAL FUNDS	ISBE PROGRAM APPROVAL DATE
CARRYOVER FUNDS	CURRENT FUNDS
BEGIN	END

BUDGET SUMMARY - *Use whole dollars only.* OMIT DECIMAL PLACES, e.g., $2536   Budget Summary/Breakdown

LINE	Function Number 1	EXPENDITURE ACCOUNT 2	SALARIES 3 (Obj. 100s)	EMPLOYEE BENEFITS 4 (Obj. 200s)	PURCHASED SERVICES 5 (Obj. 300s)	SUPPLIES & MATERIALS 6 (Obj. 400s)	TRANSFERS 9 (Obj. 700s)	TOTAL 11	ISBE USE ONLY PAYMENT SCHEDULE
7	2210	Improvement of Instruction Services							1 July-August (81)
26	4100	Payments to Other Govt. Units							2 September (82)
30		TOTAL BUDGET							3 October (83)

BUDGET BREAKDOWN - Itemize and explain each expenditure amount. Use additional pages as needed.

Function No. (1)	EXPENDITURE DESCRIPTION AND ITEMIZATION (2)	SALARIES (3)	EMPLOYEE BENEFITS (4)	PURCHASED SERVICES (5)	SUPPLIES AND MATERIALS (6)	TRANSFERS (9)	TOTAL (11)	
								4 November (84)
								5 December (85)
								6 January (86)
								7 February (87)
								8 March (88)
								9 April (89)
								10 May (90)
								11 June (91)
								12 July-August (92)
								TOTAL $

PROFESSIONAL DEVELOPMENT

ISBE 43-10 C (6/95)

Date _____   Signature of Superintendent

EXHIBIT 5.15

Budget Information, Disney Learning Partnership, Creative Learning Communities Grant Program

SAMPLE BUDGET OUTLINE

1 Salaries and Fees — Includes the amount of staff members' salaries who will be supported by grant funds. Each position (e.g. project coordinator, professional development specialist), salary, and percentage of a staff member's time devoted to the project should be identified

2 Fringe — Includes related benefits allocable to the salaries listed above

3 Consultants — Includes all fees, honoraria, and expenses paid for consulting and professional services of individuals or organizations that are not paid staff of the school or school district

4 Stipends — Includes support for teachers and other staff to direct or coordinate specific project activities

5 Temporary Staff — Includes support for substitutes to release teachers for professional development activities

6 Professional Development — Includes travel and related expenses for participation in off-campus conferences, meetings, site visits, etc.

7 Materials — Includes equipment or supplies directly related to the project

8 Other — Includes items not listed above

EXHIBIT 5.16

Program Budget

On the first page, provide a line-item budget listed by years 1, 2, and 3. For each year, list side by side the line items requested of the Mott Foundation, the costs covered by other sources, and the total cost of each line item. For example:

| | **Year 1** | | |
	Mott Request	**Other Sources**	**Total**
Salaries (#FTEs)			
Project Director	$20,000	$25,000	$45,000

On the second page, provide any details necessary to understand the line items.

Appendixes

The appendix should include:

- a summary of the applicant's institutional budget based on applicant's fiscal year, if applicant is not a major educational institution or unit of government;
- proof of tax-exempt 501(c)(3) status by the Internal Revenue Service; and
- applicant's most recent audited financial statement, or the applicant's most recent 990 tax return.

Please limit other appendixes to an annual report (or brief organizational "case statement") and a few news clips. Staff biographies are not requested.

This form shows how formatting can cause needless confusion. The line items are arrayed horizontally across the form instead of running vertically down the left side. The itemization totals are shown above the itemization itself, running counter to the usual position at the bottom of a column of figures. Finally, two sections on the form are reserved for "ISBE Use Only," creating needless clutter and occupying space that could be used to provide more space for applicants.

This budget form is designed for ease of use of the financial office and the grant maker. Typically, budget forms are designed with ease of use of the grant applicant in mind, recognizing that the average applicant is going to know how to run projects, not fill out budget forms.

Wise Guy and Wise Lady

 Wise Guy

Wow, there is a lot of detail to this! I had no idea. I just thought you listed your needs and put numbers to it. How in the world do they expect me to remember all this? What if I don't get things in just the right place—under just the right category? I am not happy. Not happy at all.

 Wise Lady

Well, we don't expect you to remember it all. That's why we've written it down. This book should be dog-eared from use—it's a reference work. And don't get tied in knots worrying about getting things in just the right place. First of all, if you are in doubt about placement of an item, you can always call the potential funder and ask *nicely* where to put it. Second, you will have a chance in the Budget Narrative (see Chapter 11) to explain where you got numbers and why the item is necessary. You will have given the potential funder enough information to place the item appropriately. Your proposal is not made or broken on one misplacement of a number. It will be read and studied as a whole. That is not to say you can get sloppy. But an honest error in budget placement between two categories, either of which is logical, will not seriously damage your chances of success.

Conclusion

This chapter could go on for literally hundreds of pages. We could illustrate one budget form after another till the exercise numbed the brain. The examples we have chosen do not show all the permutations that a grant seeker will run across. Neither do they show all the possible ways to format a budget, or lay out the figures on the page. We have, however, shown enough forms that the basics should be starting to come into focus. Several things can be said about all budget forms.

First, there are a limited number of line items that are repeated again and again. Items such as personnel and fringe appear in almost all budgets. Equipment, materials, and supplies are headings that are almost always present. This repetition of categories causes a certain similarity to all budgets regardless of the grant maker or format. This similarity should provide an applicant with confidence, because after the development of one complete budget, the next ones are all similar exercises.

Key Definition

In-Kind Contribution

In-kind is the fair market value of personnel, goods, and services contributed to the operation of a project.

Key Concepts

- A budget contains two types of costs: direct and indirect.
- Direct costs can be defined as money spent (or to be spent) that can be tracked straight to a project activity.
- Indirect costs can be defined as expense that is difficult to trace directly to a specific costing object.
- Grant projects can generate revenue and when they will, the estimated amount must be shown in the budget.
- Matching funds normally are either cash or in-kind, or a combination of both.
- A cash match limits the match to cash only.
- Analyzing budget forms with new eyes will unveil the grant maker's needs and wants.

The Three Rules of Grant Seeking

1. Read directions.
2. Follow directions.
3. Ask the slightest question.

As noted, after looking at a number of budget forms, it becomes obvious that a relatively small number of categories of direct costs are commonly used. Chapter 6 lists those categories and then defines and explains them. A concept to watch for during the rest of the book is that two distinct types of categories are used in project budgets. One type is descriptive or generic. This type of category includes line items such as equipment, personnel, and supplies. From the name of the category, we draw little to no information about the project purpose of the expense. Yes, we know that the funds will be spent, for example, on purchasing equipment, but we do not know the intended use for the equipment.

The second type of budget category is functional. A functional category explains in broad terms with its name what activities will be carried out with the funds. Examples of functional budget categories that an applicant may run across include evaluation, professional development, renovation, case management, continuation, documentation, or dissemination. If the first and the last three items in the list are unfamiliar, it might serve you well to obtain and read *Grant Seeker's Toolkit: A Comprehensive Guide to Finding Funding*, by the authors.

Chapter 6

Direct Costs: Definitions and Explanations

Nowadays people know the price of everything and the value of nothing.

Oscar Wilde, *The Picture of Dorian Gray*

This is a good time and place to explain where we are headed and how we intend to get there. We started with the simple truism that a grant project budget derives from the actions and activities of the project. Next we explained that a project derives from a problem, since from a theoretical viewpoint, a project is a solution to a problem. Once we worked our way all the way down to this beginning point of grant seeking—the problem— we began to work our way back up toward the budget. In Chapters 3 and 4, we outlined the logical process that starts with a problem and ends with a fully developed project.

In Chapter 5, we introduced basic budget concepts, looked at typical grant application budget forms, and defined the concept of direct costs. In this chapter, we divide direct costs into 10 categories and then define, explain, and give examples of costs for each category. Any and all direct costs will find a home in one of the following 10 categories:

1. Personnel.
2. Fringe.
3. Travel.
4. Equipment.
5. Capital.
6. Supplies.

7. Materials.

8. Contractual services.

9. Endowment.

10. Other/Miscellaneous.

In Chapters 7, 8, and 9, we explain how to calculate the costs of the various direct costs in the 10 categories. Several tools to help with the calculation are illustrated and explained. Working versions of the tools are found on the CD-ROM that accompanies this book. After all this preliminary work, we will be ready to put the entire process together. Chapter 10 takes all the foregoing information and uses it to generate raw budget data.

But first, we are going to define 10 categories into which any and every possible direct cost will fit. Direct costs can be grouped or categorized in two ways, by type of expense or by its function. A functional category includes the expenses derived from project actions and activities of a particular type such as evaluation, continuation, dissemination, or professional development. A "type of expense" is a simple description of an expense that carries no additional information about the use of the expense such as equipment or supplies. Both types are used by grant makers and are frequently found in combination on grant project budget forms.

With the exception of Travel, the categories in this chapter are all "types of expense." Most of the various costs of travel are actually contractual services, but the complexity and unique nature of travel and its costs demand individual treatment. Separating travel from contractual services also simplifies that category tremendously.

Personnel

First, in our case, the word "personnel" refers to the people employed by or active in the project. The direct cost category "Personnel" refers to the salaries and wages of project personnel. Importantly, from the viewpoint of the total project budget, "Personnel" refers to all personnel, whether employee, contributed, partner, or volunteer. The total project personnel cost therefore includes both the grant request and the in-kind contributions.

Personnel Costs: Plain Language Definition

Personnel costs are the salaries and wages of project personnel regardless of source.

Generally, but not by all authorities in all cases, wages are considered to be the remuneration paid to hourly employees. Similarly, a salary generally is considered to be the remuneration paid to an employee who is "exempt." An "exempt" employee does not keep or file an hourly time sheet and is not regulated by the same legal provisions as employees paid on an hourly basis. One example is overtime. State and federal guidelines mandate extra payment, typically time and a half, for hourly employees who work more than a certain number of hours in a workweek. Salaried employees have no such protection.

Salaries are usually expressed in yearly amounts such as $24,000 or $55,750, and the amount paid for a time period is determined by dividing the number of periods into the yearly total. Wages are usually expressed in hourly amounts such as $7.50 an hour or $12.75 an hour, and the amount paid for a time period is determined by multiplying the number of hours worked in that time period by the hourly wage.

The basis of all personnel cost is the time used or expended by people in project actions and activities. Payment of personnel is from two general sources: the grant and other sources. The third source of project work is unpaid personnel donated by volunteers. These descriptions yield the following list of four general sources of project personnel and the payment source for the time expended by the personnel. Important points about each of the four items are discussed in the subsections that follow the list:

1. Time for which people are paid with grant funds (grant request).
2. Time for which employees of your organization are paid by your organization (in-kind contribution).
3. Time for which employees of partner organizations are paid by partner organizations (in-kind contribution).
4. Time, the value of which, volunteers contribute (in-kind contribution).

Project Personnel: Grant Request

All the time included in this item is not necessarily expended by employees of your organization. It is certainly possible for a person paid from the grant to be an employee of an organization other than yours. While the grant funds flow initially to the fiscal agent (the legal applicant), it does not follow that all the people paid salaries or wages with grant funds will be employees of the fiscal agent. What is true is that people paid with grant funds will be employees of the project. The payroll function for different employees of the project could, conceivably, be managed by different organizations. This is not common, but at times when "turf" issues intrude, one solution is to divide equally the direct-line management of personnel between different organizations. The most concrete evidence of management authority is the source of salaries or wages. The exact flow of the funds, as long as the grant maker approves, can be determined by the needs of the project and the partnership. What is always true of this item is that it includes all the time for which grant funds pay salaries and wages.

Your Organization: In-Kind Contribution

To review, here is the definition of "in-kind," or more correctly, "in-kind contribution" to the budget of a project. Now we are confining ourselves to personnel, though soon "goods and services" will be discussed.

In-Kind: Plain Language Definition

In-kind is the fair market value of personnel, goods, and services contributed to the operation of a project.

An important concept is that there may be more than one source for the funds that provide the in-kind contribution. A county government that obtains the majority of its funding from local taxes may also receive funds from its state as well as from the federal government. If our example county also receives grant funds from a consortium of business and industry, then the time contributed by a county employee to a project could be funded, in this example, from any of four sources. The personnel time could also be funded by a combination of sources, such as a fifty-fifty split between state and federal funding. This concept comes into play with certain project budget forms that ask for the sources of other project funding. Exhibit 6.1 shows an example of a form with a request for the amount of project funding that is coming from other sources (see Item 14 Estimated Funding).

Grant makers refer to the organization that applies for a grant as the "applicant." Being the "applicant" has important legal ramifications. When

Exhibit 6.1

Partial View of Cover Sheet, ED-424 (Lower 25% of Form)

Estimated Funding

Authorized Representative Information

15. To the best of my knowledge and belief, all data in this preapplication/application are true
and correct. The document has been duly authorized by the governing body of the applicant
and the applicant will comply with the attached assurances if the assistance is awarded.

14a. Federal	$	. 00
b. Applicant	$	. 00
c. State	$	. 00
d. Local	$	. 00
e. Other	$	. 00
f. Program Income	$ 0	. 00
g. TOTAL	$	. 00

a. Typed Name of Authorized Representative

_____

b. Title: _____

c. Tel. #: (   ) _____-_____ Fax #: (   ) _____-_____

d. E-Mail Address: _____

e. Signature of Authorized Representative

_____ Date:___/___/_____

ED 424 (rev 11/12/99)

a grant is awarded, the applicant becomes the fiscal agent, responsible for the management of the funds and the implementation of the project. A successful grant proposal (one that is funded) becomes a legal contract between the applicant and the grant maker. The grant maker agrees to give money, and the applicant agrees to perform the actions and activities described in the proposal. Note the content of Item 15 in Exhibit 6.1. Here an "Authorized Representative" of the applicant must sign the grant application on behalf of the applicant organization. The person who signs this form must be able to enter into a contract for the applicant. The signature also attests that everything in the application package is "true and correct."

Partner Organizations: In-Kind Contribution

In Chapter 5, we discussed project partners and learned that partners do things. They provide concrete help with project activities. In Chapter 4, a number of partners are named during development of the example project, the Communitywide After-School Program. From this, we learn that partners can be any kind of organization or agency. They can be public or private. They can be business and industry, or they can be nonprofit. They can be big or small. They can be secular or faith-based. Project partners are limited only by the needs of the project and the imagination of the project's development team.

Project work performed by a partner's employee who then is paid for the time by the partner is an in-kind contribution by that partner to the budget of the project. If an employee of a partner performs project work for which the employee is not paid, the time is still an in-kind contribution; the source, however, is no longer the partner but becomes the individual who has volunteered the time.

Volunteers: In-Kind Contribution

Volunteers are often a major source of personnel to perform project activities. To arrive at a true project budget, the value of volunteered time must not be overlooked. The method of calculating the value of contributed time is shown in Chapter 7. For now, all that really needs to be said is that the value of contributed time is determined by the activity performed, not by the profession, education, position, or expertise of the person performing the activity.

Fringe

Without experience managing a business or organization with employees, the concept of fringe cost may be totally foreign. The way we approach the concept in our workshops is to ask, "How much money does it cost your employer to pay you a dollar?" We hasten to add that we mean cash, not indirect or hidden costs, but rather, cold hard cash paid out directly. How much does it cost your employer to pay you that dollar? Rather than answer the question with a particular amount, we then list the items that make up the cost of fringe:

- Federal Insurance Contributions Act (FICA)—

  Social Security.

  Medicare.

- State Unemployment Insurance (SUTA).
- Federal Unemployment Insurance (FUTA).
- Worker's Compensation Insurance.
- Health Insurance.
- Life Insurance.
- Retirement.

Some employers will pay only two or three of the expenses in the list. Some employers will pay all of the expenses. It is also entirely possible for an employer to have additional fringe expenses that are not listed. The amount of fringe an organization pays is expressed as a percentage of salary and wages. Experience shows that fringe expenses can run as low as 10 to 12 percent and as high as 40 to 50 percent. The vast majority of organizations pay FICA, SUTA, and Worker's Compensation Insurance. Incurring only these three expenses will result in a fringe rate toward the low end. Organizations that contribute to employee health, retirement, and life insurance plans incur a fringe rate toward the high end. The fringe rate is obtained from the people who handle payroll for your organization.

It is not at all unusual for an organization to have as many as three different fringe rates. One rate is for part-time employees. Another rate is for full-time employees with less than a defined amount of time with the organization. The third rate is for those employees who fully participate in all fringe benefits. This full participation is often called "vesting" or being "vested." Again, the people who manage an organization's payroll will know the fringe rate or rates.

Travel

The cost of travel is a legitimate project expense for many and varied reasons. One travel situation that is becoming almost commonplace is a mandatory yearly program meeting. Such meetings usually are held at a site close to the grant maker's home base. In addition, federal agencies often have regional program meetings as often as twice a year. Generally, when a grant maker requires travel, it expects to find funds in the budget to cover the expense.

Another valid reason for incurring travel expense is attending conferences either to learn something to use with the project or to teach about the project—usually part of a dissemination component. It may be necessary to visit an organization that is running a project with activities or components similar to your own and that you need to observe to gain firsthand information. It may be necessary to travel to a particular location for special training or education. More prosaically and right at home, project staff members may need simply to travel in the service area, back and forth among project activity sites. Whatever the purpose, many grant makers expect to see funds budgeted for travel.

As with so many topics in the field of grant seeking, the term "travel" can be misleading. More properly, it should read the expense of travel, lodging, and meals. The cost of travel is more than the simple cost of moving from one place to another. It includes places to stay and food to eat along with other miscellaneous expenses. The following list indicates some of the expenses a traveler may encounter.

Air travel

Scheduled airline

Charter flight

Air taxi

Ground travel

Train

Mileage

Car rental

Bus

Taxi

Shuttle

Hired car

Limousine

Rapid transit

Other travel

Watercraft

Animal

Meals

Per meal rate

Per diem

Lodging

Motel

Hotel

Bed and breakfast

Private home

Gratuities

Airport baggage
   check-in

Sky Cap

Ground travel drivers

Doormen

Hotel bell person

Valet parking

Waiters

Tolls	Courtesy expenses
Bridges	Cleaning
Tunnels	Telephone
Highways	

Parking

Airport

Overnight

Hourly

Air Travel

Most organizations or agencies to which one would report travel expenses consider the cost of air travel to consist solely of the amount paid for an airline ticket. Other expenses are almost always involved, but because of common usage we include them in other categories.

Scheduled Airlines. The most common way to travel by air is to purchase a ticket on one of the many scheduled flights offered by commercial airlines such as Delta, American, Northwest, Continental, United, and many others large and small.

Chartered Flight. Scheduled airlines often do not serve remote places or locations with small populations. In such cases, a traveler can hire an airplane from a charter airline to provide the flight. For small localities that are served by scheduled airlines, the small number of flights (perhaps only one a day) and their timing (designed to complement the hub-and-spoke system) can make the scheduled airline option less than attractive. If a charter flight is used, the schedule can often be designed specifically to meet the traveler's needs.

One aspect of charter flights can have a major effect on travel plans. Charter flights often (more often than not) fly out of different airports than the scheduled airlines. These general aviation facilities, while normally adequate for a traveler's needs, do not have all the amenities found in the large airports used by scheduled airlines. Do not expect restaurants. And most importantly, carefully arrange in advance for ground travel. At large commercial airports, ground travel is plentiful and can be arranged on the spot. At most general aviation airports, failure to arrange for ground transportation in advance can cause a long wait.

Air Taxi. Though not commonly used by ordinary travelers (or commonly available, for that matter), an air taxi can substantially decrease the time it takes to get from an airport to the center of a large city. Air taxis normally are available only in very large cities such as New York, Los Angeles, or Chicago. Unlike a taxicab, an air taxi does not deliver a traveler to a specific address. Rather, an air taxi (a helicopter), has a set delivery point, usually atop a downtown building. From that drop-off point, a traveler must obtain ground transportation to the final destination. The benefit of an air taxi is that it jumps over congested streets and highways, depositing a traveler directly into the heart of the city.

Cost Determination Principle. Determining the cost of an airline ticket up to 18 months before purchase can seem an impossible task. That is exactly what a budget developer must do, however. It is not at all unusual for the grant award process to take 6 months to complete with another month or two going by before the award is actually received. If the trip is to take place at the end of the project year, it is easy to see that a ticket may be purchased 18 months after the amount for the ticket is determined and placed in the application budget. This situation is not unique to airline tickets.

The time lapse between cost determination and the actual expenditure is a recurring and customary feature of grant projects and should not be the least surprising. What does come as a surprise is how different people and organizations respond to this absolutely predictable aspect of budgeting. First, they act as though the discovery of the time lapse is a great revelation of deep import to the budget. Next they implement a variety of methods to account for the possibility that the expenditure for an item may be larger than the budgeted amount.

That last sentence conveys two keys to this situation. First, there is only a possibility that an expenditure will be larger than the amount budgeted. Second, all the planning goes toward the likelihood that a cost will rise, none toward the possibility that a cost will decline. The truth is that the chances of a cost remaining the same or declining are about the same as the chance of a cost rising. We are conditioned to think only of rising costs, mostly by government-issued statistics on inflation. Except in clearly inflationary times, however, most items found in grant project budgets tend, over a one- to two-year time frame to remain stable or decline in cost.

This leads to a key principle of project budgeting, which is to research the current fair market value of a budget item and use that amount. Many "experts" disagree with this principle, wanting to cover any possible eventuality of an organization incurring costs during implementation of a grant project. Worry over this issue causes budgets to become bloated and unreasonable based on the here and now, which is when the budget is evaluated. That is worth repeating. The people who evaluate grant proposals and their budgets have only "the now" with which to work. If a budget is out of line with present costs, then it runs the very real risk of being rejected.

Applying this principle to airline tickets means that a budget developer simply finds the cost of a ticket now and puts that cost into the budget. It is simply impossible to know how much the ticket will cost a year from now or 18 months from now. It is easily possible, however, to know what the ticket costs now. Use that cost.

Ground Travel

Train. While the trains do not run as extensively as in former times, regularly scheduled passenger trains still serve a few densely populated areas in the country. In such areas, train travel may be attractive for both cost and time reasons. Train terminals are normally in downtown areas. Balancing the cost of additional ground transportation against driving time and parking problems and expense may make travel by train the best choice. If traveling to a suburban area, careful research of the location of the train terminal in relation to the final destination is in order.

Mileage. Typically, the cost of ground travel is determined with a mileage rate only when a private vehicle is used. If travel is done in a person's own car, then the cost is calculated with a mileage rate. Examples of private vehicle use would be driving from one project activity location to another, driving to a conference or meeting, or driving to an airport where air travel will begin.

Car Rental. Car rental agencies have become a ubiquitous travel service, even to the point of delivering a rental car directly to your door. A great advantage in renting a vehicle is the ability to get exactly what is needed. Do you need to transport several people? Rent a van. Do you need to haul a lot of equipment? Rent a truck. Do you have many hard miles to drive? Rent a luxury car. Do you just want a way to get back and forth? Rent a compact.

Several aspects of renting vehicles can impinge on project planning. All vehicle rental agencies have age limitations. A usual age limitation is that the renter must be at least 25 years old. Most rental agencies require a credit card imprint before renting a vehicle regardless of whether the rental actually will be paid by check or cash. And, as might be expected, all car rental agencies require a valid driver's license. Keep in mind these requirements for a potential vehicle renter: when a rental vehicle figures into travel planning.

Bus. Bus transportation comes in three distinct types: between cities and towns, within a city or town, and chartered. Bus service between cities and towns operates like train service. Buses travel on scheduled routes among locations. Some routes are "express," which means they stop only at large destinations, while "local" routes stop at every location the company serves. Tickets are purchased at a terminal, which usually is located close to the center of town. In very small towns, the bus terminal may be no more than a sign outside a convenient location on the highway through town.

Most towns of medium size and larger have an in-town bus service. The fee to use a city bus is paid after boarding, often by dropping the appropriate amount in coins into a special device mounted beside the driver. Bus stops are scattered around town and buses normally run continuously during operational hours.

Buses can also be rented or chartered. Charter is an exact, almost legal, term that means the hiring or leasing of an aircraft, a vessel, or other vehicle, especially for the exclusive, temporary use of a group of travelers. An important aspect of chartering is that a vehicle operator is part of the charter agreement, meaning that a bus driver comes with the charter. Chartering a bus is a reasonable option for transporting a large group of people.

Taxi. A taxi (taxicab) is an automobile that carries passengers for a fare, usually calculated by a taximeter. This is a device that measures the distance traveled along with waiting time, and computes and indicates the fare. In large cities, taxis cruise the streets or wait outside those places at which they can reasonably expect to pick up fares, such as hotels, airports, and train terminals. In smaller towns and in suburban areas, a taxi needs to be summoned with a telephone call.

In some places, Washington, D.C. being one, taxi service is based on areas or regions, not mileage or time. Travel to any location within a specific region is for a flat fee. In cities with this type of service, the fees normally are posted prominently in the vehicle and at locations at which taxis are obtained.

Shuttle. Many lodging facilities provide transportation to and from the local airport. This transportation, regardless of the type of vehicle, is commonly termed a shuttle. A shuttle was originally, and still is, the weaving device that carries the woof thread back and forth between the warp threads. The weaving shuttle eventually gave its name to regular travel back and forth over an established, usually short, route.

As the name implies, shuttles run continuously between two locations, which for our purposes are usually an airport and a lodging facility. Shuttles can be vans, minivans, or small buses. The service is normally provided at no cost. Some shuttle vehicles also offer hotel or lodge guests limited transportation to locations of their choice such as restaurants, stores, and entertainment centers (sports arenas, theaters, etc.).

Hired Car. A hired car differs from a taxi in that the cost is negotiated beforehand and is a flat fee for either a specific trip or a specified time. Hired cars usually are larger and more luxurious than taxis. A hired car differs from a rental car in that a driver (chauffeur) is provided for the hired car. It can become the preferred choice over a taxi when the trip is relatively long or a car will be needed for an extended period.

Limousine. The finances of limousine rental are the same as those for a hired car; it is simply a special type of hired car service. The fee is negotiated and set before the service is provided. The difference is in the type of vehicle. A limousine is larger than a standard car, often with a partition between the passengers and the driver. In addition to being stocked with food and beverages, it also may be equipped with television, a selection of music, telephone, and even a computer with Internet access. As should be expected, the more amenities the larger the fee.

Rapid Transit. Cities such as San Diego, Atlanta, San Francisco, Chicago, New York, and Washington, D.C. provide public, rapid transit transportation in varying form. Most rapid transit can be classified as light rail systems, which means simply that they operate on principles similar to railroads, but utilize smaller or lighter weight components. Systems vary from the highly useful (e.g., New York City, with extensive coverage) to the questionably useful (e.g., Atlanta, a city several times the geographic size of New York, with a rapid transit system that has only four spokes radiating from midtown). It is essential to know exactly what services are offered before depending on rapid transit as part of travel plans, especially if arriving at a meeting on time is part of the plan.

Other Travel

Watercraft. The most common watercraft encountered by travelers probably is the ferry, most likely the car ferry. Bridge building has brought many islands into the highway system, but ferries still provide the only automobile access to some locations. Passenger ferries also are in operation. A passenger ferry runs from New York's LaGuardia airport to Manhattan. For the traveler without extensive baggage this may be an attractive alternative.

Animal. In the United States, one does not often encounter commercial travel by horse, mule, donkey, camel, or elephant. Travel such as this tends to be undertaken for entertainment as a vacation activity. We are not the world, however. In some places, animals are still the most dependable mode of travel. From the viewpoint of calculating cost, this type of travel does not differ from any other.

Meals

The cost of eating while on a trip is calculated in one of two ways. The simplest method is to establish an amount to allocate for each person per day of the trip. The Latin phrase *per diem* (literal translation, "by the day") is often used in this context, meaning a daily rate. The alternative to a per diem rate is to estimate the cost of each meal. This method has the benefit (or detriment, based on your viewpoint) of better accuracy. For example, a person seldom consumes three meals "on the road" on the first and the last day of a trip. It is not unusual for a traveler to consume only one meal on the road on the first day of a trip and only two on the last day. A per diem rate assigns the same amount for each travel day regardless of actual meals consumed.

Lodging

Most of a traveler's lodging will be in either motels or hotels. Legitimate alternatives include bed and breakfasts and private homes. Although the difference between hotels and motels has become blurred, the hotel came first and usually provides meals and other services for travelers in addition to lodging. A motel (a word coined by combining motor and hotel) provides lodging for motorists in rooms usually having direct access to an open parking area.

Because of the blurring of the distinction between motel and hotel, the phrase "full-service hotel" has come into use to designate an establishment that provides a range of services previously associated simply with hotels. Full-service hotels usually include one or more restaurants, a cocktail lounge, room service, bell staff, concierge, and valet. Many finer motels now offer similar services.

Gratuities

A gratuity, commonly known as a "tip," is a favor or gift, usually in the form of money, given in return for service. In Chapter 8, we discuss the details of gratuities, when they are necessary and how much is appropriate. For now, it suffices to say that the larger the city, the more luxurious the service, and the more that is done for you, the more you pay in gratuities. A notable exception is Washington, D.C., a relatively small city compared with Los Angeles, Chicago, and New York, but a city in which gratuities are as much expected and as high as any place in the country. This is important to know, since many grant winners travel to Washington, D.C. for meetings.

Tolls

In many locations, it costs money to drive across bridges, through tunnels, and over highways—extra money paid in cash, over and above taxes.

These tolls can accumulate to substantial amounts and need to be part of the overall travel cost calculation. Tolls are another expense for which local knowledge is necessary.

Parking

At first glance, parking may seem to be one of those expenses too small to worry over. Two examples suffice to dispel that concern. Leaving a car in most economy long-term airport parking costs around $5.00 a day. It does not take a very long trip to accumulate a substantial parking fee. In New York City overnight parking easily can cost $30.00. Even at the regular rates for downtown parking garages in medium-size cities (an average of 75¢ an hour), it does not take many hours in meetings to accumulate a sizable parking bill.

Courtesy Expenses

People who travel for business and industry (not government) are familiar with this concept. Employers acknowledge that spending extended time away from home can be lonely, boring, and stressful. Many employers, therefore, pay for a telephone call home each day that a business traveler is on the road. Another common travel expense covered by business and industry is the cleaning of clothing. The idea is simple. One can carry along only so much clothing on a trip, especially when traveling by air. When business trips extend beyond a certain length, a traveler is expected to need to clean the limited supply of clothing. The amounts involved in these courtesy expense items are small compared with the other costs of travel. This small investment of funds, however, reaps a large return of goodwill from travelers and is well worth the relatively minor increase in overall travel costs.

Disallowed Expenses

Despite the inclusiveness of the list of legitimate travel expenses, there are a few expenses that almost no agency, organization, business, or industry will accept. The two universally disallowed travel expenses are alcoholic beverages and personal entertainment. Personal entertainment includes such items as in-room pay-for-view movies; sports events such as baseball, basketball, and football games; concerts; and amusement parks.

Equipment

The term equipment is another concept that is easy to understand but hard to put into words. Definitions of equipment usually employ one of two aspects—useful life or cost. Many people and organizations consider an item to be equipment if its useful life extends a sufficient length of time. Accountants normally use this definition, calling the item a capital or fixed asset and depreciating its value over time. Many organizations, on the other hand, simply label as equipment any item that costs over a set amount and that is clearly not an expendable.

Using cost to define equipment leads to some head-scratching situations. The electronic calculator sitting on a desk is not a piece of equipment because of its low cost. The cassette tape recorders in the audiovisual equipment room are not equipment either. They cost too little. The accounting software package, on the other hand, is equipment because it is expensive, well over the limit.

The problems in definition are inherent in any structured organization. Insistence on across-the-board, simple-to-apply solutions and definitions consistently applied in all circumstances always eventually leads to instances in which common sense stands on its head, in the corner, facing the wall.

A phrase that appears at times in the context of discussion of equipment is "furniture and fixtures." An accountant's definition is "depreciable asset consisting of office or store equipment, lighting, and showroom items. A fixture is a "fixed asset whose utility is derived from its physical attachment to a property and that usually cannot be removed without causing loss of value or damage." The usual example used for fixture is a lighting fixture, but a sink or a toilet seems even more appropriate to the definition, "whose utility is derived from its physical attachment." The point here is that an item included in the category of furniture and fixtures is probably equipment, though, as usual with this sort of thing, not always.

We can approach the definition of equipment from another angle, its purpose. One thing safely can be said of equipment. We expect an item of equipment to accomplish a task, which may be as simple as providing a place to sit or as complex as printing, collating, and binding a full-color publication. Another aspect of equipment is that it does not diminish appreciably in accomplishing its purpose, unlike, for example, a pencil or an eraser. A serious problem at this point is that a person fits the requirements so far. A person accomplishes tasks without appreciable diminution of capacity. A person, however, is not an item of equipment. Putting it all together yields the following definition:

Equipment: Plain Language Definition

Equipment is inanimate, has physical substance, can be used repeatedly to accomplish a purpose or purposes, and remains essentially unchanged after each use.

Disregarding the cost issue, this definition delineates the parameters for what constitutes an item of equipment. For the purposes of a grant proposal, our definition of equipment largely is moot, since the only definition that matters is the grantor's. Equipment is one of those troublesome items in grant seeking for which different organizations and people have different definitions. And just as is true for all the other troublesome items, all those definitions, including ours, do not matter one whit unless they just happen to agree with the only definition that counts, the grantor's.

In general, the proper approach is to use the previous plain language definition while in addition applying whatever cost rules a grantor imposes. Applicants have no problem with the items included in the equipment line in a budget. What is excluded sometimes does cause difficulties, however. Placing the items excluded from the equipment budget line into the materials and supplies budget line causes some applicants conceptual problems. It should not. As has been said several times before, and will be repeated again, words are only labels for things. Ask yourself, "As long as funding is obtained for the items needed for the project, does it matter what the items are called?" The answer is no, of course, it does not matter one little bit.

The following list contains a few items commonly included in the category of equipment. Naturally, some of the items would be excluded if a threshold value is set below which an item is not considered to be equipment:

Desk	Television
Chair	Lawn mower
Filing cabinet	Table saw
Computer	Drill press
Car	Lathe
Truck	Video camera
Van	Printer
Boat	Shelving
Airplane	Copier
Table	Microscope
Camera	Telescope

Capital

Even from the narrow viewpoint of finances within which we are working, capital can mean several things. For our purposes, however, capital is a long-term or fixed asset (capital asset). A fixed asset is an item that has physical substance and a life in excess of one year. Examples are buildings, equipment, and land. Equipment is a fixed asset. This explains the following course of events, which many of us have observed. Once an item of equipment is purchased, an organization adds the item to its inventory of capital assets, perhaps assigning a serial number. The value of the item is entered into the accounting system as a long-term asset. The piece of equipment is now "capitalized."

The item of equipment becomes a capital asset, possession of which increases the overall amount of an organization's capital or value. This is one reason, though by far not the main reason, that many grant makers severely limit the amount of a grant that can be spent on equipment. In most cases, a grant maker's purpose is to solve problems, not to increase the financial value of an applicant organization. It is understandable that many nonprofit workers take the view that increasing the value of their organization does solve problems, at least in the long run.

Equipment has its own category. Expenditures for fixed assets that belong in the capital category include the purchase of land, buildings, and improvements. The improvements can be made to either buildings or land. Improvements to buildings include such things as renovations or additions. Improvements to land include such things as grading, landscaping, roadwork, well drilling, or erosion prevention.

In the grant-seeking fraternity, this type of funding is called "brick and mortar money" or sometimes just "bricks and mortar." Funding for bricks and mortar, rare to start with, is by far the most difficult type of grant to win.

Supplies

Supplies are items expended quickly during their use. A case can be made that everything is expended by usage, to one degree or another, including even equipment. Supplies, however, are the "popcorn" of expendable items. They go the quickest. In the following list of supplies, many items can be used only once, for example, tape, glue, coffee, and food. Even for those supply items that can be used more than once, each use diminishes the item and brings measurably closer the necessity of replacement. Examples include pencils, pens, batteries, and erasers.

Rubber bands, paper clips, and a variety of other types of binding clips occupy an anomalous position among supplies. For supplies they surely are, but they are not expended by use. More likely they are expended by giving them away. They disappear as fast as any other supply. However, they are not gone totally, as is used tape or coffee. They flow from desk to desk, office to office, agency to agency—across state and national boundaries—in a chain of recycling the length of which we can only guess. The following list shows a few items that are considered to be supplies:

Batteries	Toner
Self-stick note pads	Pens
Soap	Pencils
Paper	Toilet paper
Envelopes	Trash bags
Erasers	Paint
Forms	Postage stamps
Glue	Rubber bands
Index cards	Staples
Ink	Tape
Photographic film	Fax paper
Trash bags	Food
Paper towels	Paper plates
Labels	Beverages
CD recordable disks	Printer ribbon
Coffee	Coffee machine filters
Shipping boxes	Packing materials
Highlighters	Binding combs (spirals)
Dry erase markers	Permanent markers

Materials

Materials are similar to supplies in that they also are expended. Materials are different than supplies in one or both of two ways. First, materials last longer than supplies, that is, they take longer to wear out or be expended. Examples are books, brooms, diskettes, and paintbrushes. Second, materials may become incorporated directly into a larger whole. Examples are lumber, network wiring, fiber-optic cable, and wallpaper. The following list shows some items that are considered to be materials:

Books	Lumber
Storage boxes	Paintbrushes
Clothing	Network wiring
Computer diskettes	Ring binders
Electrical wiring	Software
Fiber-optic cable	CD rewritable disks
Glassware	Audiotape

Videotape	Magneto-optic cartridges
File folders	Broom
Digital data cartridges	Mop
Removable disk cartridges	Wallpaper

Contractual Services

Service is work done by one party for another—as opposed to goods, which are commodities or wares. In the terminology of this chapter, goods are equipment, supplies, and materials. In simple personal terms, if Jim takes out the trash for Cheri, he performs a service. From the viewpoint of a project budget, if the staff of a project performs a task, the expense category is personnel. If a person or company is hired to perform the task, the expense category is services.

Although grant makers commonly use the phrase "contractual services," the term is redundant. Services inherently are contractual. In law, a contract simply is an agreement between two parties that involves an exchange of value. Only two circumstances must exist between two parties to create a contract: an agreement and an exchange. The contract exists whether the agreement is in writing or not. The exchange can be anything conceivable as long as, from the viewpoint of the involved parties, value is received. The most common exchange is goods or services for money.

The following list shows services and service providers. The first column ("Service Professions") lists several occupations or vocations. If, during a project, one or more of these people are hired to perform project activities, the funds expended belong in the category of contractual services. The second column ("People Services") contains the names of several services obviously performed by people. This type of service is the simplest to understand. The concept is straightforward. A person or company is hired to perform activities. People appear and perform the actions, and are then paid for their exertions.

The third column ("Technical Services") contains several services that often present conceptual difficulties for people mainly because of the apparent absence of people providing the service. This is why we call them technical services. Machines or electronic devices often perform these services, and the user of the service may seldom if ever see a person. Nevertheless, the service would not exist were it not for the people who create, install, maintain, and repair the devices and systems that perform the actual service.

Service Professions	People Services	Technical Services
Accountant	Advertising	Automated answering service
Architect	Catering	Database access
Artist	Construction	Insurance
Bookkeeper	Delivery	Internet access
Consultant	Drafting	Electric utility
Doctor	Installation	Equipment rental and lease
Engineer	Landscaping	Local telephone
Lawyer	Maintenance, equipment	Long-distance telephone
Musician	Maintenance, facility	Videoconferencing
Nurse	Maintenance, grounds	Water and sewer utilities
Painter	Pest control	Web site hosting
Speaker	Printing	
Therapist	Security	
Writer		

Contractors

Contractor is a term that often appears on budget forms instead of services or contractual services. A contractor is a person or business that agrees to furnish materials or perform services at a specified price. Perhaps the most common day-to-day use of the term is for companies that provide construction work such as home building or renovation. For grant project budgets, contractors are not limited to construction work. Instead, contractors provide all contractual services. For our purposes, a contractor is simply the provider of contractual services.

The expense of a contract for goods does not go in the contractual service line item but rather in a line item for equipment, materials, or supplies. That the contract may include incidental services such as installation or training does not change its fundamental nature or its proper location in the budget. Such contracts could include the purchase of computers, software, modular office furniture, or a telephone system (not telephone service).

On the other hand, many contracts for services involve the purchase and use of extensive amounts of materials and supplies. As long as the purpose of the purchased materials and supplies is the fulfillment of the service contract, the expense remains in the contractual service line item. Service contracts that may involve substantial amounts of materials and supplies include construction of a greenhouse, renovation of a facility, landscaping grounds, and training staff.

Consultants

A consultant is a person who gives expert or professional advice. Projects often use consultants to gain the benefit of their expertise and experience. Consultants typically help with or provide such services as planning, training, evaluation, and materials development (video, audio, software, or others).

From the viewpoint of the project budget, a consultant is a contractor—a person who provides contractual services. Financially, there is no distinction between a contractor and a consultant. A consultant is a contractor. It is that simple.

Contractor or Employee?

From employee wages, employers withhold income tax, Social Security and Medicare taxes, and perhaps FUTA. Employers make matching contributions to Social Security and Medicare. The withholding along with the matching amount are submitted to the federal government. Employees are issued IRS Form W-2 as a record of wages paid and the various withholding and matching amounts. In addition, state and local taxes may be withheld and submitted to appropriate state or local agencies. These amounts also appear on IRS Form W-2.

On the other hand, for a worker who is not an employee, but rather an independent contractor, an employer generally does not withhold any taxes. As a record of earnings, an employer issues to the contractor the appropriate version of IRS Form 1099.

Whether a person is a contractor or an employee is important from the viewpoint of the budget. It is even more important from the viewpoint of relations with the Internal Revenue Service. The IRS looks closely at the employee versus contractor situation. The reason is simple. It costs less to use a contractor than employ a person. Many employers would, if they could, use nothing but contractors relieving themselves of two major expenses—the cost of fringe and the indirect cost (overhead) incurred by employing a person.

Most employers are prevented from converting their employees into contractors because the IRS defines a contractor in such a way that there is large and very real difference between an employee and a contractor. In Publication 15-A, *Employer's Supplemental Tax Guide*, the IRS discusses at length, including several examples, exactly what differentiates between an employee and an independent contractor.

The issue is complex, but the following quotation from page 3 of Publication 15-A is the short form of the IRS explanation: "The general rule is that an individual is an independent contractor if you, the payer, have the right to control or direct only the result of the work and not the means and methods of accomplishing the result." If a "payer" has control over such things as where to work, what time to come to work, how long to remain at work, what tools or equipment to use, where to purchase supplies and services, what order or sequence to follow, and other such instructions about how to do work, the person being paid is an employee.

The IRS also is clear that it makes no difference what a relationship is called. Simply calling an employee a contractor will not work. Here is the way the IRS puts it on page 3 of Publication 15-A: "If you have an employer-employee relationship, it makes no difference how it is labeled. The substance of the relationship, not the label, governs the worker's status. Nor does it matter whether the individual is employed full time or part time."

In general, project budget developers will not get involved in an employee-contractor determination. Common sense applies more often than not. If the person that fills a position in a grant project will be treated as an employee, she is. If to obtain a specialized service, a company (or a person in a self-owned business) will be sought out and hired, it is a contractor. If a borderline situation appears, call in the financial people and have them make the call.

As a last comment on the subject, the IRS will make a determination for you about whether a person is an employee or a contractor. You can request a determination by completing Form SS-8, Determination of Employee Work Status and submitting it to the IRS. Form SS-8 is four pages with 19 numbered questions. The actual number of questions is much higher, however. Each numbered question has at least two parts and some have as many as seven.

In-Kind Contribution: Employee or Contractor?

When volunteers or partners will contribute time to a project, where in the budget does the value of the contribution belong? Does the value of the contributed time belong in the employee line item or in the contractual services line item? The answer is derived from the answer to an additional, hopefully simple question.

First, assume it has become necessary to pay to accomplish the activity planned for the volunteer or partner. Would the project hire an employee to get the job done, or would the project use a contractor? If the project would hire an employee, the value of the in-kind contribution belongs in the employee line item. If the project would use a contractor, the value belongs in the contractual services line item.

With that said, another consideration can be used to decide where to place the value of contributed time. Put it where it does the most good, where it is needed to meet the grant maker's needs or requirements. Generally, grant makers care only about the total amount of matching funds, perhaps stated as a percentage of the total budget. If it makes a difference, however, put the value of contributed time in the line item that best matches the grant maker's agenda.

Endowment

An endowment consists of donated funds or property that is used as a source of income. Usually, the amount an organization uses as income is only a portion (though often the greater portion) of the total earned through investment of the endowment, with the principal remaining untouched. Endowments usually are managed so the amount of invested principal grows steadily. This enables the endowment to retain its value in the face of inflation and also, over time, increases the income available for the organization.

A grant to create an endowment or augment an existing one approaches brick-and-mortar money in both rarity and difficulty of winning. Though they are few and far between, some grant makers make such grants. The best chance of obtaining a grant for an endowment probably is from a local grant maker that has a very real and personal interest in the long-term survival of your organization.

Among those grant makers that fund endowments, a common practice is to use the challenge grant concept. Simplistically, a challenge grant is an amount of money used as motivation to raise additional funds and is awarded only after the applicant raises funds to some level of match. For example, a grant maker may extend the offer of a $100,000 challenge grant award for an organization's endowment if the organization raises $200,000 for the endowment by its own efforts. The grant maker challenges the organization to raise the money. If the organization meets the challenge, the grant is awarded. There are other permutations on this same basic concept.

Other or Miscellaneous

This category is the simplest to discuss. The amount that goes in this category in every project budget remains constant regardless of the type of project or the size of the budget. The amount that belongs in this category is zero. The amount is zero unless—and this "unless" should not come as any surprise by now—the grantor includes specific items in the "other" category and your project budget includes expense for one or more of those items.

While far from common, we have worked with budget forms that include an "other" line item that is annotated with several specific budget expenses. For unfathomable reasons, printing and the cost of publications are two items that show up here with fair regularity. The obvious reason is that the people who put the budget together could not decide (or did not know) in what categories books and printing belong. We will settle the issue. Books are materials, and printing is a service.

Setting aside the rare instance when a grant maker forces the use of the other or miscellaneous category, we reassert that the proper amount for this line item is zero. Based on 40 combined years of experience, the next sentence is going to be a rare absolute statement with no modifiers, no qualifiers, and no room for misunderstanding. All possible project expenses fit in one of these nine categories: personnel, fringe, travel, equipment, capital, supplies, materials, contractual services, or endowment. With that as a given, what possible reasons are there for putting funds into this line item? From a different angle, what message do we send to the grant maker when we request funds in this line item?

The main reason funds get requested as other or miscellaneous is insecurity about the budget. When doubt creeps in about whether the budget is sufficient to run the project, it is only natural to want a cushion or a "fudge factor," often called in fine formal bureaucratic manner a contingency fund. What message does requesting a contingency fund send to the grant maker? It says, loudly and clearly, that we are not sure that we have completely thought through the project and its needs, so give us this little bit extra in case we have overlooked something. Demonstrate that you are confident in the budget you have developed. Request zero for other or miscellaneous.

Materials and Supplies Revisited

With the descriptions of the categories of direct expenses now complete, we turn to the relationship between items in different categories. Exhibit 6.2 demonstrates possible relations among equipment, materials, and supplies. For each activity listed in the left column we list a few possible needs in the three columns to the right. We have made no effort to list every possible need, just enough to indicate relationships.

EXHIBIT 6.2

Relationships between Equipment, Materials, and Supplies

Activity	Needs		
	Equipment	Materials	Supplies
Take notes	Utility table	Pen	Ballpoint refill
	Stacking chair		Pad of paper
Archive records	Filing cabinet	Hanging file folders	Labels
	Storage shelving	Storage boxes	Tape

After all the discussion of the differences between materials and supplies, a practical point needs to be made. Most grant application budget forms combine the two into a single line item.

Project Development and the Budget

Returning to the basics, we know that a project is a solution to a problem. To implement the solution, a number of activities will be undertaken. Successful accomplishment of the activities will require certain resources. The budget of a grant application organizes those needed resources into categories and quantifies them in terms of expense or cost—money.

A point not made before now is that a budget can change dramatically based on the approach or methodology chosen for the project. To illustrate, an example project is shown in Exhibit 6.3, which identifies the problem, the project (solution), and the funding source. The statement of the project contains only what is going to happen, not how it will be accomplished, the methodology, or strategy. This allows us to create three projects using three strategies, all of which might solve the problem. Developing a budget (without amounts) for each approach allows us to illustrate the drastic changes that can occur in a budget by adopting different strategies.

Operating Funds

A category of expense missing entirely from the discussion so far in this chapter is money to pay operating expenses of an organization. The

EXHIBIT 6.3

Example Project with Three Approaches

Problem: Grass, weeds, shrubs, and vines in yard continue to grow. Neighbors complain. Town levies $500 fine for zoning compliance violation.

Project: Trim, crop, prune, and cut grass, weeds, shrubs, and vines to acceptable verdure.

Funding: Foundation for Preventing the Town from Collecting Zoning Compliance Violation Fines

Project One: Applicant does the work.

Budget for Project One (without amounts)

Budget Items	Purpose of Item	Category of Item	Source
My time	Do the work	Personnel	In-kind
Lawn mower	Cut grass	Equipment	Grant request
Gas and oil	Fuel lawn mower	Supplies	In-kind
Shears, nippers, and saws	Cut shrubs and vines	Equipment	Grant request

Comment: This budget demonstrates an approach to a project that grant makers find attractive and are more likely to fund than other approaches The grant request funds only start-up costs (lawn mower and tools). The applicant absorbs those project expenses that are continuous and ongoing (personnel and supplies). This means the project has a very good chance of continuing beyond the term of the grant—very important to grant makers.

Project Two: Happy Lawn Landscaping Company does the work.

Budget for Project Two (without amounts)

Budget Items	Purpose of Item	Category of Item	Source
Landscaping company	Do all the work	Contractual service	Grant request

Comment: This budget demonstrates an approach unlikely to attract a grant maker. All the expenses of the project are concentrated in contractual services therefore the question for the grant maker is how the applicant will be able to continue the project after the flow of grant funds stops.

EXHIBIT 6.3 *(Continued)*

Project Three: Sheep and llamas do the work.

Budget for Project Three (without amounts)

Budget Items	Purpose of Item	Category of Item	Source
My time	Administer project	Personnel	In-kind
Sheep and llamas	Do all the real work	Equipment (?)	Grant request
Construction company	Build fence	Contractual service	Grant request
Additional feed	Feed animals	Supplies	Project revenue*
Veterinarian	Care for animals	Contractual services	Project revenue*

* The plan is to shear sheep and llamas yearly, sell the fleece, and use the project revenue to support continuation of the project.

Comment: This budget demonstrates an approach that uses project revenue as the primary means of continuing the project after the term of the grant. The approach would probably be considered innovative, if not lunatic (especially by the neighbors).

omission is intentional. The focus of this book is on projects and their budgets. The grants we are pursuing are project grants. By definition, the purpose of a project grant is to fill gaps, meet unmet needs, and promote innovation. Project grants are not intended to fund an organization's existing, regular, day-to-day programs. If an organization wants to innovate, to meet a need of its target population that now is not being met, or fill a gap in existing service, then a project grant is the place to start. One additional thing is necessary. The organization cannot depend on the grant to fund the effort forever. Project grants run for a set length of time and then stop. After the term of the grant, the organization is expected to continue the project on its own. Organizational operating funds, therefore fall into a different area of fund-raising than project grants, and are outside the scope of this book.

Wise Guy and Wise Lady

Wise Guy

Definitions, definitions, definitions. ARGHH! How boring! I always knew budgets were boring.

Wise Lady

Hey, if you don't know what is meant by a term, how can you work up a good budget? If you know all this, then just skip the chapter. If you know most of it, then use the chapter as a reference. But until you and the funder are defining terms the same way, you aren't communicating. If you are talking about apples and the funder is reading "eggs," then your budget is not making sense. There's a lot of difference between apples and eggs. You don't want to wind up with egg on your face, do you?

Conclusion

In this chapter, we have defined and discussed the different direct costs that can be found in a grant project budget. The purpose of gathering all the definitions and explanations together into one chapter is to streamline the rest of the book. Terms and concepts have been defined. Differences and similarities have been discussed. The basics have been covered.

Key Concepts

- Personnel costs are the salaries and wages of project personnel regardless of source.
- Fringe is the cash cost incurred by an employer when employee wages are paid.
- Equipment is inanimate, has physical substance, can be used repeatedly to accomplish a purpose or purposes, and remains essentially unchanged after each use.
- Capital is expenditure for the fixed assets of land, buildings, and improvements.

- Materials and supplies are expendable items.
- Contractual service is work done by one party for another.
- Contractors are providers of contractual services.
- Consultants are contractors.
- An endowment is a pot of money that earns money that becomes income for the holder of the endowment.
- All possible project expenses fit into one of these nine categories: personnel, fringe, travel, equipment, capital, supplies, materials, contractual services, or endowment; therefore, the proper amount for other or miscellaneous expenses is zero.
- The content of the budget is dependent on the approach, strategies, or methodologies.

In Chapters 7, 8, and 9, we move to methods of calculating and capturing budget expenses. Chapter 7 is dedicated solely to the subject of personnel expense. Chapter 8 focuses on travel expenses. In Chapter 9 are gathered the methods for calculating the remaining types of direct expenses. In these chapters, we begin to use the tools found on the CD-ROM that accompanies the book. The tools include spreadsheets for performing calculations and checklists for staying on track.

Chapter 7

Personnel Costs:
Compute and Capture

When men are employed, they are best contented; for on
the days they worked they were good-natured and cheerful,
and with the consciousness of having done a good day's
work, they spent the evening jollily; but on our idle
days they were mutinous & quarrelsome.

Benjamin Franklin, Autobiography

In conceptualizing personnel costs, it is helpful to recognize the two basic
ways that personnel are paid (salary or hourly) and the two basic ways
that funds flow to a project (the grant and other sources). This information can be placed into a two-by-two matrix as shown in Exhibit 7.1.
While many applicants are only concerned with expenses that will be
paid with grant funds, many grant makers want to know what your contribution to the project will be. This is where understanding and using in-
kind contributions becomes important. The funding under the heading
"other sources" usually will be in-kind.

This chapter is organized around the four topics defined by the matrix
of Exhibit 7.1, with an additional topic that combines all four individual
topics into a coherent whole. The topics all follow a similar process of explanation. Each topic first has introductory material, followed by an
illustration of the calculation worksheet that applies to the topic. Each
exhibit is a likeness of an actual worksheet on the CD-ROM that accompanies the book. The worksheets on the CD-ROM are automatically calculating spreadsheets. Next, we give the calculation formula that lies
at the heart of the worksheet and then define the terms used in the
worksheet and formula. Once a term is defined in one topic, the definition is not repeated even though it may be used again. The checklist that
follows the definition provides notes, warnings, and suggestions for
using the calculation worksheet (and possibly the formula) as well as instructions for completing it easily and effectively. A sample calculation

EXHIBIT 7.1

Matrix of Type of Pay against Source of Funds

	Grant	**Other Sources**
Salary	Salaried personnel paid with grant funds	Salaried personnel paid from sources other than grant funds
Hourly	Hourly wage personnel paid with grant funds	Hourly personnel paid from sources other than grant funds

worksheet is completed with several examples; the topic under discussion closes with a few concluding comments. The chapter begins, however, not with one of the four topics defined by the matrix of Exhibit 7.1, but by discussing a related personnel issue. Grant project developers will not need to become involved in the exempt/nonexempt issue, but it is worthwhile to at least know what the terms mean and what the discussion is about.

Exempt or Nonexempt Employee?

The Federal Fair Labor Standards Act (FLSA) sets minimum wage, overtime pay, equal pay, record keeping, and child labor standards requirements for employers. Oversight and enforcement of FSLA comes from the Wage and Hour Division of the Employment Standards Administration in the U.S. Department of Labor. The provisions of FLSA cover all employees; however, an employer may have employees who are exempt from certain provisions of the Act, including minimum wage and overtime pay regulations. These employees include the so-called white-collar exemptions for executive, administrative, or professional positions.

The decision to exempt an employee cannot be made arbitrarily nor can it be made based solely on the job title or the way the employee is paid. A salaried employee is not automatically exempt, though it is necessary to be salaried to qualify as exempt. The determination is based, in addition, on job duties associated with the position. The following information is derived from what the FLSA calls its "short test for high salaried employees."

An employee in an executive position may be exempt if the salary is not less than $250 per week; if the employee's primary duty is managing an enterprise, department, or subdivision; and if the employee customarily directs work of two or more employees.

135

An employee in an administrative position may be exempt if the salary is not less than $250 per week if the employee's primary duty is performing office or nonmanual work directly related to management policies, general business operations of the employer or its customers, administrative work in the academic field, or work relating to academic instruction; and the employee exercises discretion and independent judgment in performance of work.

An employee in a professional position may be exempt if the salary is not less than $250 per week and the employee's primary duty is performing work that (1) requires advanced knowledge in a field of science or learning, or (2) is original and creative in a field of artistic endeavor, or (3) involves imparting knowledge as a certified or recognized teacher.

The developers of grant project budgets generally do not need to get involved in the exempt/nonexempt issue. Since payment by salary does not necessarily make a person an exempt employee, the decision of whether to pay project personnel with salary or hourly wages can be made based on practical financial and organizational factors. If the exempt/nonexempt issue becomes important, call in the financial personnel or advisers of your organization and have them make the call.

Salaried Personnel Funded from Grant Request

Positions in which personnel are paid with a yearly salary (as opposed to hourly wages) generally are professional or management in nature. In this case, professional includes fields such as education, research, medicine, science, technology, and engineering.

Usually, though not always, a project's key personnel are salaried. "Key personnel" is a grant maker's term that refers to those few positions within a project, usually one to three, for which the qualifications of the person filling the position are key to the success of the project. Grant makers regularly require that personal information on the people who will fill the key positions be included in an application (proposal).

Exhibit 7.2 is the calculation worksheet, in shortened format, for those salaried project positions that will be funded by the grant. The full version of the worksheet, labeled CH0701A–C, is found on the CD-ROM that accompanies the book. It is a spreadsheet that automatically calculates the cost of each position and totals all the position costs at the bottom of the worksheet.

Calculation Formula

(Qty) × (Salary) × (% Involvement) = Position Cost

EXHIBIT 7.2

 CH0701A–C.XLS

Calculation Worksheet: Salaried Positions Funded from Grant Request

Position Title	Qty	Yearly Salary	% Involvement	Position Cost
Grant Request Salaried Positions Total				

Definitions

Position Title

Descriptive title of the position.

Examples: Project Director, Principal Investigator, Events Coordinator, Counselor, or Therapist.

Qty

Quantity: the number of personnel in the position (with the position title).

Note: While "Qty" is most often simply one, multiple project positions occur frequently enough that inserting this multiplier is worthwhile. Using a quantity multiplier removes the necessity of entering data in multiple separate lines when more than one person will be hired for a particular position. One line is sufficient for all personnel with the same title, salary, and % FTE.

Yearly Salary

The total yearly salary for the position.

Examples: $80,000, $18,000, or $42,575.

% Involvement

This item indicates the percentage of a person's time that will be covered by the grant-funded salary.

Examples: 100% is a full-time employee, 50% is a half-time employee, 25% is a quarter-time employee.

Position Cost

The result of application of the calculation formula.

Note: Calculation occurs automatically on worksheet CH0701.

Grant Request Salaried Positions Total

The sum (total) of all Position Costs.

1. When a person's time commitments are totaled, they may not exceed 100 percent. If a person is committed full-time to one project, that person may not be committed for any time for any other project. Or, for example, if 75 percent of a person's time is committed to one project, then 50 percent cannot be committed to another project, 25 percent is the maximum involvement. Total involvement may not exceed 100 percent.

2. More often than not, grant makers require that an applicant not supplant existing salary. The phrase they use to signal this requirement is "supplement not supplant." To supplant is to take the place of or replace. When salary is supplanted, it means that grant funds are used in the place of existing funding. The funds previously dedicated for salary are now free to use for any purpose the applicant chooses. Supplanting salary is a ruse to convert grant funds from a specific purpose to general purpose. If a grant maker intended to make a grant for general purposes, it would do so. Supplanting existing funds converts a grant maker's funds from the purpose intended by the grant maker to any purpose the grant winner wishes. Most grant makers do not allow the supplanting of existing funding. The idea that supplanting is appropriate comes from the experience of research in higher education, in which grants at times pay the salary of staff. This does not change the generality that most grant makers, in most cases, do not allow supplanting of existing funding. Grant funds are to supplement not supplant. See Exhibits 7.3 and 7.4.

Salaried Personnel Funded from Other Sources

By "other sources," we mean any funding source other than the grant request. This category collects the in-kind contributions of salaried personnel

EXHIBIT 7.3

Salaried Positions Funded from Grant Request Calculation Worksheet Checklist

- ☐ 1. Position title is descriptive—conveys a sense of the purpose of the position.
- ☐ 2. If "Qty" is more than one (1), "Salary" and "% Involvement" the same for all positions.
- ☐ 3. No person's involvement exceeds 100%.
- ☐ 4. Existing funding is not supplanted.

time to the budget of the project (see Exhibit 7.5). The sources of this funding are the applicant, the project partners, and project volunteers. Also included in "other sources" is the relatively rare circumstance in which an applicant or project consortium or partnership must make a cash match. In reality, the difference between a cash match and an in-kind contribution is one of bookkeeping, since someone ultimately pays in cash for contributed personnel time, goods, and services. The only instance in which in-kind contributions do not incur a cash outlay is when the claim is spurious. If in-kind contributions are included in a budget but no actual project activities take place, there is no diversion of personnel time, goods, or services to the project; then no cash is expended. Otherwise, someone pays for the in-kind contribution. In the case of volunteers, the payment is in time denied to the volunteer for use in other activities.

EXHIBIT 7.4

Example of Completed Worksheet CH0701, Calculation Worksheet: Salaried Positions Funded from Grant Request

Position Title	Qty	Yearly Salary	% Involvement	Position Cost
Project Director	1	$42,000.00	100	$ 42,000.00
Counselors	3	34,500.00	100	103,500.00
Site Coordinators	3	28,000.00	50	42,000.00
Grant Request Salaried Positions Total				$187,500.00

EXHIBIT 7.5

CH0702A–B.XLS

Calculation Worksheet: Salaried Positions Funded from Other Sources

Position Title	Funding		Qty	Yearly Salary	% Involvement	Position Cost
	Type	Source				
Other Sources Salaried Positions Total						

	Key to Funding Source
1	
2	
3	
4	

Calculation Formula

(Qty) × (Salary) × (% Involvement) = Position Cost

Definitions

Funding Type

Designation of the type of funding, either cash or in-kind.

Funding Source

The source of the cash or in-kind that will bear the cost of the position.

Examples: applicant, local government, state government, foundation, corporation, partner, or volunteers.

Exhibit 7.6

Salaried Positions Funded from Other Sources Calculation Worksheet Checklist

☐ 1. Position title is descriptive—conveys a sense of the purpose of the position.

☐ 2. If "Qty" is more than one (1), "Salary" and "% Involvement" the same for all positions.

☐ 3. No person's involvement exceeds 100%.

☐ 4. Involvement percentages of partner personnel are realistic.

☐ 5. Existing funding is not supplanted.

% Involvement

The percentage of the person's total work time that will be dedicated to working on project activities.

In the example (Exhibit 7.7), a contribution of 5 percent of salary is shown for the Executive Director of the applicant. Elsewhere in the proposal, probably in both the project narrative and the budget justification, the purpose of this contribution will be explained. The 5 percent contribution likely is for the oversight and leadership provided by the director to the proposed project. Here is a case where the percentage of involvement claimed must be reasonable and realistic, as noted in item 4 in the checklist (Exhibit 7.6). Five percent of a 40-hour work week is 2 hours. For the Executive Director to spend two hours each week in oversight of a project is not unreasonable, assuming the project is big enough. If the budget for the proposed project is just several thousand dollars, no one will believe it will take 2 hours every week of the director's time. If, however, the budget for the project is hundreds of thousands of dollars, it is quite reasonable that the director dedicate 2 hours a week to the project's care.

Hourly Wage Personnel Funded from Grant Request

Personnel doing technical, secretarial, or vocational work generally are paid hourly wages (as opposed to a yearly salary). There are, however, no hard-and-fast rules about the types of positions paid with salary and those paid with hourly wages.

EXHIBIT 7.7

Example of Completed Worksheet CH0702, Calculation Worksheet: Salaried Positions Funded from Other Sources

Position Title	Funding Type[1]	Source[2]	Qty	Yearly Salary	% Involvement	Position Cost
Executive Director	I	1	1	$65,000.00	5	$ 3,250.00
Speech Therapist	I	1	2	38,000.00	25	9,000.00
Director of Recreation	I	2	1	26,000.00	15	3,900.00
Language Arts Tutor	I	3	10	32,000.00	10	32,000.00
Nurse Practitioner	I	4	1	40,000.00	20	8,000.00
[1]C = cash; I = in-kind		Other Sources Salaried Positions Total				$52,900.00

[2]Key to Funding Source	
1	Applicant
2	County Parks and Recreation Division
3	Local School District
4	County Hospital

Exhibit 7.8 shows, in shortened format, the calculation worksheet for those hourly wage project positions that will be funded by the grant. The full version (worksheet CH0703) is on the CD-ROM that accompanies the book. This spreadsheet automatically calculates the cost of each position and totals all the position costs at the bottom of the worksheet.

Calculation Formula

(Qty) × (Hourly Wage) × (Hours per Week) × (Weeks per Year) = Position Cost

Definitions

Hourly Wage

The amount paid for an hour's work during a standard full-time workday (not weekends, holidays, or after normal hours and not overtime).

Examples: $7.50, $12.25, $9.89.

EXHIBIT 7.8

Calculation Worksheet: Hourly Wage Personnel Funded from Grant Request

Position Title	Qty	Hourly Wage	Hours/ Week	Weeks/ Year	Position Cost
Grant Request Hourly Wage Positions Total					

Hours/Week

The anticipated number of hours per week that the person in this position will work.

Note: Wage-and-hour regulations forbid an employer from establishing a normal workweek of more than 40 hours.

Examples: 20 hours per week is a half-time person, 10 hours per week is a quarter-time person.

Weeks/Year

The number of weeks per year for which the person in this position will be paid.

Note: For most organizations in the private sector this number will be 52, however, the work year of many employees of school systems (and other organizations with seasonal schedules) less than 52 weeks.

See Exhibits 7.9 and 7.10.

EXHIBIT 7.9

Hourly Wage Positions Funded from Grant Request Calculation Worksheet Checklist

- ☐ 1. Position title is descriptive—conveys a sense of the purpose of the position.
- ☐ 2. If "Qty" is more than one (1), Wage, Hours, and Weeks the same for all positions.
- ☐ 3. No person's involvement exceeds 100%.
- ☐ 4. Existing funding is not supplanted.
- ☐ 5. Hours per week do not exceed 40.

Hourly Wage Personnel Funded from Other Sources

The information to arrive at the position cost and the calculation performed remain the same in this worksheet as in the last. What changes is the source of the support. We need to know two new items of information, the source of the support and the type of support (see Exhibit 7.11). After going through the three previous versions of a worksheet that calculates

EXHIBIT 7.10

Example of Completed Worksheet CH0703, Calculation Worksheet: Hourly Wage Personnel Funded from Grant Request

Position Title	Qty	Hourly Wage	Hours/ Week	Weeks/ Year	Position Cost
Project Secretary	1	$12.25	40	52	$25,480.00
Technician	1	13.50	40	52	28,080.00
Scheduling Secretary	1	10.25	20	32	6,560.00
Grant Request Hourly Wage Positions Total					$60,120.00

EXHIBIT 7.11

 CH0704A–B.XLS

Calculation Worksheet: Hourly Wage Personnel Funded from Other Sources

Position Title	Funding Type[1]	Source[2]	Qty	Hourly Wage	Hours/ Week	Weeks/ Year	Position Cost
[1]C = cash; I = in-kind	Other Sources Hourly Wage Personnel Total						

[2]**Key to Funding Source**	
1	
2	
3	
4	

personnel expense, you will find this one does not spring any surprises (see Exhibits 7.12 and 7.13).

Calculation Formula

(Qty) × (Hourly Wage) × (Hours per Week) × (Weeks per Year) = Position Cost

Personnel Fringe (One Rate)

The expense of personnel fringe, at times called fringe benefits, is an amount expended in cash by an employer when an employee is paid salary or wages. An employer must match the amount withheld from employee wages for Social Security and Medicare. Employers may pay additional

EXHIBIT 7.12

Hourly Wage Personnel Funded from Other Sources Calculation Worksheet Checklist

☐ 1. Position title is descriptive—conveys a sense of the purpose of the position.

☐ 2. If "Qty" is more than one (1), Wage, Hours, and Weeks the same for all positions.

☐ 3. No person's involvement exceeds 100%.

☐ 4. Existing funding is not supplanted.

☐ 5. Hours per week do not exceed 40.

☐ 6. In the table appended to the bottom of the worksheet, enter a descriptive identifier of the source of the support for each position.

EXHIBIT 7.13

Example of Completed Worksheet CH0704, Calculation Worksheet: Hourly Wage Personnel Funded from Other Sources

Position Title	Funding Type[1]	Source[2]	Qty	Hourly Wage	Hours/ Week	Weeks/ Year	Position Cost
Bus Driver	I	1	3	8.50	10	42	$10,710.00
Computer Technician	I	2	1	12.75	5	42	2,677.50
Network Administrator	I	3	1	17.50	5	42	3,675.00
Project Evaluator	I	4	2	20.25	20	4	3,240.00
Homework Monitors	I	5	30	7.00	5	42	44,400.00
Mentors	I	6	25	7.00	2	42	14,700.00
[1]C = cash; I = in-kind		Other Sources Hourly Wage Personnel Total					$79,402.50

[2]Key to Funding Source	
1	Municipal Transit Authority
2	Maintenance Div., County Government
3	Network Solutions, Inc.
4	State University, Our Town Campus
5	Volunteers, Parent Teacher Assoc. Chip In Program
6	Volunteers, Chamber of Commerce Leadership Program

EXHIBIT 7.14 CH0705.XLS

Calculation Worksheet: Personnel Fringe (One Rate)

Descriptions	Amounts
Grant Request Salaried Positions Total	
Grant Request Hourly Wage Positions Total	
Other Sources Salaried Positions Total	
Other Sources Salaried Positions Total	
Total Personnel Expense	
Fringe Rate	
Personnel Fringe	

expenses based on employee wages. A few examples are worker's compensation insurance, state unemployment insurance, federal unemployment insurance, health insurance, life insurance, retirement plan, and other possibilities. These payments are a cash expense to an employer. Grant makers almost always allow applicants to include the expense of fringe in the grant request.

Exhibit 7.14 shows the calculation worksheet for personnel fringe. The full version (worksheet CH0705), is on the CD-ROM that accompanies the book. This spreadsheet automatically calculates the expense of personnel fringe (see Exhibits 7.15 and 7.16).

EXHIBIT 7.15

Personnel Fringe (One Rate) Calculation Worksheet Checklist

☐ 1.
☐ 2.
☐ 3.
☐ 4.
☐ 5.
☐ 6.
☐ 7.
☐ 8.
☐ 9.

Exhibit 7.16

Personnel Fringe (One Rate) Calculation Worksheet

Descriptions	Amounts
Grant Request Salaried Positions Total	$ 50,000.00
Grant Request Hourly Wage Positions Total	12,500.00
Other Sources Salaried Positions Total	55,500.00
Other Sources Salaried Positions Total	15,750.00
Total Budget Personnel Expense	$133,750.00
Fringe Rate	19.720%
Personnel Fringe	$ 26,375.50

Calculation Formula

(Fringe Rate) × (Total Budget Personnel Expense) = Fringe

Definitions

Fringe Rate

The percentage of employee salaries and wages an employer pays, in addition to salaries and wages, for expenses such as Social Security, Medicare, worker's compensation insurance, unemployment insurance, health insurance, retirement, and possibly others.

Examples: 12 percent is a very low fringe rate; 50 percent is a very high fringe rate.

Personnel Fringe (More than One Rate)

More than one fringe rate may be encountered. A project partner, for example, may have a vastly different fringe rate than the applicant organization. Also, it is not unusual for an organization to utilize two fringe rates, one rate for full-time employees and another for part-time workers. Where a grant applicant needs a large amount of matching funds, it might be important to use a partner's higher fringe rate. Many organizations have fringe rates of over 30 percent. The addition to the contributed value of salaries and wages can be substantial and can help greatly with the accumulation of needed matching funds.

Exhibit 7.17 shows the calculation worksheet for personnel fringe. The full version (Worksheet CH0706) on the CD-ROM that accompanies

EXHIBIT 7.17

 CH0706.XLS

Calculation Worksheet: Personnel Fringe (More than One Rate) for Hourly Wage Positions Funded from Other Sources

Position Title	Funding		Qty	Hrly Wage	Hrs/ Wk	Wks/ Yr	Position Cost	Fringe Rate	Fringe Amount
	T[1]	S[2]							
Other Sources Hourly Wage Personnel Totals									

[1] Type Funding with C = cash & I = in-kind
[2] Source

Key to Funding Source	
1	
2	
3	
4	

the book is a spreadsheet that automatically calculates the expense of personnel fringe. The calculation of fringe has been added to only one of the worksheets previously illustrated—the one for hourly wage personnel funded from sources other than the grant. The principle of calculating fringe is the same for the other three worksheets, all of which can be found on the CD-ROM (see Exhibits 7.18 and 7.19).

Calculation Formula

(Qty) × (Hourly Wage) × (Hrs/Wk) × (Wk/Yr) = Position Cost
(Position Cost) × (Fringe Rate) = Fringe Amount

EXHIBIT 7.18

Personnel Fringe (More than One Rate) for Calculation Worksheet: Hourly Wage Positions Funded from Other Sources

☐ 1. Position title is descriptive—conveys a sense of the purpose of the position.

☐ 2. Funding Type (T) is noted (C for cash and I for in-kind).

☐ 3. A number indicating the Funding Source (S) is entered and a corresponding organization or agency name is entered into appropriately numbered row of "Key to Funding Source" section at bottom of worksheet—name each partner separately and specifically.

☐ 4. If "Qty" is more than one (1), Hourly Wage, Hours per Week, and Weeks per Year must be the same for all individuals with the position title.

Enter as a whole number such as 1, 2, or 3 (no fractions or decimals).

☐ 5. Hourly Wage is in line with wages normally paid in your locality for comparable work performed by persons with comparable background (education and experience) to those established for the project.

Enter as follows: dd.cc, with d = dollars and c = cents—do not use dollar sign ($).

Examples: 7.50, 10.25, 13.33.

☐ 6. Hrs/Wk (Hours per Week) may not exceed forty (40).

Enter as follows: h.m with h = hours and m = fraction of hour.

Examples: 20, 10, 2, 2.5.

☐ 7. Weeks per Year may not exceed fifty-two (52).

Enter as whole number only in the range of zero to 52; note that zero will return $0.00 as Position cost.

☐ 8. Position cost is calculated and entered automatically by the worksheet when Qty, Hourly Wage, Hrs/Wk, and Wks/Yr all have been entered.

☐ 9. Obtain Fringe Rates from the personnel that handle an organization's finances.

Enter as a number smaller than one; the spreadsheet converts the number to a percentage.

Examples: 25% is entered as 0.25; 19.752% is entered as 0.19752.

☐ 10. Fringe Amount is calculated and entered automatically by the worksheet when a Position Cost is calculated and Fringe Amount is entered.

☐ 11. The sum of all Position Costs will be automatically calculated and entered in the bottom cell in that column.

☐ 12. The sum of all Fringe Amounts will be automatically calculated and entered in the bottom cell in that column.

EXHIBIT 7.19

Calculation Worksheet: Personnel Fringe (More than One Rate) for Hourly Wage Positions Funded from Other Sources

Position Title	Funding T[1]	Funding S[2]	Qty	Hrly Wage	Hrs/ Wk	Wks/ Yr	Position Cost	Fringe Rate	Fringe Amount
Bus Drivers	I	1	3	$ 8.50	10	42	$10,710.00	13.600%	$1,456.56
Computer Tech	I	2	1	12.75	5	42	2,677.50	38.525	1,031.51
Network Admin	I	3	1	17.50	5	42	3,675.00	19.752	725.89
Other Sources Hourly Wage Personnel Totals							$17,062.50		$3,213.95

[1] Type Funding: C = cash; I = in-kind

[2] Key to Funding Source	
1	Municipal Transit Authority
2	Maintenance Div., County Government
3	Network Solutions, Inc.
4	

Definitions

T (under "Funding")

Stands for Type of Funding, with the two possible types being cash and in-kind contribution.

S (under "Funding")

Stands for Source of Funding—the three major sources of funding are the applicant, project partners, and volunteers; make a separate entry for each partner; entries for volunteers should reflect the source and purpose of the volunteers.

Hrs/Wk

Abbreviation for Hours per Week, which means the number of hours a person spends each week on project activities.

Wks/Yr

Abbreviation for Weeks per Year, which means the number of weeks in the course of a year that a person will spend the hours per week of the previous column on project activities.

Fringe Rate

A fringe rate is a percentage of salary or wages.

Fringe Amount

Fringe amount is the employer cash expenditure that occurs when salary and wages are paid to an employee.

Combined Personnel Expense Calculation Worksheet

So far in this chapter, to make it easier to absorb the details of calculating the cost of personnel, we demonstrated the various permutations of salary, wage, and fringe calculations in separate worksheets. These individual worksheets are handy for quick calculations of a particular expense. The problem with this approach is that several worksheets are needed to calculate all personnel and fringe expense for the typical project. A more elegant solution would be a single spreadsheet that combines the functions of the individual worksheets into one integrated and unified worksheet. That worksheet (CH0707 on the CD-ROM) is illustrated in Exhibit 7.20.

This worksheet provides substantial opportunity for confusion and mistakes because it incorporates all the data necessary for calculating both salaried and hourly wage positions. Therefore, careful attention to detail is going to be very important. An excellent method is to have a rough idea of what an amount should be before having the worksheet calculate it for you. For example, if you expect a Position Cost to come in somewhere around $5,000 but the worksheet returns $22,000, something is wrong. It could be that your estimate is wrong, but more likely, one of the pieces of information has been entered incorrectly or the information itself is wrong.

The simple expedient of asking yourself whether an amount is reasonable will avoid many problems. Generally, you have an idea of how much you intend to pay for a position. When the worksheet returns an amount vastly different, whether smaller or larger, revisit the individual pieces of data that the formula uses in its calculation. The old computer truism

EXHIBIT 7.20

Personnel and Fringe Expense Calculation Worksheet

CH0707.XLS

Position Title	Fund Source Key	Qty	Salaried Positions		Hourly Wage Positions				Position Cost	Fringe Rate (%)	Fringe Amount
			Salary	% Involve	Hrly Wage	Hr/ Wk	Wk/ Yr	% Involve			

Positions Supported by Grant Request:

	1										
	1										
	1										
	1										

Totals Supported by Grant

Positions Supported by Sources Other than Grant Request:

Totals Supported by Sources Other than Grant

Fund Source Information

Key	Identity of Source	Type
1	Grant Request	C
2	Applicant	I
3		
4		
5		
6		
7		
8		
9		
10		

Project Totals

Personnel Expense ☐

Fringe Expense ☐

"Garbage In Garbage Out" (GIGO) applies nowhere more than with a worksheet that does calculations for you.

Another possibility is that the underlying formulas in the worksheet may have been modified or changed inadvertently. If you suspect that is the cause of a faulty calculation, obtain a new copy of the worksheet from the CD-ROM, and begin again. One of the handiest aspects of regular CD-ROM is that the contents cannot be changed by accident. A clean copy awaits the user at all times.

It will pay dividends to carefully peruse Worksheet CH0707 (Exhibit 7.20). Check Definitions to ensure understanding of all the terms used as column headers. Read the Checklist for additional information on the use of the worksheet (Exhibit 7.21). Finally, Exhibit 7.22 illustrates a completed worksheet. The point is to understand the meaning of each entry on this key worksheet, including where the information came from and its purpose.

Calculation Formulas

Salaried Positions

(Qty) × (Salary) × (% Involvement) = Position Cost

Hourly Wage Positions

(Qty) × (Hourly Wage) × (Hours per Week) × (Weeks per Year) = Position Cost

Personnel Fringe

(Fringe Rate) × (Personnel Cost) = Fringe

Definitions

Positions Supported by Grant Request

The top portion of the worksheet is used to collect the data and calculate the personnel expenses for positions that will be funded from the grant, both salaried and hourly wage positions.

Positions Supported by Sources Other than Grant Request

The bottom portion of the worksheet is used to collect the data and calculate the personnel expenses for positions that will be funded from sources other than the grant, both salaried and hourly wage positions.

Position Title

Descriptive name of the position for which expenses are to be calculated on that row of the worksheet.

Fund Source Key

This column provides space to enter a number that keys to the Fund Source Information Table appended to the bottom of the worksheet.

Exhibit 7.21

Checklist, Personnel Expense Calculation Worksheet

☐ 1. **Position Title** is descriptive, conveys a sense of the purpose of the position.

☐ 2. **Fund Source Key** is a number that keys to a row in the Fund Source Information Table appended to the bottom of the worksheet; each Position Title must have a Fund Source key number assigned; if one cannot be assigned, it means there is no information about the source of funding for the position; is it practical to assume that a position will actually exist if no idea of a funding source exists?

☐ 3. **Qty** is the number of persons who will carry the same position title and be paid exactly the same.

☐ 4. **Salary** is expressed in normal U.S. currency notation.

   Enter as dd.cc, with d = dollars and c = cents; do NOT enter a dollar sign ($).

   Examples: 42,000.00, 32,500.00, 17,235.75.

☐ 5. **Salaried Positions % Involve** is a percentage.

   Enter the whole number one (1) for 100%; all other percentages are entered as numbers less than one; they begin with a decimal point.

   Examples: for 10%, enter 0.1, for 25%, enter 0.25, for 50%, enter 0.5, for 75.5%, enter .755, for 19.752%, enter 0.19752.

   Do NOT enter the percent sign; the worksheet will translate the number you enter into a percentage.

   Warning: While the worksheet will accept percentages larger than 100%, grant makers do not permit a person's involvement to exceed 100%.

☐ 6. **Hourly Wage** is expressed in normal U.S. currency notation.

   Enter as dd.cc, with d = dollars and c = cents; do NOT enter a dollar sign ($).

   Examples: 7.55, 10.33, 17.50.

☐ 7. **Hr/Wk** is expressed as a whole number such as 5, 10, or 20; any decimal amounts entered will be truncated to the whole number; for example entering 5.5 will result in a value of 5 in the cell.

☐ 8. **Wk/Yr** is expressed as a whole number such as 10, 26, or 52; any decimal amounts entered will be truncated.

☐ 9. **Hourly Wage Positions % Involve** is a percentage.

   Usually, the amount of involvement is determined by the hours per week and the weeks per year; it is possible to use a percentage involvement for hourly wage positions, but this is rare.

   Use checklist points from Item 5.

☐ 10. **Position Cost** will calculate and display automatically as soon as sufficient data has been entered in a row; for a salaried position: Salary and % Involve; for an hourly wage position: Hourly wage, Hr/Wk, Wk/Yr, and % Involve.

(continued)

Exhibit 7.21 *(Continued)*

☐ 11. **Fringe Rate** is a percentage displayed to three decimal places.

For 100%, enter one (1); it will display as 100.000%.

Enter all other percentages as numbers less than zero (beginning with a decimal point).

Examples: for 19.752%, enter 0.19752; for 33.5% enter 0.335.

Warning: The worksheet will allow a percentage larger than 100%.

☐ 12. **Fringe Amount** will calculate and display automatically as soon as a Position Cost and a Fringe Rate are entered.

☐ 12. **Totals Supported by Grant** and **Totals Supported by Sources Other than Grant** label the locations of the automatically calculated totals of the Position Costs and Fringe Amounts for each main section of the worksheet.

As soon as one Position Cost or Fringe Amount is calculated, it will automatically reflect as a Total; each newly calculated Position Cost or Fringe Amount is added automatically to the existing Total to create a new Total.

☐ 13. **Project Totals** labels the locations of the automatically calculated grand totals, the sums of all Position Costs and Fringe Amounts regardless of source of support.

☐ 13. **Fund Source Information Table** contains the identity of the source of support for a personnel position along with the type of support, cash or in-kind.

☐ 14. **Key** is a number corresponding to a number entered in the "Fund Source" column in the main body of the worksheet; the number links or keys the information in the Fund Source Information table to Positions in the main body of the worksheet.

☐ 15. **Identity of Source** is a descriptive name of the source of the support for a position; remember that the three categories of funding sources are the grant, the applicant, project partners, and volunteers.

Note that two Identities of Source are preentered, the grant request and the applicant. This means that positions funded by the grant request are keyed with the number one (1); and in-kind contributions from the applicant are coded with a two (2).

☐ 16. **Type** indicates whether the support from a source is cash or in-kind:

C = cash; I = in-kind

A grant is normally cash.

EXHIBIT 7.22

Worksheet CH0707 Personnel Expense Calculation Worksheet

Position Title	Fund Source Key	Salaried Positions			Hourly Wage Positions				Position Cost	Fringe Rate (%)	Fringe Amount
		Qty	Salary	% Involve	Hrly Wage	Hr/Wk	Wk/Yr	% Involve			
Positions Supported by Grant Request:											
Project Director	1	1	$42,000.00	100					$42,000.00	14.255	$ 5,987.10
Counselors	1	3	34,500.00	50					51,750.00	14.255	7,376.96
Site Coordinators	1	3	28,000.00	100					84,000.00	14.255	11,974.20
Project Secretary	1	1			12.25	40	26	100	12,740.00	14.255	1,816.09
								Totals Supported by Grant	$190,490.00		$27,154.35
Positions Supported by Sources Other than Grant Request:											
Executive Director	2	1	$65,000.00	5					$ 3,250.00	14.255	$ 463.29
Counselors	5	3	34,500.00	50					51,750.00	19.852	10,273.41
Sports/Recreation Coordinator	4	1	26,000.00	15					3,900.00	32.750	1,277.25
Language Arts Teachers	5	6	32,000.00	10					19,200.00	19.852	3,811.58
Nurse Practitioner	3	1	40,000.00	20					8,000.00	36.555	2,924.40
Bus Drivers	6	3			8.50	10	42	100	10,710.00	26.450	2,832.80
Project Secretary	2	1			12.25	40	26	100	12,740.00	14.255	1,813.09
Scheduling Secretary	2	1			10.25	20	42	100	8,610.00	14.255	1,227.36
Network Administrator	7	1			17.50	5	42	100	3,675.00	12.600	463.05
Technician	4	1			13.50	40	52	100	28,080.00	32.750	9,196.20
Homework Monitors	8	30			7.00	5	42	100	44,400.00	14.255	6,286.46
Mentors	9	25			8.50	2	42	100	17,850.00	14.255	2,544.52
Assessment and Evaluation	10	1			18.75	20	10	100	3,750.00	44.855	1,682.06
								Totals Supported by Sources Other than Grant	$215,615.00		$44,798.45

	Personnel Expense	Fringe Expense
Project Totals	$406,105.00	$71,952.80

Fund Source Information

Key	Identity of Source	Type
1	Grant Request	C
2	Applicant	I
3	County Hospital	I
4	County Parks and Recreation Division	I
5	School District	I
6	Municipal Transit Authority	I
7	Networks Solutions, Inc.	I
8	Volunteers, PTA Chip In Program	I
9	Volunteers, C of C Leadership Program	I
10	State University, Our Town Campus	I

C = cash
I = in-kind

Qty

The quantity or number of persons that will be utilized in the position.

Salaried Positions

Enter data in the appropriate row in the two columns beneath this heading (Salary and % Involve), if the position on that row is to be paid with a yearly salary.

Salary

The amount of the position's yearly salary.

% Involve

Percentage of involvement: the proportion of a person's time, represented by salary, dedicated to project activities.

Hourly Wage Positions

Enter data in the appropriate row in the three columns beneath this heading (Hourly Wage, Hr/Wk, Wk/Yr), if the position on that row is to paid with an hourly wage.

Hourly Wage

The amount paid for an hour's work in this position during a normal workday (not after hours, not weekends or holidays, and not overtime).

Hr/Wk

Hours per week: the number of hours per week that a person in this position will work.

Wk/Yr

Weeks per year: the number of weeks in a year that a person in this position will work.

% Involve

Percentage of involvement: the proportion of a person's time, represented by wages, dedicated to project activities; for hourly wage positions, this percentage is normally 100% (preentered in the worksheet).

Position Cost

The expense or cost of a position.

Fringe Rate

A fringe rate is a percentage of salary or wages.

Fringe Amount

Fringe amount is the employer cash expenditure that occurs when salary and wages are paid to an employee.

**Totals Supported by Grant
and
Totals Supported by Sources Other than Grant**

Position Costs and Fringe Amounts are totaled in the cells indicated by this heading.

Project Totals

Cell labeled Personnel Expense contains the sum of all Position Costs. Cell labeled Fringe Expense contains the sum of all Fringe Amounts.

Fund Source Information

This is the heading for the table of information about the type and source of funding for personnel positions.

Key

A number entered into the "Fund Source" column in the body of the worksheet that corresponds to a numbered row in the Fund Source Information Table.

Identity of Source

An identifying name of the organization or agency that will provide the funding for the position to which this row is keyed.

Type
Indication of the type of funding: cash or in-kind.

An amazing amount can be discerned from budget figures. The example illustrated in Exhibit 7.22 is not even a complete project budget, only personnel and fringe expenses, but still, a great deal about the project can be seen. For example, the amount of the grant request is smaller than the amount contributed to the project by the applicant and other members of the community partnership. This concretely demonstrates community involvement. Also, the grant amount requested for two of the positions covers only half of the total expense. Counselors and Project Secretary are found in both the grant request section and the support from other sources section. Half of the support for these positions comes from each.

Providing for the expense of project personnel is the most difficult hurdle to continuing a project after the term of the grant. One concrete way to demonstrate the ability to continue a project after the grant runs out is for the applicant to absorb a good portion of the personnel costs at the beginning. Additional proof of capability to continue the project is demonstrated by decreasing the amount of the grant request to support personnel in next year's project budget, while also increasing the amount of support from the applicant and partners. Continue to decrease the size of the grant request to support personnel for each project year of funding. This concretely demonstrates to the grant maker that the applicant and the partnership have the capacity to continue the project after the term of the grant.

Many grant applicants will be concerned only with the amount of the grant request and have no interest in the total project budget. For those that fit this description, we include a worksheet dedicated only to personnel and fringe expenses that will be supported by the grant request. This grant request only worksheet is found on the CD-ROM as CH0703B. The companion worksheet dedicated to personnel support from sources other than the grant request is named CH0704B. Exhibit 7.23 provides a complete list of all the calculation worksheets for determining the expense of personnel and fringe.

Exhibit 7.23

Complete List of Calculation Worksheets for Expense of Personnel and Fringe

Worksheet File Name	Purpose of Worksheet
	Expense of:
CH0701	Salaried Positions Funded from Grant Request
CH0702	Salaried Positions Funded from Sources Other than the Grant
CH0703	Hourly Wage Positions Funded from Grant Request
CH0704	Hourly Wage Positions Funded from Sources Other than the Grant
	Expense of:
CH0705	Personnel Fringe (One Rate)
	Expense of Personnel Fringe (More than One Rate) for:
CH0706	Salaried Positions Funded from Grant Request
CH0707	Salaried Positions Funded from Sources Other than the Grant
CH0703B	Hourly Wage Positions Funded from Grant Request
CH0704B	Hourly Wage Positions Funded from Sources Other than the Grant
	Combined Personnel and Fringe Expense for:
CH0701B	Both Grant Request and Other Sources
CH0701C	Only Grant Request
CH0702B	Only Other Sources

Wise Guy and Wise Lady

Wise Guy

Now we're talking—here's where I plug in the numbers! I can use the worksheets and spreadsheets on that CD for sure. Last year, the state threatened to eliminate a couple of positions—they said we didn't really need them. I am just going to go to the funder and transfer those jobs to them. I like having them around—it means I don't have to do so much work!

Wise Lady

Well, on the one hand I like your response to the worksheets and spreadsheets. They will be a big help for sure. But, I'm not happy with your ideas about personnel. Your personnel must fit your project. Grant funders are not just going to fund positions because you want to have less work! They're not going to supplant state funding—meaning that they're not going to let you take a position that is normally funded at the state level and transfer it to your budget sheet. Grant funders are funding innovative projects that operate effectively to solve a problem for the target population. *You* are not the target population. How tired you are is not of concern to the funder!

Conclusion

In this chapter, we demonstrated the use of the calculation worksheets for personnel and fringe expenses and contributions. A variety of calculation worksheets are provided on the CD-ROM. One of the worksheets will meet the needs of all but a small minority of grant applicants wanting to calculate the expenses of personnel and fringe. Introduced in this chapter is a principle that is fundamental to grant project management after a grant has been won, but that also carries great importance in budget development. The principle is that grant funds are intended to supplement not supplant.

Key Principle

Supplement *Not* Supplant
Supplanting replaces (substitutes) existing funding with grant funding. The formerly committed funds, having been replaced, are now available for any purpose. Supplanting converts grant funds that are dedicated to a specific purpose into general-purpose funds free for any use the supplanting organization chooses. Supplanting subverts a grant maker's intentions—at best it amounts to a serious misunderstanding of the purpose of project grants, and at worst it amounts to fraud.

Although the methods of calculating the expense of personnel positions cause seemingly duplicative calculation worksheets, differences, both small and large, exist between all the various worksheets and processes illustrated and explained in this chapter.

Key Concepts

- The two categories of funding (the grant request and sources other than the grant request) and the two ways to pay employees (salary and hourly wages) create four distinct aspects of calculating personnel expense:

  Salaried personnel paid with grant funds.

  Hourly wage personnel paid with grant funds.

  Salaried personnel paid with funds from sources other than the grant.

  Hourly wage personnel paid with funds from sources other than the grant.

- The cost of a salaried position is calculated with the following formula and data:

  Position Cost = (Qty) × (Salary) × (% Involvement)

  Qty = Number of people who will be employed in the position

  Salary = Yearly remuneration

  % Involvement = The percentage of employer paid time, expressed in terms of salary, that is dedicated to project activities

- The cost of an hourly wage position is calculated with the following formula and data:

Position Cost = (Qty) × (Hourly Wage) × (Hours per Week) × (Weeks per Year)

Qty = Number of people who will be employed in the position

Hourly wage = Amount paid for a normal work hour

Hours per week = Number of hours a week the position offers employment

Weeks per Year = Number of weeks a year the position offers employment

In Chapter 8, we investigate the estimation of the expense of travel. Travel is a complex topic, while the amount of grant funds normally expended on travel amounts to a relatively small percentage. When compared with other direct costs such as personnel, equipment, and contractual services or when compared with such functional topics as evaluation and professional development, the expense of travel usually is much smaller. It is, therefore, legitimate to ask if the topic merits a chapter's worth of attention. The answer is an unequivocal yes.

While small in comparison to the grant request, the amount of money spent on travel can be substantial. When the expense is underestimated, the shortfall must be covered from some source. Experience shows that two main sources bear the cost, either the applicant organization or project staff members. Either way, the results are bad. Using precious organizational funds to cover a shortfall in a category for which the grant maker would have paid all the expenses is simply poor fiscal management. Relying on loyal employees to dig into their own pockets to make up the shortfall is all too normal and is also poor management, in both fiscal and personal areas. When the expense of travel is estimated accurately, neither the organization nor its staff suffer.

Travel Costs:
Compute and Capture

However much I travel I shall not travel fast.
Horses and cars and yachts and planes:
I've no more use for such:
For in three years of war's alarms I've hurried far too much.

Norman Davey, By the Canal in Flanders

This chapter describes a method for accurately determining the cost of travel, whether the trip will be far or near, one day or several. At first look, the cost of travel may seem simple to estimate. After all, the expenses of a trip originate from only three basic sources: the travel itself (air, ground, or both), lodging, and meals. As noted in Chapter 6, however, many and varied expenses are involved in each of these three seemingly simple sources.

Accurately estimating the cost of travel can be organized into a process and divided into its major steps. Each major step then can be divided further into smaller steps. Along the way, discrete items of data must be collected. Approaching the process methodically and step-by-step may appear at first blush to be overkill. Underestimating the expense of travel, however, is one of the most common faults in project budgets. Grant makers do not make up the amount of underestimated travel expenses. An organization and its staff make up the shortfall. Follow the procedure shown in this chapter and the amount requested for travel expenses will cover the cost of the travel. We divide the process of estimating the cost of travel into three major steps:

1. Initial Planning.
2. Calculating.
3. Compiling and summing.

The following numbered steps lead through the initial planning phase, followed by calculation, and then compilation. The whole thing may seem complicated, however, it takes less time (and is easier) to do the actual work of estimating the expense of a trip than it does to explain it. Complete the process thoroughly and completely only once and the logic (and utility) of it becomes obvious. Subsequent iterations move along quickly.

Initial Travel Planning

Accurately estimating the cost of a trip involves many variables and a degree of complexity. The work-flow process is detailed in Exhibit 8.1. The Travel Planning Questionnaire (Exhibit 8.2) and companion Travel Planning Worksheet (Exhibit 8.3), capture the variables and break the complexity into manageably small pieces called travel segments. Once travel data is gathered on the Travel Planning Worksheet, the appropriate calculation worksheets (discussed later in this chapter) can be used to compute the cost of the trip.

The Travel Planning Worksheet is found on the CD-ROM as Worksheet CH0801. The CD-ROM contains a second Travel Planning Worksheet

EXHIBIT 8.1

Initial Planning Work Flow

1. Open the Travel Planning Questionnaire (filename 08.01), illustrated in Exhibit 8.2.
2. Print a copy of the questionnaire.
3. Open the Travel Planning Worksheet (08.02), illustrated in Exhibit 8.3.
4. If a copy of the completed worksheet is desired, perform a "Save As" and give the worksheet a name descriptive of the trip being planned.
5. Answer the questions from the Travel Planning Questionnaire.
6. Enter the answers to the questions into the open worksheet.
7. Perform a "Save" if appropriate.
8. Print a copy of the completed worksheet.
9. Guided by information from the completed Travel Planning Worksheet and the transition question portion of the Travel Planning Questionnaire, select the appropriate calculation worksheets.
10. Once work begins with the worksheets, the process moves into the next major step, Calculation.

EXHIBIT 8.2

CH0801.XLS

Travel Planning Questionnaire

Travel Planning Questionnaire

Setup Questions

Questions	Directions
In what month or months will the trip take place?	In Row 1, enter the month or months.
On what dates will the trip take place?	In Row 2, enter the dates, one per column.
On what days of the week will the trip take place?	In Row 3, enter the days of the week.
How many days will the trip take including partial days?	In Row 13, enter the length of the trip in days.
How many people will travel?	In Row 14, enter the number of people traveling.
Will lodging be single occupancy?	In Row 15, enter the number of people per room.

Travel Questions

For each day, will there be:	Directions If answer is YES, then:
Air travel?	In Row 4, for each day, enter the number of persons traveling by air (zero if none).
Ground travel only?[1]	In Row 5, for each day, enter the number of persons traveling by ground (zero if none).
Lodging?	In Row 6, for each day, enter the number of persons spending the night (zero if none).
Morning meal?	In Row 7, for each day, enter the number of persons eating breakfast (zero if none).
Midday meal?	In Row 8, for each day, enter the number of persons eating midday meal (zero if none).
Evening meal?	In Row 9, for each day, enter the number of persons eating evening meal (zero if none).

[1] The automatic assumption is that any day with travel by air also has travel by ground; therefore, this question pertains only to those days without air travel. Remember that getting back and forth from lodging to meeting sites or meals involves ground travel.

The data entered in the first three rows of the Travel Planning Worksheet in Exhibit 8.3 shows that the trip would take place from Tuesday through Saturday, August 8–12. The numbers in Row 10 illustrate that the trip takes all or part of 5 days.

EXHIBIT 8.3

 CH0802.XLS

Example of Completed Worksheet CH0802, Travel Planning Worksheet

Travel Planning Worksheet

1	Month(s)	August								
2	Date	8	9	10	11	12				
3	Day of Week	Tues	Wed	Thur	Fri	Sat				**Totals**
4	Air Travel	1	0	1	0	1				3
5	Ground Travel	0	1	0	1	0				2
6	Lodging	1	1	1	1	0				4
7	Breakfast	0	1	1	1	1				4
8	Midday Meal	0	1	1	1	0				3
9	Evening Meal	1	1	1	1	0				4
10	**Travel Day**	**1**	**2**	**3**	**4**	**5**	**6**	**7**	**8**	
11	**Air Travel**									
12	**Ground Travel**									
13	Length of Trip in Days	5								
14	Number of People on Trip	1								
15	People per Lodging Room	1								

(filename CH0802). Experience shows that the vast majority of trips planned for grant project purposes entail a stay of three days or less. Worksheet CH0801 is designed for this length trip. Worksheet CH0802 is designed for those rare situations when a project trip entails an extended stay.

The Travel Planning Questionnaire, illustrated in Exhibit 8.2, is found on the CD-ROM with filename CH0801. An example trip adds a degree of realism to the process illustrated in this chapter. The completed worksheets shown in exhibits in this chapter derive their information from the example trip.

Example Trip

The Project Director of the Communitywide After-School Program (CAP) is planning a trip for the project's Technology Coordinator. A new teleconferencing capability is being brought online that will be coupled with two newly obtained assistive technologies, one for hearing-impaired children and the other for the sight-impaired. The Technology Coordinator will spend a day visiting a project operating in another state. This project has implemented an effort similar to one planned by CAP to multiply the efforts of the specialists trained to work with sight- and hearing-impaired children through teleconferencing combined with assistive technologies. After a day of travel to another city, the Technology Coordinator will attend a one-day training course by the vendor from which CAP is purchasing the assistive technologies. On the day following the training, the Technology Coordinator will return home.

Completing a Travel Planning Worksheet

Read the questions and directions in the illustration of the Travel Planning Questionnaire (Exhibit 8.2). Pause at the end of each direction, and note the requisite information entered on the completed example (Exhibit 8.3). In estimating the cost of the Example Trip (described earlier in this chapter), we lack many facts required by the process. When that is the case, simply fabricate the facts.

A properly completed Travel Planning Worksheet is the focal point of estimating accurately the expense of a trip as well as the automatic calculation of several travel expenses. The worksheets are linked so that information flows between them. This linked relationship causes one problem. The worksheets cannot be renamed or the links will be lost. The simplest method of working with the worksheets is to copy all of them, as is, from the CD-ROM to a newly created folder (directory) on a hard drive. Give the newly created folder or directory a descriptive name that identifies its contents with the project for which a budget is being developed. The fact that the worksheets have generic names should not cause problems using this technique.

The calculation worksheets on the CD-ROM are substantially larger than the illustrations in the book. They all have more space than is illustrated (rows or columns or both as appropriate). Generally, one copy of a worksheet is sufficient to collect all the data for even a long and complicated trip.

To allow the travel worksheets to work together to simplify your work, follow carefully the directions in the Master Checklist for Travel (CH0803), illustrated in Exhibit 8.4. This checklist, along with a completed Travel Planning Worksheet (CH0802), allows you to easily, simply, and accurately estimate the total expense of a trip.

Calculation Worksheet: Ground Travel by Private Vehicle

The first type of ground travel is by private vehicle, defined as a vehicle owned by an individual (in our case an individual performing work for the grant project). When the travel performed is necessary to the completion of

Exhibit 8.4

Illustration of CH0803, Master Checklist for Travel

☐ 1. Copy all Chapter 8 worksheets into a newly created folder (directory) on a hard drive.

Be careful not to change the names of any worksheets. For the links between worksheets to work properly, all file names must remain unchanged.

Chapter 8 worksheets all begin with W08 followed by a dot (decimal point) and a two-digit file number ranging from .01 to .10.

☐ 2. Complete a Travel Planning Worksheet (TPW), W08.01.

Printing a copy of the completed Travel Planning Worksheet makes the rest of the process easier to follow for some people.

☐ 3. Print a copy of this Master Checklist for Travel, C08.01.

☐ 4. Consult Row 4 of Travel Day 1 on the completed Travel Planning Worksheet (TPW).

If air travel is indicated, open and complete Worksheet W08.07A.

Note that there are four copies of the TPW lettered A through D.

☐ 5. Consult Rows 4 and 5 of Travel Day 2 on the completed TPW.

If air travel is indicated, open and complete the next W08.07 worksheet, moving A to B to C to D.

If ground travel only is indicated, open and complete the appropriate ground travel worksheet.

If necessary, open and complete more than one type of ground travel worksheet.

☐ 6. Consult Rows 4 and 5 of the next Travel Day.

Continue to open and complete versions of W08.07 if indicated.

If ground travel only is indicated, continue to enter information into the open Ground Travel worksheets. They will hold a large number of ground travel segments.

☐ 7. Continue to consult Rows 4 and 5 of each Travel Day.

Open and complete worksheets or continue to enter information in worksheets as appropriate.

☐ 8. Once air and ground travel is exhausted for all travel days, open and complete a Meals Worksheet, dependent on the method used (per meal or per day).

☐ 9. Open and complete Lodging Worksheet, W09.09.

☐ 10. Open the Miscellaneous Expense Worksheet and consult the list of commonly overlooked expenses.

Enter any expenses not previously entered on another worksheet.

☐ 11. Open Compile and Total Worksheet, W08.11.

If all the links between worksheets work properly, this worksheet will be completed automatically when it is opened.

Worksheet W08.11 displays the total from each worksheet and computes a total for all travel expenses for the trip analyzed.

project activities, the worker may be compensated for the use of a private vehicle. Compensation usually is based on a value established for each mile the private vehicle is driven for the purpose of completing project activities. The calculation is done simply by multiplying the number of miles driven by the amount established for each mile. Other costs may be incurred when using a private vehicle. Adding the costs of any tolls, parking, and tips to amount accumulated through the miles driven provides a total of expenses incurred during a ground travel segment via private vehicle (see Exhibit 8.5).

Formula

[(Rate) × (Miles)] + Tolls + Parking + Tips = Trip Expense

Read each numbered item in the checklist in Exhibit 8.6. Pause at the end of each item and note the appropriate entry or entries in the completed worksheet illustrated in Exhibit 8.7.

A useful technique for working your way through any of these travel worksheets is simply to take the trip in your mind. Visualize or imagine preparing your vehicle for the drive. Are there any costs involved in getting your vehicle, such as a parking fee or tip for a parking attendant? Visualize or imagine driving away from the starting point of a segment. Will there be tolls before reaching the segment destination? Once you arrive at the destination for the segment, will costs be incurred in depositing your vehicle, or will the charges be deferred to the beginning of the next ground travel segment? Keep mentally moving along the travel path noting every instance in which you incur any expense.

Techniques for determining the actual cost of the various expense items in this worksheet and all the others are described in Chapter 9.

EXHIBIT 8.5

Calculation Worksheet: Ground Travel by Private Vehicle

Travel Day	Trip Segment		Rate $/mile	Miles	Tolls	Parking	Tips	Totals
	From	To						
							TOTAL	

Exhibit 8.6

Checklist for Calculation Worksheet: Ground Travel by Private Vehicle

☐ 1. In the "Travel Day" column, enter the number from Row 10, Travel Day, of the Travel Planning Worksheet that corresponds to the day on which the ground travel will take place.

A single worksheet may be used for more than a single day's ground travel.

☐ 2. Enter the starting location of a trip segment in the "From" column.

The location can be generically descriptive such as "hotel" or "meeting site."

Note that the "From" on the second row (and all the rows that follow) is the same as the "To" on the row just above—it may be possible to develop a scenario in which this is not true, but generally a vehicle is driven away from where it previously stopped.

☐ 3. Enter the ending location of a trip segment in the "To" column.

☐ 4. Enter the mileage rate in the "Rate $/mile" column.

This rate is expressed as a number of cents per mile, for example 35¢/mile.

☐ 5. Enter the estimated segment mileage in the "Miles" column.

This is estimation, so use whole numbers (no tenths).

☐ 6. Enter anticipated tolls: Roads, bridges, and tunnels.

☐ 7. Enter the cost of parking.

It does not matter whether the expense of parking is entered when the vehicle is parked or when it is retrieved, as long as the expense is not entered at both ends.

☐ 8. Enter the cost of any anticipated tips.

Tips may be incurred when arriving at or departing from lodging.

It does not matter whether the tips are recorded on this worksheet or on the lodging worksheet as long as the expense is not entered on both.

Valet and attended parking will incur tips on both depositing and retrieving the vehicle.

☐ 9. The result of the application of the formula appears automatically in the "Totals" column.

As shown in Exhibit 8.7, the traveler in the example trip is using a private vehicle on the first day of the trip to drive from work to the airport and on the last day of the trip to drive from the airport to home. We know that the drive to the airport crosses a bridge with a toll. As is common for bridges, the toll is levied in only one direction. The vehicle will be parked in long-term parking. Using the Travel Planning Worksheet, Exhibit 8.3,

EXHIBIT 8.7

Completed Example of CH0803, Calculation Worksheet: Ground Travel by Private Vehicle

Travel Day	Trip Segment		Rate $/mile	Miles	Tolls	Parking	Tips	Totals
	From	To						
1	Work	Airport	$0.36	38	0	0	0	$13.68
5	Airport	Home	0.36	52	$1.25	$17.00	0	36.97
							TOTAL	$50.65

to count days, we find that the vehicle will spend four days and a few hours in long-term parking.

The total expense of $50.65 certainly will not loom large in budget considerations for almost any size grant. However, for the individual staff member who gets compensated with over 50 dollars, the amount along with the intangible effects of working for a thorough, professional, and caring organization will loom large indeed. The brief time expended to arrive at the amount of this expense will pay large dividends in the attitude, morale, and loyalty of the staff of your organization. The amount is legitimate. A grant maker generally will allow the expense. There truly is no excuse for not calculating the expense and including it in the grant request.

Calculation Worksheet: Ground Travel by Rental Vehicle

Renting a vehicle typically consists of two costs: (1) the amount charged by the rental company and (2) fuel, if only to return it with a full tank to avoid the five-dollar a gallon gas so thoughtfully and with such kindness provided by rental companies. In addition to these expenses, the travel may incur tolls, parking fees, and gratuities (see Exhibit 8.8). The formula with which to calculate the total expense for a trip segment is simply the total of all the various expenses incurred.

Formula

Rental Cost + Gas + Tolls + Parking + Tips = Trip Expense

The daily rate quoted by a rental company may not include taxes, which can be substantial in some parts of the country. To arrive at a reasonable

Exhibit 8.8

Calculation Worksheet: Ground Travel by Rental Vehicle

Travel Day	Trip Segment		Rental Cost	Gas	Tolls	Parking	Tips	Totals
	From	To						
						TOTAL		

estimate of the expense of fuel, estimate the miles the rental vehicle will be driven. Using an industry standard miles per gallon rate for the type of vehicle rented, compute the estimated gallons of fuel used. Multiplying the number of gallons by the cost of fuel in the driving area provides the fuel expense. Worksheet CH0805, illustrated in Exhibit 8.9, is provided to aid with this calculation. Enter the number of miles anticipated to be driven. Enter the fuel efficiency of the vehicle. The worksheet calculates and displays the gallons of fuel used. Enter the cost of fuel. The worksheet calculates and displays the expense of the fuel.

Read each item in the Rental Vehicle Checklist (Exhibit 8.10) and compare it with the completed worksheet for our example trip (Exhibit 8.11).

Exhibit 8.9

Completed Example of CH0805, Calculation Worksheet: Fuel Expense from Miles Driven

Description	Units	Values	Source of Value
Estimated mileage	Miles	150	User enters
Fuel efficiency	Miles/Gallon	18.5	User enters
Fuel used	Gallons	8.1	Worksheet computes and enters
Cost of fuel	Dollars/Gallon	$1.65	User enters
Fuel Expense	Dollars	$13.37	Worksheet computes and enters

EXHIBIT 8.10

Checklist for Calculation Worksheet: Ground Travel by Rental Vehicle

☐ 1. In the "Travel Day" column, enter the number from Row 10 of the Travel Planning Worksheet that corresponds to the day on which the ground travel will take place.

   A single worksheet may be used for more than a single day's ground travel.

☐ 2. Enter the starting location of a trip segment in the "From" column.

   The location can be generically descriptive such as "hotel" or "meeting site."

   Note that the "From" on the second row (and all the rows that follow) is the same as the "To" on the row just above—it may be possible to develop a scenario in which this is not true, but generally a vehicle is driven away from where it previously stopped.

☐ 3. Enter the ending location of a trip segment in the "To" column.

☐ 4. Enter the cost of the rental vehicle in the "Rental Cost" column.

   This amount will be a lump sum that covers one or more days.

☐ 5. In the "Gas" column, enter the estimated cost of fuel purchased during the duration of the rental.

   See worksheet W08.05 for help with this calculation.

☐ 6. Enter anticipated tolls: Roads, bridges, and tunnels.

☐ 7. Enter the cost of parking.

   It does not matter whether the expense of parking is entered when the vehicle is parked or when it is retrieved, as long as the expense is not entered at both ends.

☐ 8. Enter the cost of any anticipated tips.

   Tips may be incurred when arriving at or departing from lodging.

   It does not matter whether the tips are recorded on this worksheet or on the lodging worksheet as long as the expense is not entered on both.

   Valet and attended parking incurs tips on both depositing and retrieving a vehicle.

☐ 9. The result of the application of the formula appears automatically in the "Totals" column.

EXHIBIT 8.11

Completed Example of CH0805, Calculation Worksheet: Ground Travel by Rental Vehicle

Travel Day	Trip Segment From	To	Rental Cost	Gas	Tolls	Parking	Tips	Totals
1	Airport	Lodging 1						
2	Lodging 1	Site						
2	Site	Lodging 1				$10.00		$10.00
3	Lodging 1	Airport	$72.50	$10.00				82.50
							TOTAL	$92.50

From the Travel Planning Worksheet (Exhibit 8.3), we see that ground travel, in addition to the travel by private vehicle already analyzed, is necessary during every day of the trip. The choice is to utilize a rental vehicle during the stay in the first city and a series of different hired vehicles in the second city. On Day 1, the traveler must get from the airport to the lodging facility in the first city visited on the trip. This is shown in the example in Exhibit 8.11 on the Day 1 row. The two rows for Day 2 show the travel back and forth to the site being visited. The row for Day 3 shows the travel to the airport to meet the flight to the second city to be visited on the trip.

No tolls will be encountered during the ground travel analyzed on the worksheet of Exhibit 8.11. The only parking fee will be for the parking garage downtown near the site being visited. The lodging facility has no services necessitating tipping associated with a vehicle, and parking is provided gratis.

Many cells for entering expenses are blank. It might be tempting to shortcut the process and only use rows on which expenses will be incurred. This defeats the purpose of the process. The thinking through of each travel segment is an important part of the process. Although it may not eliminate missed or forgotten expenses, it goes a long way toward preventing them because the column headings stare you in the face, mutely asking the questions. Will you buy gas? Will you pay tolls? Will you pay for parking? Will you tip a valet or attendant or doorman? The worksheets are not only for calculating, but also for prodding, reminding, and probing for as much detail as possible. The more detailed your analysis of the trip, the fewer expenses you will overlook.

Calculation Worksheet: Ground Travel by Hired Vehicle (Shuttle, Taxi, Hired Car, Limousine, Bus, or Rapid Transit)

The significant difference between a rental vehicle and a hired vehicle is that a hired vehicle comes with a driver. When using a hired car, a limousine, a bus, or rapid transit, normally the fare is flat and established beforehand either by established policy or through negotiations. A shuttle works the same except that many shuttles have no fare, are free. Taxis are the exception. In most cities, taxis charge by the mileage traveled with additional fees for time spent waiting. Exhibit 8.12 illustrates a worksheet for ground travel by hired vehicles.

Formula

Fare + Wait Fees + Tolls & Parking + Tips = Trip Expense

Read each item in the Hired Vehicle Checklist (Exhibit 8.13), and compare it with the information in the Completed Example Worksheet (Exhibit 8.14). At first glance, the checklist will appear to be the same as previous checklists. It is not. Differences between this checklist and the others—some small, some large; some subtle, some obvious—tailor this checklist specifically to hired vehicles.

When our traveler arrives in city number two in the afternoon or early evening of Travel Day 3, the lodging facility's free shuttle provides ground transportation from the airport to lodging. We allocate $2.00 as a tip for the shuttle driver to handle our luggage. Some shuttle drivers never

EXHIBIT 8.12

 CH0806.XLS

Illustration of CH0806, Calculation Worksheet: Ground Travel by Hired Vehicle

Travel Day	Trip Segment		Type	Fare	Wait Fees	Tolls & Parking	Tips	Totals
	From	To						
							TOTAL	

EXHIBIT **8.13**

Checklist for Calculation Worksheet: Ground Travel by Hired Vehicle

☐ 1. In the "Travel Day" column, enter the number from Row 10, of the Travel Planning Worksheet that corresponds to the day on which the ground travel will take place.

    A single worksheet may be used for more than a single day's ground travel.

☐ 2. Enter the starting location of a trip segment in the "From" column.

    The location can be generically descriptive such as "hotel" or "meeting site."

    Note that the "From" on the second row (and all the rows that follow) is the same as the "To" on the row just above—it may be possible to develop a scenario in which this is not true, but generally a vehicle is driven away from where it previously stopped.

☐ 3. Enter the ending location of a trip segment in the "To" column.

☐ 4. Enter the type of hired vehicle that will be utilized.

    This will help with visualizing the potential fees involved with the trip.

☐ 5. Enter the cost of the hired vehicle in the "Fare" column.

    This amount may be zero.

    Many lodging facilities provide free shuttle service to and from airports.

    Some hired vehicles such as taxis compute the Fare based on mileage.

    Some compute based on time, and some have flat fees for specific trips.

☐ 6. In the "Wait Fees" column enter the estimated cost incurred while the hired vehicle waits.

    A Wait Fee may be incurred when a traveler asks a hired vehicle to wait while making a purchase, making a delivery, or any other such task.

    Local knowledge is necessary to estimate this amount.

☐ 7. Enter the anticipated cost of tolls and parking.

    Hired vehicles normally handle parking fees transparently within the fare.

    Tolls normally are added directly to the fare.

☐ 8. Enter the cost of any anticipated tips.

    Drivers of hired vehicles generally are tipped only if they either handle luggage or packages or perform a special service.

☐ 9. The result of the application of the formula for calculating ground travel by hired vehicle appears automatically in the "Totals" column.

Exhibit 8.14

Completed Example of CH0806, Calculation Worksheet: Ground Travel by Hired Vehicle

Travel Day	Trip Segment		Type	Fare	Wait Fees	Tolls & Parking	Tips	Totals
	From	To						
3	Airport	Lodging 2	Shuttle	$ 0.00			$2.00	$ 2.00
4	Lodging 2	Training site	Metro	3.50				3.50
4	Training site	Lodging 2	Metro	3.50				3.50
5	Lodging 2	Airport	Taxi	18.00	$6.00	[$22.50]	3.00	49.50
							TOTAL	$58.50

leave their seat. They do not deserve a tip. A driver who comes outside the shuttle and helps with your luggage is deserving of a gratuity.

Many people disdain the help of drivers, doormen, bell persons, porters, and skycaps. Some people think the whole tipping thing is a racket, a con game, a hustle—just another somewhat disreputable way to separate cash from the traveler who is basically helpless in the face of the organized, semilegitimate extortion. Other travelers feel awkward and inadequate when faced with a tipping situation. How much to tip creates the most insecurity, and the physical aspects of transferring the cash contribute also.

A change of attitude might be in order. Let people help you. Even in many medium-size cities, if you so choose, you need never touch your bags until you unpack them in your room. Yes, it costs a bit, a dollar a bag is about right for each person who handles your luggage along the way. At the end of a long tiring trip, especially after several days on the road, it helps both the back and the attitude to let someone else do the hard physical work.

On Day 4 of the trip, our traveler takes the Metro (rapid transit) to and from the training site. On the morning of the final day of the trip, the departure time of the flight home requires traveling to the airport before the operating hours of the shuttle. A taxi is the choice. Also, during the training, our example traveler has accumulated a large box of documentation and is shipping it directly back to the office. This is reflected by the $6.00 charged by the taxi to wait outside the delivery company while the box is sealed, labeled, and accepted for shipment.

One could legitimately ask, where is the delivery fee? We put the cost of the delivery in brackets in the column for Tolls & Parking. But, one might continue legitimately, delivery of a bunch of manuals and documentation is not a travel expense. Fair enough. In an exact sense, it might not be, but we incurred the expense as a result of the travel. The travel was undertaken for the benefit of the project. Almost any expense not for luxuries or personal entertainment becomes a legitimate travel expense.

Calculation Worksheet: Air Travel

By "air travel segment," we mean that portion of a trip that occurs between one destination and another. Examples would be the travel from home in Colorado Springs to a hotel in San Francisco, the travel from the hotel in San Francisco to a hotel in Sante Fe, and the travel from the hotel in Sante Fe to return home in Colorado Springs. The three air travel segments combine to make a complete trip beginning and ending at home.

For our purposes, it does not matter that a segment may consist of more than one flight. For example, to fly from Colorado Springs to San Francisco, a traveler may make a connection, changing planes, in Salt Lake City. It matters a great deal when the travel is taking place, but for expense estimation, it is disregarded.

It can be said predictably that a traveler begins an air travel segment in one place and ends in another. After all, that is how we define an air travel segment. It also can be said with a fair degree of confidence and certainty that air travel segments take place only in three possible permutations:

1. Home to destination.
2. Destination to destination.
3. Destination to home.

It can be argued that there is only one valid permutation, destination to destination, since home, without too much of a stretch, can be categorized as a destination. All air travel follows a predictable flow, as illustrated by the diagram in Exhibit 8.15. What is predictable is that a traveler will begin the travel from someplace, probably home. The trip to the airport almost certainly will use one of three methods of ground travel: the traveler's private vehicle, a hired contrivance, or a free ride, for example, from a friend or fellow worker. Once at the airport, baggage is checked unless carried onboard the aircraft by the traveler. After the flight arrives, baggage is retrieved, if only from an overhead bin. The trip

EXHIBIT 8.15

Flow of an Air Travel Segment

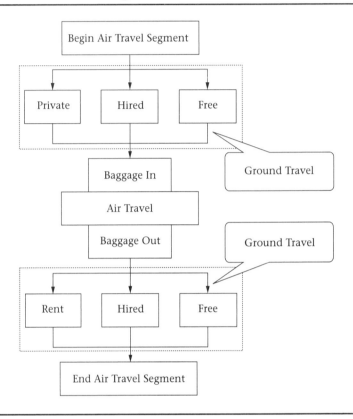

from the airport to the ground destination will almost certainly use one of three methods of ground travel: rented vehicle, hired transportation, or a free ride such as a hotel shuttle or a friend's or business acquaintance's vehicle.

The predictability in the vast majority of air travel segments allows the creation of a Calculation Worksheet for Air Travel, CH0807 (see Exhibit 8.16). The column on the far left of the worksheet contains row numbers. Rows run across the page. The top row of the worksheet contains column numbers. Columns run up and down the page. The shading in a few blocks of Worksheet CH0807 indicates visually that no information is required for that location.

Read each step in the Air Travel Segment Worksheet Checklist (Exhibit 8.17) carefully. This checklist differs dramatically from all precious checklists. The entire concept is different. The outcome of following the directions in the checklist is illustrated in the completed example in

EXHIBIT 8.16

 CH0807A-E.XLS

Calculation Worksheet: Air Travel

Row #	Column 1	Column 2 Reference Information		Column 3 Totals
1.	Departure Location			
2.	Travel Day			
3.	Ground Travel Worksheet			
		Column 2A No. Traveling	Column 2B Cost	
4.	Check-in expense			
5.	Airline Ticket Expense			
6.	Check-out expense			
7.	Ground Travel Worksheet			
8.	Destination Location			
9.	Air Travel Segment Total			

Exhibit 8.18. The purpose of following the directions in the Air Travel Checklist and completing an air travel worksheet is to calculate the estimated expense of air travel and its associated ground travel.

Repeat the process described in the checklist for each Travel Day that contains an air travel segment as shown on the Travel Planning Worksheet, CH0801, (Exhibit 8.3). Be sure to /enter the airfare only once. Though we estimate expenses for each air travel segment, tickets for air travel usually are purchased as complete trips (roundtrip) for one price. If the trip for which you are estimating the cost will require two or more unlinked one-way tickets, the cost of each ticket must be entered into the appropriate Air Travel Worksheet.

Calculation Worksheet: Meal Expense

The anticipated cost of meals can be estimated in two ways, per day or per meal. The worksheet for calculating the expense of meals using the per meal method, CH0808, is illustrated in Exhibit 8.19. The Number Eating Meal is obtained from Travel Planning Worksheet CH0802, and is transferred automatically to the Per Meal Calculation Worksheet, CH0808.

The only action necessary is to enter values into the "Cost Allocated for Meal" column, one value for each meal, morning, midday, and

EXHIBIT 8.17

Air Travel Segment Worksheet Checklist

☐ 1. In Row 1, Column 2, enter a descriptive name of the location from which the traveler is departing.

Examples: home, office, lodging, or meeting site.

☐ 2. In Row 2, Column 2, enter the Travel Day number from Row 10 of W08.01, Travel Planning Worksheet.

☐ 3. In Row 3, Column 2, enter the filename of the ground travel worksheet to be used to calculate an estimate of ground travel expense between the Departure Location in Block 1 and the airport:

W08.03 for Private Vehicle.

W08.04 for Rental Vehicle.

W08.06 for Hired Vehicle.

☐ 4. In Row 4, Column 2A, enter the number of people making the trip.

The worksheet automatically places the number entered into Row 4, Column 2A into the same column in Rows 5 and 6.

☐ 5. In Row 4, Column 2B, enter the anticipated expense of check-in at the airport for one person.

Examples of check-in expenses are: tip for outside luggage check-in; tip for skycap; or tip for parking attendant.

The total will be computed automatically and displayed in Column 3.

☐ 6. If this is the first Air Travel Worksheet completed for this trip, then.

In Row 5, Column 2B, enter the cost of an airline ticket.

A total will be computed automatically and displayed in Column 3.

☐ 7. If this is the second or third Air Travel Worksheet completed for this trip and the cost of the airline ticket has been entered into a previously completed worksheet, leave Row 5, Column 2B blank—make no entry (zero is okay).

☐ 8. In Row 6, Column 2B, enter the anticipated expenses of getting out of the airport for one person.

An example of these expenses includes a tip for a skycap.

A total will be computed automatically and displayed in Column 3.

☐ 9. In Row 7, Column 2, enter the filename of the ground travel worksheet to be used to calculate an estimate of ground travel expense between the Airport and the Destination Location in Block 8:

W08.03 for Private Vehicle.

W08.04 for Rental Vehicle.

W08.06 for Hired Vehicle.

☐ 10. In Row 8, Column 2, enter a descriptive name of the destination of this travel segment: Examples: home, office, lodging, or meeting site.

Exhibit 8.17 *(Continued)*

☐ 11. Complete the Ground Travel Worksheet indicated in Row 3, Column 2, and enter the total from the worksheet in Row 3, Column 3.

☐ 12. Complete the Ground Travel Worksheet indicated in Row 7, Column 2, and enter the total from the worksheet in Row 7, Column 3.

☐ 13. The Air Travel Worksheet will sum the amounts entered in Row 3 and display the total in Row 9, Column 3.

---

evening. Once a cost is entered, the worksheet will automatically compute and display totals.

The worksheet for calculating an estimated meal expense for a trip using the per day method, CH0808, is illustrated in Exhibit 8.20. Note that three items of information are needed, the number of people on the trip, the length of the trip in days, and the cost allocated for a day's meals. The Total automatically calculates and displays once all three values have been entered.

The Number Eating Meals and the Length of Trip in Days is entered automatically from the Travel Planning Worksheet, CH0802 (Exhibit 8.3).

Exhibit 8.18

Completed Example of CH0807, Calculation Worksheet: Air Travel

Row #	Column 1	Column 2 Reference Information		Column 3 Totals
1.	Departure Location	Miami, FL		n/a
2.	Travel Day	1		n/a
3.	Ground Travel Worksheet	1		n/a
		Column 2A No. Traveling	Column 2B Cost	
4.	Check-in expense	2	$ 10	$ 20.00
5.	Airline Ticket Expense	2	573.22	1,146.44
6.	Check-out expense	2	$ 10	20.00
7.	Ground Travel Worksheet	1		58.00
8.	Destination Location	Atlanta, GA		n/a
9.	Air Travel Segment Total			$1,244.44

EXHIBIT 8.19

 CH0808.XLS

Calculation Worksheet: Meals (per Meal)

	Number Eating Meal	Cost Allocated for Meal	Totals
Morning Meal			
Midday Meal			
Evening Meal			
Meal Expense Total			

When a daily allocated cost is entered, the Total will be automatically calculated and displayed.

Calculation Worksheet: Lodging

Only two items of information are necessary to calculate the expense of lodging. The first item is the Number of Lodging Nights. This figure is the number of people spending the night times the number of nights lodging. The number is obtained automatically from the Travel Planning Worksheet, CH0802.doc (Exhibit 8.3). The second value necessary is the night lodging rate. Once the Nightly Rate is entered, the worksheet automatically computes and displays the Total Lodging Expense (see Exhibit 8.21).

An assumption goes into the calculation of the Number of Lodging Nights. That assumption is single occupancy, one person per lodging room. If two people will share a room, it must be noted on the Travel Planning Worksheet in Row 13.

EXHIBIT 8.20

 CH0808.XLS

Illustration of CH0808, Calculation Worksheet: Meals (Per Day)

Number Eating Meal	Length of Trip in Days	Cost Allocated for Day	Totals

EXHIBIT 8.21

Illustration of CH0809, Calculation Worksheet: Lodging

Number of Lodging Nights	Nightly Rate	Total Lodging Expense

Compiling Expenses

If all the necessary worksheets have been completed, and if they are all open, they will link their totals to the Compile and Total Worksheet. If a worksheet computes a total and is open, but the total does not appear on this worksheet, check that the name of the worksheet has not changed. If none of the worksheet totals appear, check that the name of this worksheet has not changed. No amount is displayed in the Total Returned column if a worksheet is unused or not open.

Wise Guy and Wise Lady

 Wise Guy

Travel. There is so much involved! I will just hire a travel agent and be done with it. I hate trying to figure it all out.

Wise Lady

Well, you can hire a travel agent. There's nothing wrong with that, but that agent has to give you the figures to plug into your budget. You can't just write in the proposal "$2,000 for travel—see my travel agent!" Travel is one place where a lot of money is spent quickly. It costs a great deal to ship folks from one side of the country to another, house, and feed them. It is also an area where there is frequently a lot of abuse. If you don't want travel cut from the budget by the reviewer, then be very careful to get accurate figures and fully justify the expense.

Conclusion

The general predictability of the activities involved in travel make it possible to create a system that will simply, easily, and accurately capture the expenses of a trip. A few basic formulas used repeatedly provide the mathematical underpinnings of the process. Also, the ability to link data from one worksheet to another means that the further along the process a person progresses, the less work there is to do. Much of the needed data will already have been entered or calculated.

Key Concepts

- The expenses of travel can be divided into four categories:
  1. Ground Travel.
  2. Air Travel.
  3. Lodging.
  4. Meals.
- All ground travel can be calculated by three sets of worksheets:
  1. Private vehicle.
  2. Rental vehicle.
  3. Hired vehicle.
- Air travel follows a predictable flow:
  1. Ground travel to airport.
  2. Check-in.
  3. Flight.
  4. Check-out.
  5. Ground travel to destination.
- The expense of meals is calculated using one of two methods:
  1. Per meal rate.
  2. Per day rate.

The remaining direct costs include equipment, contractual services, material and supplies, and others. Chapter 9 finishes the job of establishing a system for calculating the cost (expense) of direct costs. It also includes a section on how to obtain realistic costs and prices to feed into the worksheets—after all, garbage in, garbage out. If the cost figures entered into the worksheets are not accurate, then it does not matter how thorough, complete, or accurate the process or system is, the results will bear no resemblance to reality.

Chapter 9

Other Direct
Costs and Prices

**For which of you intending to build a tower,
sitteth not down first, and counteth the cost,
whether he have sufficient to finish it?**

Luke 14:28

This chapter covers two main topics. First, we cover the method of calculating the direct costs, not yet covered in previous chapters. Worksheets are provided to simplify these calculations. Second, we cover how to find prices. All the worksheets are not much help if the costs entered are not as accurate as possible. The last half of this chapter provides guidance on tracking down accurate prices for direct costs such as personnel, equipment, supplies, and contractual services. The direct costs covered in this chapter are:

- Equipment.
- Materials and supplies.
- Contractual services.
- Other/Miscellaneous.
- Endowment.
- Capital.

Materials and supplies are grouped together because most grant makers do so, and the discussion of them for the purposes of calculation is identical. The category "Other/Miscellaneous" is included only for the sake of completeness. Since the proper budget amount for this category is always zero, a worksheet is not truly necessary. To serve, however, as a place to collect miscellaneous project expenses in the short term before a home for them is found, we include a worksheet. The calculation for endowment is an interesting special case, much different from the rest of the chapter, though simple and short to explain and discuss.

Following the sections on the worksheets, a long discussion of prices concludes the chapter.

The Calculation

A salient fact becomes obvious when comparing the worksheets in this chapter. The underlying mathematical formula is the same for all of them, with one exception—endowment. We have left behind any interesting math, if indeed we ever actually encountered any. To calculate the remaining direct costs, we need only three facts: the unit of measure, or sale or purchase; the unit cost; and, how many units the project requires.

Unit of Purchase

The concept of a unit of purchase or sale is one with which everyone is familiar. A large group of items exist that normally are not sold individually. A common example is a letter-size envelope. In special circumstances, a single envelope can be purchased, for example, prestamped at the Post Office, but usually envelopes are purchased in a box of 50, or 100, or for business purposes, more often in a box of 500. The unit of purchase is the box. The purchaser knows beforehand that the purchase of one box is going to yield 50, or a 100, or 500 envelopes. The envelopes are not priced individually, but by the box. A box becomes the unit of measure or sale or purchase.

Many common quantities of individual items are grouped and sold as a unit. We encounter so many that they fade into the background and we do not even think twice about how common it is to purchase one unit of a thing while in fact we are purchasing several of the items. Exhibit 9.1 lists a few common examples. Note the variety of quantities of individual items commonly available as units.

When items are used for their normal purpose, usually though not always, they are used individually. Many items, however, are purchased in bulk, a large quantity at one time. Some items that we commonly purchase in bulk, we no longer even think of in terms of one item or piece. Paper is a good example. Seldom, if ever, when considering the purchase of paper does the issue of the number of sheets arise. Paper is thought of in terms of reams or cases.

When developing project budgets, as in any other purchasing situation, knowing how many items are actually being purchased is important. Everyone has seen the situation in which someone misunderstood the unit of measure. It can be comic, or it can be tragic. The delivery of 12 screwdrivers becomes a farce when 12 gross of screwdrivers show up. The

EXHIBIT 9.1

Examples of a Variety of Units of Sale or Purchase

Quantity	Item	Unit
2	Scissors	Pair (a little joke)
4	Toilet paper	
6	Soft drinks and beer	Six-pack (4 six-packs = case)
8	Crayons	Box (one-row)
12	Soft drinks and beer	Twelve-pack (2 twelve-packs = 1 case)
12	Pencils	Sleeve (12 sleeves = 1 gross)
12	Donuts	Dozen
16	Crayons	Box (two rows)
24	Soft drinks and beer	Case
24	Crayons	Box (three rows)
64	Crayons	Box (four two-row boxes in one box)
100	Index cards	Pack
144	Pencils	Gross (a dozen dozens)
500	Paper, sheet	Ream (10 reams = 1 case)
5,000	Paper, sheet	Case

overnight rush delivery of a box of 100 transparencies for the big presentation that night becomes tragic (or at least frantic) when there are only 50 in the box.

The formula for all the worksheets in this chapter is about as simple as a formula can get. It is used daily by almost everybody, if only to arrive at a rough estimate. It is how we know approximately how much money to pull out to pay for the three soft drinks. We multiply the cost of one drink by the number we ordered, in this case three, and arrive at a mental approximation of the amount the cash register will calculate exactly. When the server asks for an amount, we recognize the amount as being correct because it is close to our estimate. We have the correct amount of money ready. All goes well.

We all see this formula at work on order forms. The form requires that we enter the unit cost of our purchase. Next we enter the quantity we want to order. Finally, a column labeled something such as "Total Cost" requires us to multiply the quantity times the unit cost to arrive at a total cost for that item. Nomenclature may change. For example, "Number of Units" is often shortened to "Quantity," which is further abbreviated to "Qty."

Formula

(Unit Cost) × (Number of Units) = Cost

Equipment

Equipment covers a broad range of items as discussed previously. In addition, equipment is often not a single "thing," but a collection of things. Consider the ubiquitous computer. The computer is actually just a box with the hard drive in it. A metal (or cheerfully colored plastic) rectangular box. That's it. But it's not really "it," is it? One should have a monitor, speakers, keyboard, and cabling for a printer at the very least. You can list each of these pieces under separate categories if you wish. You certainly should get costs for each item because they may not be "packaged" as a whole. But you may want to bundle them together for purposes of working with budget spreadsheets and budget itemization. Note the way we treated the "computer" on the first line of the spreadsheet shown in Exhibit 9.2. A spreadsheet is, in its simplest form, a way of organizing information in a table so it is easily understood. The computer has made it

EXHIBIT 9.2   CH0901.XLS

Illustration of CH0901, Calculation Worksheet, Equipment

Description	Fund Source	Unit Cost	Qty	Cost
Equipment: Grant Request				
Desktop PC Computer System	1	$ 2,230.00	3	$ 6,690.00
Laser Printers	1	323.00	3	969.00
Adult Clinic Examining Table	1	4,236.00	1	4,236.00
Portable X-Ray Unit	1	25,643.00	1	25,643.00
Equipment: Grant Request Total				$37,538.00
Equipment: Other Sources				
High-Speed Commercial Copier	2	10,435.00	1	$10,435.00
Desk Units	2	786.00	3	2,358.00
Sink and Cabinet Unit	3	1,034.00	1	1,034.00
Refrigerator	3	1,554.00	1	1,554.00
Equipment: Other Sources Total				$15,381.00

Source	Identity
1	Grant Request
2	Applicant
3	Weefixit Hospital
4	
5	

Equipment Total	$52,919.00

much more by adding calculating ability to the various "boxes" in the spreadsheet. It is almost magic.

Suppose your grant project is to create an outstationed medical examining room and office in a very poor neighborhood where residents have no means of transportation to come to the city clinic for regular health exams. The office setup should be such that the information system is linked with the hospital clinic to diagnose, treat, and track patients. A portion of your budget worksheet might look something like Exhibit 9.2.

The first column is for a *Description* of the item in the budget. Then comes the *Source* of the funds. As previously stressed, it is important to separate funds. No one grant is likely to fund all costs. Grant makers want to see local investment to ensure project success and continuation, so you must show them the funds all partners are contributing as well as the portion of the budget you want to fund with the grant. Always keep in mind the source of the funds, even when using worksheets. *Unit Cost* is the next logical piece of information needed, followed by the *Quantity,* or number of items you need and then the *Cost* of all the items you have listed under that item *Description*. The first set of boxes appears under the heading *Equipment: Grant Request*. The items listed here are the ones you will ask for from the potential funder. The second set of boxes falls under the heading *Equipment: Other Sources;* the items shown here will be provided by you, the applicant, and the other partners. All that remains is to add the columns—the magic.

Materials and Supplies

The category of materials and supplies covers a multitude of items from the very simple to the highly complex. You must be careful to identify what the "unit" is when you are applying costs. Everyone who has been involved in purchasing can tell you a funny story or two about orders that have gone awry. You intended to get one box of paper clips and wound up buried in little boxes or you wanted to order a box of pencils and wound up with one. It works both ways.

Now suppose your grant project is to make a photographic history of a historic neighborhood that is to be torn down to make way for a shopping mall. Even if this project is a one-person operation, you need to purchase many materials and supplies. More than you probably would expect.

The materials and supplies category is where you plug in such things as software needs, computer disks, and other supplies, general office supplies, and even reference books. Unless it relates to people or contractual services, if you don't know where to put an item, it probably belongs in the materials and supplies category.

Contractual Services

Contractual Services is a difficult category because such services are contracted out at such different units of measure. You must be really careful that you understand the contractor's costing method and that the two of you agree on what the costing units include. Many errors in budgeting come from a misunderstanding between the contractor and person doing the hiring. As previously stated, it is imperative to develop a precise statement of work before getting bids from contractors. This cuts down on the confusion.

Many things in everyday life that one takes for granted are actually contracted services. Some of these are local telephone service, long-distance telephone service, television cable services, and any construction or maintenance type activity.

Your project is to establish and operate a centralized information system for area senior citizens such that they can call in to an information attendant or log into your computer system to get answers to questions of importance to them. The project will be housed in a community center and staffed by volunteers under the guidance of a full-time professional staff.

Exhibit 9.4 shows a partial spreadsheet that covers the following different types of things:

Item	Unit
Telephone service	Fee per line per month
Office leasing	Fee per square foot per month
Internet site license	Access fee per month
Telephone system leasing	Monthly fee based on hardware and number of units
Technical support, hardware	Hourly fee for labor
Technical support, software	Hourly fee for labor
News clipping service	Flat fee for a certain number of articles a month
Rewiring and renovation	Hourly rate for labor

Other/Miscellaneous

This is easy. When you finish putting together your final budget, there should not be an entry in this worksheet. It is simply a place to "park" items until you figure out what category best fits. Some trouble items are listed in Exhibit 9.5. Check out the quiz answers provided in Exhibit 9.6 to see if you can figure out where the items should go.

EXHIBIT 9.3

Illustration of CH0902, Calculation Worksheet, Materials and Supplies

Description	Fund Source	Unit Cost	Qty	Cost
Material and Supplies: Grant Request				
FotoShoot Software	1	$202.00	1	$ 202.00
FotoArchive Software	1	179.00	1	179.00
CD Recordable Disks	1	1.89	4	7.56
Steno Pads	1	5.79	2	11.58
Materials and Supplies: Grant Request Total				$ 400.14
Material and Supplies: Other Sources				
Laser Printer Toner Cartridge	2	123.00	6	$ 738.00
Photo Print Paper	2	19.03	10	190.30
Our County in Maps, Reference Book	4	41.11	1	41.11
Nonacid Archive Film	3	25.32	4	101.28
Materials and Supplies: Other Sources Total				$1,070.69

Source	Identity
1	Grant Request
2	Applicant
3	Progressville Historic Council
4	Progressville Planning Agency
5	
6	

Materials and Supplies Total	$1,470.83

Endowment

Probably, most endowments just show up, not necessarily out of the blue, but still the receiving organization is not in control, the contributor is. Seldom is there much if any control over the size of an endowment when it appears. An organization can, however, set a goal for itself of creating an endowment and set about raising funds to create the fund. One question to answer during planning is the size of the target. How large an endowment is needed or wanted?

The answer begins at the other end with another question. What is the amount of funding we expect the endowment to produce? Once we settle on how much income from the endowment we want, the next issue

CH0903.XLS

EXHIBIT 9.4

Illustration of CH0903, Calculation Worksheet, Contractual Services

Description	Fund Source	Unit Cost	Qty	Cost
Contractual Services: Grant Request				
Monthly local telephone service, 3 lines	1	$ 24.56	3	$ 73.68
Office leasing	1	325.00	12	3,900.00
Internet site license	1	40.00	12	480.00
Telephone system leasing	1	654.00	12	7,848.00
Contractual Services: Grant Request Total				$12,301.68
Contractual Services: Other Sources				
Technical support, hardware	2	60.00	60	$ 3,600.00
Technical support, software	2	100.00	240	24,000.00
News clipping service	3	125.00	12	1,500.00
Rewiring, renovation of facility	4	40.00	38	1,520.00
Contractual Services: Other Sources Total				$30,620.00

Source	Identity
1	Grant Request
2	Applicant
3	Senior Council
4	Healthy Life Community Center
5	
6	

Contractual Services Total	$42,921.00

is how much the endowment can reasonably be expected to earn. Different investments earn different returns. Different investment strategies produce different returns. Once a reasonable return on investment is set, it becomes a simple math problem.

Financial consultants may cringe at our worksheet. It ignores some financial factors that affect the actual return on investment, such as compounded interest (a positive) and investment fees and taxes (negatives). The little worksheet, CH0905, is only intended to provide rough guidance, not financial advice. In Exhibit 9.7 is a completed example of the worksheet. We started by supposing that we want a yearly income from our endowment of $5,000, so that amount is entered in the first column. We assume that we can earn a 5 percent return on our investment. That figure is entered in the middle column. As soon as both amounts are

EXHIBIT 9.5

Illustration of CH0904, Calculation Worksheet, Miscellaneous

Description	Fund Source	Unit Cost	Qty	Cost
Miscellaneous: Grant Request				
Set of Photographic Reference Books	1	$2,436.00	1	$2,436.00
Fresh Flowers	1	85.00	12	1,020.00
Dog Biscuits	1	40.00	12	480.00
Set of Professional Cookware	1	1,320.00	1	1,320.00
Miscellaneous: Grant Request Total				**$5,256.00**
Miscellaneous: Other Sources				
Automobile Travel Club Membership	2	$ 120.00	1	$ 120.00
Business License	2	1,060.00	1	1,060.00
Insurance on Building Contents	2	115.00	12	1,380.00
Parcel Pickup	2	12.00	52	624.00
Miscellaneous Other Sources Total				**$3,184.00**

Source	Identity
1	Grant Request
2	Applicant
3	
4	
5	

Miscellaneous Total	**$8,440.00**

entered, the worksheet calculates and displays that it will take an endowment of $100,000 to provide the income we desire at the earning rate we envision.

One of the values of worksheets (and spreadsheets in general) is the ability to play with numbers while the heavy lifting of the mathematics is done for you. In Exhibits 9.8, 9.9, and 9.10, we do just that. In Exhibit 9.8, we continue to want a $5,000 yearly income, but we think we can get a higher return on investment; 6 percent is our new estimate. Increasing the return on investment by 1 percent decreased by $16,777 the size of the endowment necessary to provide our target yearly income.

That worked out really well. What happens if we make an even larger return on investment? Exhibit 9.9 shows that when we enter 7.5 percent as the rate of return, the size of the endowment we need drops to $66,667.

Okay, now let's get realistic. Assume a 5 percent return on investment, which is probably sustainable on average over a number of years,

EXHIBIT 9.6

Quiz

Can you determine where the Miscellaneous items in Exhibit 9.5 really belong?

Answers:

Set of Photographic Reference Books	Materials and Supplies
Fresh Flowers	Materials and Supplies or Contractual Services depending on whether you have a service that regularly provides the flowers or if you schlep down to the local store yourself
Dog Biscuits	You may say, "Materials and Supplies, of course," but what if it's part of the contractual agreement to pay the therapy dogs in dog biscuits? Never thought of that, did you?
Set of Professional Cookware	Materials and Supplies—it doesn't meet all the requirements for equipment even though it is expensive.
Automobile Travel Club Membership	Contractual Services
Business License	Contractual Services
Insurance on Building Contents	Contractual Services
Parcel Pickup	Contractual Services

EXHIBIT 9.7

 CH0905.XLS

Completed Example of CH0905, Calculation Worksheet Endowment

Yearly Income Desired	Rate of Return	Endowment Needed
$5,000	5%	$100,000

EXHIBIT 9.8

Completed Example of CH0905, Calculation Worksheet Endowment

Yearly Income Desired	Rate of Return	Endowment Needed
$5,000	6%	$83,333

with some years' returns dipping below and some years' returns rising above. Our organization needs $100,000 a year as a base from which to operate. This does not allow us to provide all our services, but it keeps the doors open and keeps us in business regardless of what else happens. The worksheet illustrated in Exhibit 9.10 shows that we need an endowment of two million dollars.

When an organization begins allocating cash or convertible assets into an endowment fund, almost invariably a vexing problem arises. People, mostly well meaning, serious, and concerned people, will question the ethics of diverting resources from the critical needs of today to provide for the contingencies of an uncertain, perhaps even unknown future. As with most problems of this sort, it is easier to avoid by proper planning than to solve once it appears.

Unless your organization has the good fortune to be endowed by a donor, creating an endowment will be long hard work. It will be a project. Part of the planning for any project must be preemptive, that is, you must identify potential problems and develop a plan of action to head them off before they have the opportunity to develop fully. These plans of action almost invariably center on efforts to educate and inform, since most resistance to projects tends to come from people who misunderstand the need, the method, or the intended outcome.

EXHIBIT 9.9

Completed Example of CH0905, Calculation Worksheet Endowment

Yearly Income Desired	Rate of Return	Endowment Needed
$5,000	7.5%	$66,667

EXHIBIT 9.10

Completed Example of CH0905, Calculation Worksheet Endowment

Yearly Income Desired	Rate of Return	Endowment Needed
$100,000	5%	$2,000,000

Capital

A worksheet is not needed for the calculation of the cost involved in the purchase of land, buildings, or improvements. When the purchase of land or a building is contemplated, it is essential to obtain the services of a qualified professional, in fact, perhaps more than one. Rely on them to provide the costs involved.

The same applies to improvement to land or buildings. Obtain the services of a person qualified to manage the work of contractors.

Finding Prices

Finding prices is a little like being a detective. You have to learn to ask yourself the right questions and you need to know how to ask other people the right questions. If you are generally good at using resources and finding information, you will not have problems with pricing things. If you are one of those many people who, when trying to find something tend to stand in the middle of the floor and turn on one foot, it would be good to get someone else to perform these tasks.

What questions do you need to ask?

- I do not have the information, but who would?
- Who has to collect that information as a part of their normal job activity?
- Who would publish that information?
- Will I have to have a plan or blueprint before I can get costing information?
- What sales representative would have information about that item?
- What discrete parts of the item have to be figured separately?

- What supportive or peripheral things will have to be changed and therefore will incur a cost, if we acquire an item?
- Will the item require maintenance?
- Will the item entail insurance?
- What keyword(s) can I use to search for information online?

Personnel

If the position you are requesting or listing in the overall budget is like a position you already have in your organization, then you're home free. There should be documentation of entry level and higher level salaries for the position in question. Ask for the wage and salary information from the person in your organization who is responsible for personnel. If the position is a new one, then you could ask someone in another organization who has a staff member in roughly the same type position for an entry level or higher level starting salary figure. You can also ask your local or state Employment Security Commission (ESC) what they list for a starting salary for a person in the same or a similar position. To guide the ESC person, you will need to supply either a job function title that is common to a lot of organizations or a succinct job function description.

Also there are books published of comparative wages and salaries such as *The American Almanac of Jobs and Salaries,* published each year by Avon Books and *American Salaries and Wages Survey: Statistical Data* published by Gale Research. These are available in bookstores and libraries. These books are very helpful if there is no locally derived information on the particular job you are including in your proposal.

The Department of Labor at the state level has information on wage and salary comparisons. This information can be accessed online at the state department of labor Web site or by calling or writing for the information. In some cases, the state Employment Security Commission has information on wages and salaries by job function. Again, the ESC can be reached on their Web site or by telephone.

Fringe

If the position you are requesting or listing in the overall budget is like a position you already have in your organization, then once again, you're home free. The same person who is in charge of personnel will have the information about the fringe percentages. Fringe figures will be similar across the board on your organization's personnel. But what if you are setting up an entirely new organization? You can get fringe benefit information by calling your state Employment Security Commission and asking for the person who works in the "labor market information" division or area.

The IRS has good information on requirements for fringe benefits as well, but we don't recommend you call them. You can access the national IRS Web site at http://www.irs.gov. Information is searchable, so if you enter "fringe benefits" you will find the IRS publications on that topic.

Travel

Air Travel

You can call an airline or two and ask for a rate. If you intend to do this, then be sure you first think out the information you need. You need to choose a date of departure and a return date. Of course, you probably do not know exact dates of travel, but you will not get information from an airline without a definite date. So pick a date within the next week or two. If it is likely that the person traveling will be leaving and returning on a weekday during the same week then make a weekday choice—say Monday, March 5 and a return date of say Friday, March 9. The fares will be the same if the person leaves Monday and returns on Tuesday or Wednesday or Thursday. For purposes of listing prices in a budget, the rates will be the same if it is March or July. As previously discussed, the funder knows that some prices can change, especially those connected with travel.

If the travel event is likely to begin during a weekday and end on Sunday, then the fares will be vastly different because of travel over a Saturday night. This is the way airlines work. A person traveling on a "business-type" schedule (i.e., departing on a weekday or Sunday and returning the same week), pays a premium. If a traveler departs on either a weekend or a weekday, however and does not travel back until after a Saturday night has passed, then the fares are significantly better to accommodate "tourist" travelers. Yes, businesses are carrying most of the burden of the cost of air travel.

Do not ask for special rates; get standard rate quotes. Some fares booked at least 21 days prior to travel qualify for reduced rates. You do not know if you will be able to book the actual flight that far ahead so you do not want to include a rate that may be a great deal lower than the one you will have to pay. This is why we say, "Pick a date within the next week or two."

Also don't let the airline representative give you the "restricted" rate. You want the rate for an "unrestricted" ticket. A restricted ticket costs less, but you must use it on the date and for the flight listed or pay a penalty for any change. You do not know that your traveler will have the luxury of being able to purchase a "restricted" ticket—s/he may need to change plans at the last minute so you want to get the higher, "unrestricted" ticket rate for budget purposes.

One more thing—if the city you are traveling from or to has multiple airports, you will need to tell the airline what airport you will be flying from or to. The rates may differ depending on the airport. If you don't know whether there is more than one airport and the airline representative asks you into which airport you will be flying, then be prepared to ask the right question. If your traveler must fly jet service instead of very small planes, then you will want the one that handles jet aircraft. Some cities have municipal airports that only accommodate very small commercial airplanes. Many people avoid flying into municipal airports because services such as taxis and baggage assistance are limited. However, you should be aware that the airline representative might ask you about it. If the choice is between two large airports or jetports, then a good question might be, "Which one is located closer to the city?" Or you might ask, "Which one is nearest Interstate 80?" The representative should be able to answer such questions. Depending on the answer, make your choice of airports.

Next, there is the selection of "class" of ticket. There are three major classes. The least expensive and most popular ticket is Coach Class. Then there is First Class, which is significantly more expensive than Coach Class. First Class is like "box seats" in a stadium with special seating and service. Finally, there is Business Class seating, which offers amenities somewhere between Coach and First Class. It is more expensive than Coach Class and is only available on long flights and only with certain planes and airlines. Undoubtedly, you will be requesting tickets for Coach Class.

There are sometimes special rates under some circumstances for certain government agencies. Your agency may be one of those. It may be worth the effort to ask the airline if there are special rates for your agency. However, these rates are usually on "standby" or with some other restriction that limits service. We recommend that you get pricing for regular tickets rather than those that have any restrictions.

Here is an appropriately worded request when calling for ticket price information.

> I would like the price of an unrestricted round-trip ticket Coach Class from Pleasantville Central Airport, Utah, to Washington, DC, Dulles International Airport, departing Pleasantville on Monday, March 5 and returning on Friday, March 9.

You can get prices online at a number of sites. The most direct way is to go to the airline Web sites of the airlines that serve your airport. You then enter the information requested by the site and receive itinerary options and prices. If you are adept at online searches, this may be the quickest way for you to obtain information. We suggest that you avoid sites that are travel agencies for purposes of costing airline tickets because you are likely to get a special rate that might not be available when the actual travel takes place. Some airlines (American is one), provide information for flights available from a variety of airlines in addition to their own schedule. These sites can be a valuable tool in checking costs for a budget.

Airlines also provide bound documents listing their flight schedules and other information. If your agency generally uses a particular airline, acquiring this document might be a helpful addition to your grants library. Most of this information is also online.

Ground Travel—Private Vehicle or Car Rental

When we speak of automobile travel, we usually are discussing an amount for mileage per mile. This varies from agency to agency or company to company. We suggest that you first call the funder and ask if they have a required rate for mileage. If they don't have a rate, then ask the person in charge of finances in your organization for your company rate. If that rate is not available, then call the financial person in an agency most like the one you are proposing to establish and ask what rate they use. If you are working with a potential government funder, it will most likely have a set rate. A foundation may or may not have a set rate. A potential corporate funder usually has an established mileage rate.

Under certain circumstances, you might want to get a quotation for renting a vehicle for a trip. Usually a good case can be made for doing this if the traveler will be driving a long distance, if there is a group traveling together, or if a lot of materials or equipment must be transported to the event. If there is a long distance to drive, it is unreasonable for an individual to use a personal vehicle because of the undue wear and tear. If a group is traveling together, it is frequently more cost-effective to lease a large vehicle to transport everyone than to pay individual mileage. If a large amount of materials are being transported, as to a conference, then it may be more cost-effective or convenient to transport them by automobile or truck than to ship them.

To get a quote for leasing a vehicle, first determine what kind of vehicle you need and for how long. Determine if you have a brand preference. Vehicle leasing agencies lease by the day or by the week. Some have special packages for certain vehicles or certain combinations of days. If you are leasing for four or five days, a weekly rate may be the better deal. Determine if your organization has insurance that covers staff members traveling in leased vehicles. You can call the person who handles your financial affairs to ask. Also, if you are a nonprofit organization or government entity, you may get special rates. Ask your financial person whether the company gets special rates from any area leasing agencies.

Call two or three vehicle leasing agencies that lease the kind of vehicle you need. Ask for the daily rate for that vehicle with any discounts for which your agency may be eligible; include insurance if your agency doesn't carry it, and tell them about the insurance you do carry if that is appropriate. If you are leasing for several days, ask for the weekly rate.

Ask for the difference between a daily rate with unlimited mileage and one with limited mileage. Unlimited mileage agreements may cost a little more on the front end but be more effective for your trip if it is over a fairly long distance. Limited mileage agreements are lower on the front end but have a rather stiff penalty for using more miles than the agreement covers. Be sure you consider distances when you agree to a lease.

Most agencies lease vehicles with a full tank of gas; you need to return it with a full tank or you will be charged a premium for the difference in gas between when you received it and when you return it.

Even if you are leasing a vehicle for the trip, you still need to charge mileage or you will need to figure about how much gas will cost to make the trip you are planning. This is because the lease agreement does not include gas. A motoring association such as AAA is valuable to establish routes and mileage between sites.

Motoring associations such as AAA also have online sites that provide mileage and other travel information to members. A selected membership may be valuable if you travel frequently yourself or must develop grant budgets with travel information.

Leasing agencies also have Web sites. If you are familiar with the automobile leasing agencies in your area, then you can check rates at their sites online. You will need to supply much the same information as when booking airline tickets: the departure date and the arrival date as well as the cities traveling from and to. Since you probably will not know these dates, you need to make up dates to get the appropriate information to plug into the budget.

Ground Travel—Train

If train travel is available within and between large cities, schedules and fares are posted and available through the agency responsible for managing the trains. Organizations such as New Jersey Transit produce schedules in print. Regional organizations sometimes post schedules online. Amtrak schedules and fares can be accessed online at http://www.amtrak.com. You can find numbers to call for information through the telephone directory. Many state transportation agencies list main contact information for various mass transit resources. These can often be found online through the state transportation agency Web site.

Ground Travel—Bus

Like airlines and trains, bus lines publish schedules. Look up the nearest bus terminal and call for information. Local bus lines may post their schedules and rates online and regional bus lines publish or post schedules as well.

But what if you need to lease a bus for a trip? Organizations that lease buses for groups are generally listed in the telephone directory. Here are the things to consider:

- How many people will be transported?
- What insurance will I need and does the bus leasing agency provide it? What is my liability?
- Do I need to provide the driver and what are the licensing requirements?
- If I provide the driver, where do I find licensed bus drivers?
- If the leasing agency provides drivers, what licenses do they have and how do I check their driving record?
- How much does the bus cost in day rates, mileage, and gasoline?
- How much does the leasing agency charge for the licensed driver? What arrangements are made and charges incurred if the bus trip requires overnight stay for the driver?

Ground Travel—Taxi, Shuttle, Limousine, or Hired Car

Taxi service differs greatly from city to city. Some cities do not have taxi service. The quickest way to get information on taxi or shuttle service is to contact the Travelers Bureau, Tourist Bureau, or Chamber of Commerce in the city to which you are traveling. These agencies have taxi and shuttle information or can tell you the names of taxi or shuttle services so you can contact them for rates. Be sure you know where your travelers will likely be using taxi or shuttle services to and from before you call.

If the travel in question is to and from the airport and the hotel, then call the hotel Concierge, Information, or Reservations staff and ask if there is a free shuttle. Many hotels and motels have free shuttle service to and from airports.

If the city to which your travelers are going has a consolidated area where there is dining and entertainment, then there may be free shuttles to and from this area. The Travelers Bureau, Tourist Bureau, or Chamber of Commerce can give you this information.

A motoring association such as AAA can also provide much of this information either in print or online.

Ground Travel—Mass Transit (Train, Subway, or Bus)

The Travelers Bureau, Tourist Bureau, Chamber of Commerce, or a motoring association is the best source of information about mass transit systems. Be sure to tell the representative where your people will be traveling from and to determine whether mass transit is available. Then ask the rates. As previously stated, many of these bureaus have Web sites.

Meals

First carefully read proposal instructions or ask the potential funder if they prefer a per meal or a per diem rate. If you are submitting a proposal to a government agency, that agency may have a meal policy. Ask the potential funder. If not, it is likely your agency has a meal policy. Call your financial specialist and ask what it is and follow it. If neither the potential funder nor your agency has a meal policy, call the financial person within an agency that most closely resembles yours or the one you are establishing in your proposal and ask for their meal policy.

If there is a choice, it is a good idea to allow more for meals if the travelers will be going to a large city than if they are traveling to a smaller one. If you are still in doubt, the Travelers Bureau, Tourist Bureau, or Chamber of Commerce will be able to send you booklets, brochures, or other information regarding average meal prices in the city.

Lodging

Contact the city's Travelers Bureau, Tourist Bureau, Chamber of Commerce, or a motoring association for lodging information. They will send brochures, lists, and booklets. Contact the lodging facility of choice and ask for room rates for the number of weekdays and weekend days for which you want costs. Rates may be different for weekdays and weekend days. Be sure to ask for rates including taxes and other charges. These can be significant. If you are with a nonprofit or governmental agency, ask if there are special rates and also ask if there are restrictions. We suggest that you go with standard rates rather than discounted rates with restrictions.

Gratuities

Read directions carefully or ask the potential funder if gratuities are allowable. Some agencies do not allow for gratuities and some do not allow for them unless they appear on a receipt. Most full-service hotels have arrangements for giving a receipt even for gratuities. Ask. Certainly ground transportation representatives provide receipts as well as valet parking, waiters, and bell persons. Others may be a problem. If receipts are required, just estimate costs for those that are likely to provide receipts.

Gratuities are usually between 17 percent and 22 percent for meals and $1 a bag or parcel for baggage carriers and handlers. Tips for taxi service range between 15 percent and 20 percent up to 50 percent depending on how long or short the trip. If your travelers are taking taxis for a few blocks, then the tip should be higher because the short trip has "robbed" the taxi driver of a larger fare. If the trip is longer, then the tip is in the lower percentage range. Add another dollar or two if the driver handles bags.

If the trip requires lodging in a full-service hotel, there will frequently be two persons handling bags, one at the door and one to carry bags to the room. Both require tips.

Tolls

If travel is by automobile, then tolls must be considered in many parts of the country and overseas. These are for bridges, tunnels, and highways. If you are unfamiliar with the roadways, then contact the Travelers Bureau, Tourist Bureau, or Chamber of Commerce, or a motoring association and ask about tolls. In some very large cities, when taking taxis, travelers will cross toll areas and must pay the toll in addition to the taxi fare. This should also be considered in costing for travel.

Parking

Airport parking fees should be considered for those traveling by plane. Contact the airport information service and ask rates. As with automobile leasing, check the differences in daily and weekly rates if appropriate.

Courtesy Expenses

Some hotels have surcharges on both local and long distance calls. If your travelers are expected to keep in communication during their trips either by e-mail or by telephone, it is a good idea to check with the hotel or motel for these charges. They can sometimes be significant. You can contact the Concierge or the Information or Reservation personnel for this information.

Equipment

Equipment is a big category. There are many ways to find costs for equipment. Grant seekers are collectors of catalogs for this reason. One of the best ways to cost equipment is to have current catalogs from equipment dealers and providers. Most companies provide free catalogs, and you simply look up the items you are requesting in the budget.

Many equipment dealers and providers now have Web sites where you can get prices for some items. The entire line of items shown in a catalog rarely appears on the Web site; information may be limited there and is sometimes harder to find.

For complicated, expensive, or larger quantity equipment purchases, it may be necessary to contact a sales representative to itemize equipment parts and provide a bid. Many organizations have a bid list of items you can access by contacting your agency, area, or state purchasing department. These bids are usually firm until a specified date, so you can use the information with confidence.

In getting costs from sales representatives, be sure you have provided all the information and that you get quotes on all necessary pieces of equipment. Do not get a quote for "computers" and forget that the quote probably does not include monitors. Be sure cabling is either bid separately or included. Be sure installation and setup is either bid separately or included. Again, you need to ask the right questions.

Get an itemized bid. Do not get a bid that says something like "for a complete computer workstation, the cost per is $10,000." Define all words. What constitutes a workstation? What is "complete?" Know what you need before you go to get a quote.

Specialized equipment may have only one or two dealers. More common equipment may have hundreds. Be sure you are getting a quote from a dealer that has a good track record and will be there when your grant comes through. Nothing is more frustrating than getting a good quote and then when the time comes for purchase, discovering that the bidder is out of business and the other available dealers are twice as expensive.

Capital

Land Purchase

If you need to purchase land as a part of the project, again, you have to know what questions to ask. What kind of land do you need? How much of it is needed? What location is desirable? What access or improvements are necessary on the land before you will consider purchase (i.e., well, sewer access, road access, cable access)? Armed with your list of needs, price comparable land. You can do this by Internet through realtor Web sites and multiple listing services or you can go to the city or county records and check recent sales of land with the same general description as the land you need.

You can also go to a realtor and ask for a sampling of land that fits your description. Or you can target a particular property and get an actual sales price on that piece of land. The way you go about getting costs for land depends entirely on your use and how specific your needs are. If you just need two flat acres with good drainage in the county, you may not really need a realtor to get a cost per acre. This research can usually be done on the Internet.

Building Purchase

If you need to purchase buildings, you need to know your exact specifications. What square footage? What condition? What amenities? What surrounding land is necessary for your use? What kind of access is desired? Armed with your needs, ask realtors to provide a list of sources of various price ranges that fit your description. If you have a specific building in mind, a sales price should be easily accessible. Realtors are usually the key to information about building sales although individuals occasionally sell property on their own. In either case, you may be asked to provide appraisals or other key information to prove that the property is worth what you will be paying for it. You may also need to provide proof that the building meets all appropriate codes (electrical, soil, structural, safety, etc.). Grant makers will want to know their money is invested wisely. Most of this information can be provided by the realtor but you may need to have the building inspected prior to requesting funds in your proposal.

Land Improvement

This usually involves contracting, so please read that section carefully. Land improvement includes grading; landscaping; adding highway access; clearing; and installing sewer, water, and electric lines. These are all contractual services. Once again, the key is in preparation. You must know what you want before you seek contractors. Once you are sure of the details, then the telephone directory is as good a start as any. Your agency may already have a list of approved contractors, but if not, then almost any contracting agency can provide an estimate of costs if they have enough information. In complex improvement situations, it may be hard to assess costs without expending money to obtain a professional architectural or landscape site plan. So if land improvement is a part of your proposal, start your project development early enough to get the appropriate plans drawn up so that contractors can accurately assess costs. It is not reasonable to ask a funder to buy a "pig in a poke" as the saying goes. This means that funders want no hidden costs and no surprises. They want some assurance that budget costs are reasonable and accurate. This is most important where foundational activities or structures are at stake. Foundational activities are those that provide a foundation for other project components. Land improvement would be a foundational activity. Any funder will ask this sort of question, "How did you know it would cost $XX for grading. Did you have a site plan developed?"

For further information about landscape contractors, there are various associations including the Associated Landscape Contractors of America with a Web site at http://www.alca.org as well as state and area landscape and grading contractors associations.

Building Improvement

Building improvement can be complex or simple depending on the task involved. It can be as simple as upgrading light fixtures or as complex as installing new electrical wiring. You must have specific ideas and images of the work that has to be done—where, when, how, how much, and why. As with land improvement, if the activity is major, a plan will be necessary and will be funded up front, before your proposal is developed. With most improvements, building codes and contractors' licenses come into play. Construction or improvement must be "to code," meaning that it must meet area minimum guidelines for the way the work is done. The people doing the construction or improvement must be licensed to do it by the appropriate regulatory agencies. Your organization may have a list of approved contractors. This would be the first place to start in seeking prices. The person in charge of maintenance and/or operations is the most likely person to know about approved contractors.

If there is not a list, then again, check the yellow pages for contractors. A good online resource is the Blue Book of Building and Construction, published by the Contractor's Register, Inc., at http://www.thebluebook.com. This site provides a searchable database (by type of contractor and region) of 800,000 contractors. There are also area building contractor associations in every region of the country. Those associations can be found in telephone directory yellow pages under "Associations" or online using a good search engine and the keywords "building contractor association <your state>."

There are various directories of contractors. The best and most up-to-date ones are published locally and are available in your local library. An industrial directory or business and industry directory is published in each state. Copies of this directory are available in public libraries and are purchasable from the state resource that developed the directory. Developers vary state-to-state and include state development boards, state chambers of commerce, and state industry development associations.

Supplies and Materials

Again, as with equipment, your best ally is a good set of catalogs. There are many office supply companies and healthcare supply companies, and all of them have catalogs available for free. Collect a good up-to-date assortment. If your agency only uses certain suppliers, then get catalogs from those suppliers.

For many suppliers, Web sites provide an alternate way of getting information. Good search engines to find suppliers include Buyers Index at http://www.buyersindex.com and Global Biz Directory at http://www .globalbizdir.com. Again, as with equipment, the number of items and the variety within a category will likely be limited online. Catalogs still provide more extensive listings.

You can provide a list of items to be purchased and get quotations from sales representatives. However, it is a good idea to know brands or at least the terminology for the quality and look of the items you want. Sales representatives are frequently under pressure from suppliers to quote a particular product.They may get a bigger commission on a particular item. There may be a larger inventory of a particular item and that may encourage sales representatives to recommend it over another item that is in short supply. It is better to feed the exact information to sales representatives, including all necessary details, and even brand if possible, than to just provide a category of supply and leave sales representatives to their own devices.

Contractual Services

The first question you must answer is, for what, exactly, do you need contractual services? *Exactly* is the keyword. You must think through the job needed completely before you ask for a quote for contractual services. This means writing what is commonly known as a "statement of work." Statements of work include such things as:

- Type of work to be done (i.e., digging trenches, painting floors and ceilings, running cable, building non-load-bearing walls).
- Amount of work to be done:

    Dig 1-foot deep rectangular trenches around two 8- by 10-foot garden plots.

    Paint floors and ceilings in two 9- by 12-foot rooms.

Run 60 feet of cable between two rooms and under tile in a dropped ceiling.

Build two non-load-bearing walls 8 feet long and 7 feet high connecting two load-bearing walls.

- Time frame for work to be done (i.e., work to be started no later than May 1 and completed no later than May 5).
- Special requirements and/or materials:

Dig around oak tree roots to avoid damaging the trees.

Paint floors and ceilings using semigloss enamel.

Use twisted pair, class five cable.

Match paneling of new walls with paneling of the existing walls.

- Licensing and code requirements (i.e., all work to be done by state and locally licensed electricians and to maximum electrical code specifications).

Once you write up the statement of work, then get bids for the contractual work to be done. You may get bids from contractors already on your agency bid list or you may have to "shop" for contractors. If you must shop, the yellow pages of the phone directory is as good a place as any to start. If the job requires a specialized contractor, then the Internet is a valuable tool. Use a good search engine such as Google (http://www.google.com) or Ask Jeeves at http://www.askjeeves.com for assistance. There are many sites with contractor information including the Associated Builders and Contractors at http://www.abc.org /index.html and the Software Contractors Guild at http://www.scguild .com.

Wise Guy and Wise Lady

Wise Guy

Statement of work! I never thought of that. I have always felt at the mercy of contractors. I'd say something like, "We need this room renovated to support a computer lab," and BAM! Back comes a bid that equals half the National Debt! I never knew how to stop that! Statement of work! Okay, that's a very good thing to know.

> ### Wise Lady
>
> WOW! A compliment from you! Businesses and industries use Statements of Work all the time—they put together very detailed "Bid Packets" for every job. It really helps keep down costs and confusion as well as stress. But nonprofits of all types frequently don't think of this. Many managers have not been trained to do this sort of thing. That's why we keep harping on project development. It's up to you to tell the contractors what has to be done: They are the experts on how it's to be done, but you need to take leadership on the what. After all, if you are an expert on computer labs and someone says "set up this lab," it's natural for you to do everything you always wanted to do to the very top-level quantity and quality. And yes, that would be nice, but most often one has to settle for something workable but less ideal because of other demands on budgeted funds. That's where your good management skills come in. That's the reason for the Statement of Work.

Conclusion

The calculation worksheet introduced in this chapter can be used to capture the costs of just about anything that can be purchased. As long as the goods or services can be defined with measurable units and the cost of a unit can be determined, a total cost can be calculated.

Key Principle

> ### Cost Calculation
>
> A cost, regardless of its number of components or its complexity, eventually comes down to the determination of only three facts even though the determination may be repeated many times:
>
> **1.** Quantity of an item needed.
> **2.** Quantity of the item in a unit of purchase.
> **3.** Cost of a unit of purchase.

Also fundamental to the accurate estimation of expenses is using correct prices. The resources for price finding are large and numerous. After all, sellers want people to know the price. Asking a vendor is one of the simplest and easiest ways to learn more about pricing than you will ever need to know. The lure of a sale makes it worth a vendor's while to be as accommodating as possible.

Key Concepts

- A unit of purchase may contain more than one of the item being purchased.
- The basic formula to calculate most direct costs is
  (Units Needed) × (Unit Cost) = Cost.
- Determining the price of an item is simply basic research.
- Who needs to know? Who makes it their business to know? Who has a stake in knowing? Whose business depends on knowing? Answer these questions and you identify the place to get the information you need.

We have now all the pieces. We know that a budget is a formal presentation of the expense involved in performing the activities necessary to accomplish the mission of a project. We know how to design and develop a project. We understand basic concepts such as direct costs, indirect costs, and in-kind contributions. We have the tools for calculating the various direct costs. All that remains is to put the pieces together in a coherent whole. In Chapter 10, we put together all the pieces and produce a budget.

Reporting
Your Budgets

Chapter 10

Putting It All Together: Developing a Finished Budget

Let no act be done at haphazard, nor otherwise than according to the finished rules that govern its kind.

Marcus Aurelius Antoninus, *Meditations IV,* Chapter 2

For nine chapters, we have been accumulating knowledge and developing concepts, processes, and tools for creating project budgets. Now is the time to put it all together. When we apply what we have learned, however, the result is not a budget, but a mass of raw budget data. It still remains to craft this data into an actual project budget. Shaping raw budget data into a project budget is the purpose of Chapter 11. This chapter picks up and weaves together strands that we developed earlier but left hanging. We explain how we join these disparate pieces to develop our raw budget data.

How to develop raw budget data is simple to state. Thoroughly and exhaustively complete Activity Analysis Worksheets for all project activities. The Activity Analysis Worksheet was introduced in Chapter 4 and is found on the CD-ROM as Worksheet CH0403. Before Activity Analysis Worksheets can be completed, however, the goals and objectives of the proposed project must be fully developed. Therefore, the first step in creating raw budget data is to develop your project to the level of completed goals and objectives. In Chapters 3 and 4, we presented a much shortened version of this task. The complete, detailed process of project design and development, along with worksheets and checklists, can be found in *Grant Seeker's Toolkit: A Comprehensive Guide to Finding Funding,* also by the authors; it is another volume in the Wiley Nonprofit series.

Activity Analysis Worksheet

The starting point for developing raw budget data is a set of completed goals and objectives (see Chapter 4). At its most basic, the purpose of the Activity Analysis Worksheet is to break down project objectives into their constituent activities and, along the way, to list key aspects of the activity. Those aspects include the answers to the following questions:

- When does the activity occur (time line with a start and a stop)?
- Who is responsible for seeing that the activity is accomplished?
- What personnel are needed to accomplish the activities?
- What is the expense of the personnel?
- What facilities are needed to accomplish the activities?
- What is the expense of facilities?
- What other resources are needed to accomplish the activities?
- What is the expense of the other resources?

These major questions along with other more detailed questions are formalized in the Activity Analysis Checklist, found on the CD-ROM as file CH1001. The Activity Analysis Checklist is the guide or road map to activity analysis. It provides the structure and consistency to ensure, as much as possible, that no resource necessary for successful accomplishment of project activities has been overlooked. Of course, something always gets overlooked, but the chance of neglecting something critical is greatly lessened by using a formalized, step-by-step procedure.

The Activity Analysis Checklist is illustrated in Exhibit 10.1. We strongly suggest that you read the checklist carefully while continually consulting the Activity Analysis Worksheet illustrated in Exhibit 10.2. It might pay additional dividends to print a copy of each from the CD-ROM so they will be full size and easier to manipulate.

Because CH1001 is an Activity Analysis Checklist, with emphasis on Activity, we have not included directions such as print as many pages as you need, number the pages, enter the goal of the activities being analyzed, or enter the objective of the activities being analyzed. We include only checklist items that deal directly with activities.

Before getting started on the checklist, here is a list of six strategies for approaching activity analysis and for using the activity analysis worksheet:

1. When entering an activity, ignore grammar. Ignore incomplete thoughts. Ignore lack of clarity. Get the heart of the activity down.

Exhibit 10.1  CH1001.DOC

Illustration of CH1001, Activity Analysis Checklist

☐ 1. Enter an activity that must be performed to accomplish the objective.

Personnel

☐ 2. Who is responsible that the activity takes place?
Use a Position Title such as Project Director or Site Coordinator.

☐ 3. Who performs the work?
Use Position Titles such as Counselor or Therapist or Mentor.

Thought Provokers

Is it absolutely necessary that this person be paid from the grant?
Search for alternatives to spending grant funds on personnel.
Who is positively the best, most logical person (position)?
Realistically, does the person have the time?
What about existing personnel in our organization?
What about personnel from partners?
What about a temporary worker?
What about contracting to have it done (contractual services)?
What about volunteers?

Facilities

☐ 4. Where will the activity take place?

Thought Provokers

Our facility?
A partner's facility?
A rented or leased facility?
A remote facility?
Will travel to the facility be necessary?
Will the facility need preparation?
Will the facility need cleaning before and/or after?
Will security be an issue?

Other Resources

☐ 5. What other resources will be needed to accomplish the activity?

Thought Provokers

Equipment we have?
Equipment we can borrow?
Equipment we can rent or lease?
Equipment a partner can provide?
Materials?
Supplies?
Outside services such as printing, installation, renovation, or training?
Consultants?

(continued)

EXHIBIT 10.1   *(Continued)*

Cost

☐ 6. What personnel expense will this activity incur?

☐ 7. What facility expense will this activity incur?

☐ 8. What expense for other resources will this activity incur?

Thought Provokers

What part of the expense must be paid with grant funds?
What part can be covered with in-kind contributions?
Partner in-kind?
Volunteer in-kind?

Time Line

☐ 9. When will this activity begin?

☐ 10. When will this activity end?

Thought Provokers

Some activities begin when the project starts and end when the project stops.
Some activities are repeated at intervals. They have multiple starts and stops.
Use Project Months, Quarters, and Years.

Completing the analysis will help flesh out the activity. The beginning point of an activity description can be as simple as the following examples: newsletter, publicity, recruit, or committee. Let the details and the complexity come to you over time.

2. At the start, ignore the order in which activities will occur. It just slows you down. The order will become obvious as planning progresses. This strategy is reflected in the Activity Analysis Checklist by placing the Time Line questions last.

3. Use as many lines on a worksheet as you need for each activity. It may take several or many lines to list the personnel and resources needed for the activity. While you are new to the process, it may be worthwhile to use a new worksheet page for each activity. It is often useful to drop below the lines used to initially describe the activity to enter items in the Personnel, Facilities, and Other Resources columns. This allows you to make notes in the Activity Description column concerning that item. Note the worksheet in Exhibit 10.2 for examples.

4. Use project time not calendar time for the Time Line. Project time is measured from the start of the project, when the money arrives. Project time begins at zero when the grant arrives and counts forward

EXHIBIT 10.2

Illustration of CH0403, Activity Analysis Worksheet

Goal One—During PM 1, establish project organization and logistical foundation through a plan of action to accommodate XX participants so that the plan is complete and adequate to ensure successfu project implementation.

Objective B—Prepare indoor and outdoor facilities to accommodate project activities, ensuring all regulations and codes are met, by the end of PM 4 so that all sites are ready to fully, adequately, and safely accommodate XX participants.

Activity Description	Time Line Start	Time Line End	Personnel Needed Describe	Personnel Needed Cost	Facilities Needed Describe	Facilities Needed Cost	Other Resources Needed Describe	Other Resources Needed Cost
Run conduits 3 rooms for computers	3/1	3/10	Tech Services, Inc.	$1,250				
Pave 3 basketball half-courts	3/1	4/12	Jones Construct.	3,640				
Install three-prong outlets (22 each)	3/7	3/8	In-house	220				
Resurface gym floor	3/1	4/1	Tom's Paint Co.	4,350				
Fence playground area	3/7	3/14	In-house	750			Posts, Concrete, Wire	$1,400
Repair light fixtures (2 each)	3/14	3/14	In-house	20			Light Units	70
Install light fixtures (5 each)	3/18	3/19	In-house	200			Fixtures, drills	520
Install window air conditioner (1 each)	3/20	3/20	In-house	50			Air conditioner	350
Loosen stuck windows (18 each)	3/21	3/21	In-house	90				
Clean 4 rooms	3/22	3/22	In-house	320			Cleaning products	80
Paint 4 rooms	3/25	4/10	In-house	740			Paint, brush, etc.	424

through the project in whatever increment is appropriate, days, weeks, months, quarters, and years. For example the first month of a project is Project Month One or PM1. The first three months of a project are Project Quarter One, or PQ1. The first year of a project is Project Year One, or PY1.

5. When more than one person is listed in Personnel Needed, track across to Activity Description and on the line with the person put the aspect of the activity the person is to do.

6. Every activity will not provide an answer for every question on the Activity Analysis Checklist. The questions take into consideration a wide range of possibilities.

Develop All the Data

Before moving forward with developing raw budget data, we need to reintroduce and reinforce a key point made in Chapter 1. The key concept is that a project budget is always larger than the grant request. The expense of participation in project activities that is incurred or contributed by the applicant, project partners, and volunteers always makes the total expenditures on a project larger than the amount of grant that is requested.

Key Concept

> A project budget is always larger than the grant request.

Many grant makers, in their application procedure, require only an accounting of how the grant request will be expended, not a complete accounting of the project. This is especially true for small grants and local grant makers. When application is made to large national programs—federal, foundation, or corporate—it is much more likely that the grant makers will require, in effect, two budgets; the project budget and the grant request budget.

A key purpose of this requirement is to ensure grant makers that an applicant is committed to the project. The only sure method of demonstrating commitment is through the contribution of time and resources. Letters extolling the value of the project and the intention of applicant's management to "place the highest priority on the proposed project" will fall on deaf ears if not accompanied by concrete demonstrations of that priority. Concrete demonstrations take the form of time and resources, money expended.

The following quotation from the application guidelines for the Technology Innovation Challenge Grant program, is an example of a grant maker wanting to see the entire project budget. In addition, this grant maker instructs applicants that their share must "significantly exceed" the grant request. What that means in terms of a percentage can be debated, but what is completely clear is that the support from sources other than the grant must, in aggregate, be larger than the grant itself. The match is, therefore, greater than 100 percent:

> The total value of commitments made by members of the consortium should significantly exceed the funds provided by the grant.
>
> —"Application Guidelines," Technology Innovation Challenge Grant

Note in the quotation the phrase "total value of commitments." This is grant-speak meaning that in-kind contributions may be used to make the financial match. This is normally true. In fact, the only time in-kind contributions may not be used as matching funds is when a grant maker uses the phrase "cash match."

A budget form that can be used to fulfill a grant maker's requirement to show the contributions of the applicant and the project partners is illustrated in Exhibit 10.3. Note the column headed "Requested." This column contains amounts being requested from the grant maker. The column headed "Support from other sources" contains the amounts being contributed by the applicant and its project partners. The two amounts are summed in the third column ("Total") to yield the actual budget of the project.

A Short but Advanced Discussion of Goals and Objectives

Over the years, in discussions with grant seekers, project developers, and evaluation specialists, we have run across three strongly held and interesting "takes" on project planning. Although the people who explain these points are trying to set things right and clear up confusion, confusion often grows rather than dissipates.

One of the viewpoints is that there is a difference between an objective and the activities employed to accomplish one. These people point out that an objective is a state after which to seek (a goal, if you will), while activities are actions. One expresses an outcome, while the other expresses means. The second point these people make is that there is also a difference between the activities to be undertaken and a strategy that provides the overall direction or guidance for what is done. Activities are

Exhibit 10.3

Example Summary Budget

Project Budget Summary

A. Direct Costs	Requested	Support from Other Sources	Total
1. Salaries (professional and clerical)			
2. Employee Benefits			
3. Employee Travel			
4. Equipment (purchase)			
5. Materials and Supplies			
6. Consultants and Contracts			
7. Other (equip. rental, printing, etc.)			
8. Total Direct Costs			
B. Indirect Costs			
C. TOTALS			

actions, whereas a strategy is a direction and a guidance that gives the activities a meaning and stability. Another viewpoint often expressed is that measurability absolutely must be built into the evaluation component of the project. These three points, by the way, are all true and correct. The points, however, miss the mark. They see trees while missing the forest all around.

Exhibit 10.4 illustrates the worksheet we use for creating goals and objectives. The column headings have been expanded to more than just a couple words to clarify what is meant by each of the parts of a goal or an objective. Note that the middle column is used to establish the time line for goals, but it records personnel issues for objectives. The other four columns remain the same for both goals and objectives. Also, a top row has been added that numbers the columns. This makes identifying the columns much easier in the following short discussion.

We return now to the possible misunderstandings about, or shortcomings with, project planning. First, when the word goal or the word objective is used to label one of the major organizational steps of a project plan,

EXHIBIT 10.4

Partial, Modified Worksheet for Development of Goals and Objectives

1	2	3	4	5
What is to be done?	Methodology (How is it done?)	(Goal) When is it done?	For how many is it done, or how much is done?	What will be the result or outcome of having done it?
		(Objective) Who is responsible and who does it?		

the word loses much of its dictionary meaning and certainly does not retain the meaning held by all the different specialties and fields of learning. Rather, goal and objective are simply words that label the parts into which a project is divided so it can be better understood, planned, and implemented.

When people worry over the difference between an objective or a goal and the means to accomplish either or both, they miss the point. A goal should have an outcome or purpose built into it as an integral part of the whole. In our process, that is found in column 5, labeled in Exhibit 10.4, "What will be the result or outcome of having done it" ("it" being the action described in column 1)?

The issue of strategy, while true and correct, again misses the point. A stated outcome and a bunch of activities do not, in and of themselves, constitute much of a plan, except for lots of action with not much result. The activities must be driven and informed by a unifying and directional methodology or strategy that shapes and guides the actions taken. In our model, this aspect of a goal or an objective is found in column 2. The methodology or strategy is an integral part of the whole.

When people, especially evaluation specialists preach about measurability, they often are already too late. If the "how many or how much" does not get addressed until the evaluation part of the project is developed, things are already out of control. The logical place—in fact, the only reasonable place—for the initial measurability is as an integral part of each goal and objective. Exhibit 10.4 shows that we place this information in column 4.

For project planning purposes, a goal and an objective are not simply things toward which to strive, but are multifaceted parts of the project itself. They are a totally integrated part of the project. After all, each contains and expresses all the key high-level concepts inherent to project organization:

- An expected outcome provides the reason for the actions (column 5).
- Actions provide the means of accomplishing the outcome (column 1).
- A methodology or strategy guides and directs the actions (column 2).
- Setting the time frame for actions and activities establishes the implementation relations between different aspects of the project (column 3 for a goal).
- Naming the person assigned responsibility and the people assigned to perform the activities gives impetus to getting things done (column 3 for an objective).
- Establishing the "how many or how much" provides the means to measure the level of accomplishment (column 4).

From Objective to Activities

A problem for just about everyone who develops projects is failing to include in the project plan all the activities or actions that it will take to accomplish objectives. This is easy to do because even relatively simple activities can incorporate an amazing number of discrete tasks. It is important not to overlook tasks or activities because when a task is left out, the resources necessary to accomplish the task are also left out. These unexpected expenses of time, equipment, materials, supplies, and perhaps money that pop up once a project is already in implementation can wreck a budget and, when serious enough, bring into doubt the very future of the project.

Because thinking through and incorporating into the project plan all the necessary activities for accomplishing project objectives is so important, we created a checklist to use whenever developing a project down to the activity level. The Activity Checklist is illustrated in Exhibit 10.5 and is found on the CD-ROM as Checklist CH1002. The concept that drives the content of this checklist is simple. From a process viewpoint (not subject matter content), there are relatively few types of project activities. Enough experience with project development allows a person to list those activities. The Activity Checklist directs the attention of the project planner

Exhibit 10.5

Activity Checklist

 CH1002.DOC

Potential Activity Topics

☐ Mentor	☐ Test
☐ Recruit	☐ Order
☐ Meet	☐ Purchase
☐ Train	☐ Install
☐ Develop materials	☐ Wire
☐ Interview	☐ Landscape
☐ Tutor	☐ Compare
☐ Travel	☐ Chart
☐ Set Up Conference	☐ Track
☐ Present	☐ Teach
☐ Program	☐ Print
☐ Audio Tape	☐ Distribute
☐ Video Tape	☐ Participate
☐ Write	☐ Compose
☐ Plan	☐ Hire
☐ Schedule	☐ Cater
☐ Contract	☐ Advise
☐ Paint	☐ Consult
☐ Build	☐ Archive
☐ Measure and Sew	☐ Link
☐ Plant	☐ Deliver
☐ Harvest	☐ Package
☐ Examine	☐ Ship
☐ Treat	

toward the possible types of activities, allowing the planner to decide whether particular activities need to be incorporated into a project.

The purpose of this checklist is totally different from the purpose of the Activity Analysis Checklist, CH1001. The analysis checklist aids in digging into the internal complexities of an activity. This checklist simply provides a selection of potential activities to help along the process of breaking an objective into its constituent parts.

Using the Calculation Worksheets

On an Activity Analysis Worksheet, three columns await a project planner's estimation of the cost or expense involved in project activities. We need information about the cost of personnel, facilities, and other resources. From the earlier discussion of direct cost (Chapter 6), we know that the "other resources" category on the Activity Analysis Worksheet covers a lot of ground including travel, equipment, materials, supplies, and contractual services.

This is where the calculation worksheets that were introduced and explained in Chapters 7, 8, and 9 can be useful. For example, when the analysis of an activity shows that travel will be necessary, the appropriate travel calculation worksheets can be used to estimate the cost.

More than one method can be used, but it works well to use a computer and the calculation worksheets. They are spreadsheets and perform the calculations automatically. Next, perform a "Save As" of the worksheet into a folder (directory) specially created for the project. This allows the worksheet to be reopened and quantities changed as necessary. Third, print a copy of the worksheet and attach it to the Activity Analysis Worksheet. Our experience is that a team does a much better job of planning a project than a person working alone. Our experience also is that, regardless of advances in groupware and shared work environment software, a team works best when computers are left out of it.

One additional comment about calculation worksheets is that there will be plenty of times when they are not needed. A cost may be obvious. The subject may be one about which one of the project developers has great experience and can speak with authority about costs. The worksheets are aids. They are supposed to save time, not bog you down with manipulating worksheets just for the sake of the manipulation. If you need them, use them. Otherwise, move on.

We have attempted to develop a system sufficiently structured to provide guidance to those most in need. At the same time, we have broken the system into discrete blocks (worksheets and checklists) each of which, to some degree, stands on its own. This allows the more experienced budget developer to pick and choose those aspects of the system that can provide help where needed.

A Practical Matter

Identifying all the activities that must take place to accomplish a project's objectives will take a lot of time and a lot of paper. The next step of analyzing the identified activities and deciding what resources each one will need and the expense involved also will take a lot of time and a lot of paper. If you are in the habit of spending a few minutes filling in a grant application budget form with numbers drawn directly from your brain, all this will seem to be a tremendous amount of work. It is only natural to ask whether the extra work is worth the investment of time, effort, and resources.

If your organization wants to be competitive, to place its proposals in the top 10 percent of applicants, which is where the competition takes place, then, yes, it is worth it. If your organization wants to compete for and win one or more of those million-dollar-a-year grants, yes, it is worth it. A well crafted and fully developed budget goes a very long way toward convincing the evaluators of grant proposals that the applicant is capable of handling the project it has proposed.

Think hard on this last point. If a project budget is not practical, complete, and realistic, the message is sends loud and clear to the grant maker is that the applicant does not possess the financial knowledge or skill to handle the project. Think on this from the grant maker's position. In fact, go further and put yourself in the grant maker's position. Imagine that you are making the decision about who is awarded a million dollars a year for five years. Which applicant wins—the applicant whose budget reflects directly and accurately the purposes and activities of the project, or the applicant whose budget raises more issues than it resolves? The answer is obvious.

Also, when a project budget is small, $100,000 or less, budget mistakes normally remain manageable. Take that same budget mistake and scale it up to a million dollars and the problem can become formidable. This is especially the case if the problem is a shortfall in funds that must be covered by your organization. Scraping together a few thousand dollars to cover a small mistake is one thing. Coming up with tens of thousands of dollars to correct the same level of mistake in a million-dollar budget is quite another.

The work that is necessary to develop a solid budget is an investment in a successful future. One of the more interesting things we have observed over the years is how often a careful and thorough investigation of the budget has brought light to major flaws in a project. This can result in making important changes or even in scrapping the entire idea. This is one of those old "stitch in time saves nine" situations.

Master Budget Development Checklist

To move project planning from the relatively simple objective level to the much more complex level of activities requires a systematic approach.

Projects usually have only 4 to 5 goals. Goals generally have only 3 to 7 objectives. Each objective, on the other hand, can have 10, 20, 30, 40, or more activities, and each activity may have several steps or tasks. This amount of detail simply cannot be handled without a system that both records what has been done and guides the way so gaps do not develop. At some point, the mind alone becomes unable to keep track of all the details. The system must be able to step up and help.

For the project planner-developer, the system developed in this book offers guidance and direction for recording, saving, and retrieving information. It provides an organization for the project plan. And, it almost totally eliminates mathematical calculations. All the pieces are in place. The need now is for an overall organizational scheme. This is provided by the Master Budget Development Checklist, illustrated in Exhibit 10.6 and found on the CD-ROM as file CH1003.

EXHIBIT 10.6

 CH1003.DOC

Master Budget Development Checklist

☐ 1. The project's mission defines clearly the target population and the intended outcome.

☐ 2. A set of goals describe a clear path to accomplishing the mission.

☐ 3. Each goal includes a method or strategy, a time frame, measurability, and the expected outcome.

☐ 4. A set of objectives describe a clear path to accomplishing each goal.

☐ 5. Each objective includes a method or strategy, who is responsible, measurability, and the expected outcome.

☐ 6. A set of activities describe a clear path to accomplishing each objective.

☐ 7. Each activity includes a time frame, personnel responsible and personnel to do the work, facilities and other resources needed, and the associated expenses for all resources (Activity Analysis Worksheet).

☐ 8. Calculation Worksheets are used when necessary.

☐ 9. Costs from Activity Analysis Worksheets are collected into line items as defined by grant maker's budget form (Budget Worksheet).

☐ 10. Line item totals are entered into grant maker's budget form.

☐ 11. Budget narrative is crafted to explain the budget figures.

Preparing to Complete a Budget Form

All the activities for all the objectives are analyzed and all the costs are calculated. The pieces are in hand to complete a budget. A small difficulty may exist, however. The budget form divides expenses into different categories than our system does. A grant maker can devise its budget form any way it chooses, and a grant maker's choices may not match our choices. The differences will be cosmetic only, involving arrangement naming, or grouping. A common grouping is to lump equipment, materials, and supplies together while adding a note to the effect that any item valued over a certain amount, say $500, must be explained.

The most helpful tool is the one you construct yourself. Taking the time to duplicate the grant maker's budget form with a spreadsheet will pay handsome dividends. You do not need to worry with making the worksheet look similar to the budget form. Only you will see it. Your worksheet needs to have the same line items and the same columns all in the same order as the budget form. Enter the formulas for the calculation of fringe and indirect cost. In the cells in the spreadsheet that correspond to the subtotal and total blocks of the budget form, enter summing formulas. Now you have a powerful budget tool. We cannot do this for you. The closest we can come is a generic sort of budget summing device to overcome the problem that grant makers use an almost infinitely variety of budget forms.

Budget Worksheet is designed to help with this last hurdle. The worksheet is partially illustrated in Exhibit 10.7. This worksheet sums along rows. Column C displays the sum of all quantities entered along the same row to its right. The quantities entered into Columns D, E, F, G (not shown), and so on, will all be reflected in the sum displayed in

EXHIBIT 10.7

Illustration of Budget Worksheet

	A	B	C	D	E	F
1	#	**Line Item**	**Total**			
2						
3						
4						
5						
6						

Column C, assuming, of course that they are all on the same row. This worksheet sums along rows, beginning with Column D and running to the right.

Here is how to use the worksheet. Enter in the cells in Column A, the line item numbers from the budget form. Enter in Column B, the corresponding names of the line items. You might want to leave a line or two between each budget line item. It is up to you. Columns A and B now identify a row as one of the line items on your budget form. Any quantity entered into that row beginning in Column D and working to the right is assigned to that line item and sums in Column C. As you collect expenses, you can simply enter them into a new column.

Showing a blank copy of this particular worksheet may not be very helpful since it consists mostly of blank spaces. Explaining the utility of the worksheet probably is best done with an example. To give something with which to work, a sample budget form that should be familiar by now is illustrated in Exhibit 10.8.

The budget form of Exhibit 10.8 displays three totals for each line item, the grant request, the support from other sources, and the total of those two. As a result, we will want to use two rows on our worksheet to collect amounts for the grant request and for the support from other sources. We can sum the two later. Look at Rows 2 and 3 in the example in

EXHIBIT 10.8

Example Summary Budget

Project Budget Summary

A. Direct Costs	Requested	Support from Other Sources	Total
1. Salaries			
2. Employee Benefits			
3. Employee Travel			
4. Equipment			
5. Materials and Supplies			
6. Consultants and Contracts			
7. Other			
8. Total Direct Costs			
B. Indirect Costs			
C. TOTALS			

Exhibit 10.9 to see how this is done. We continue with the same process for each line item, skipping number 7 since our total for that item is always zero. We skip a row between each line item to distinguish visually and clearly between the items.

After we identify the line items, we begin to enter amounts we have previously calculated and can now collect into one place. Rows 2 and 3 with salaries and Rows 11 and 12 with equipment illustrate how this looks.

The layout of Exhibit 10.9 has the benefit of grouping like budget items together so the line item totals display one on top of the other. The layout has the drawback of mixing together, alternating actually, project expenses to be paid out of the grant and project expenses to be supported from sources other than the grant. Usually, when a grant maker requires figures on in-kind contributions, it is because some level of matching is involved. Comparing the total grant request to the total of other support quickly shows whether the match is made or not. With this layout, we can compare individual line items but not the overall totals.

EXHIBIT 10.9

Illustration of Budget Worksheet

	A	B	C	D	E	F
1	#	**Line Item**	**Total**			
2	1	Salaries from Grant Request	$42,500	$20,000	$15,000	$ 7,500
3	1	Salaries from Other Sources	43,000	12,500	12,500	18,000
4						
5	2	Employee Benefits from Grant Request				
6	2	Employee Benefits from Other Sources				
7						
8	3	Employee Travel from Grant Request				
9	3	Employee Travel from Other Sources				
10						
11	4	Equipment from Grant Request	85,000	85,000		
12	4	Equipment from Other Sources	95,500	35,000	15,500	45,000
13						
14	5	M & S from Grant Request				
15	5	M & S from Other Sources				
16						
17	6	C & C from Grant Request				
18	6	C & C from Other Sources				
19						

Completing a Budget Form

One of the most helpful tools a budget developer can have is a spreadsheet that duplicates the organization of the budget form, but not necessarily its exact appearance, and that calculates automatically. Once the spreadsheet is set up to calculate fringe and indirect cost and to sum columns and rows in the appropriate cells (blocks), it becomes a powerful tool for manipulating numbers and working with financial matters. The result of changing an amount is instantly shown in the totals. This allows for free and easy sessions of creativity, seeing how various options work out, all without the strain and pain of calculation. It really is worthwhile to learn how to use a spreadsheet. If you will be doing much budget work, it most certainly will be well worth your while to learn how to use a spreadsheet, or more precisely a spreadsheet program.

Without a spreadsheet specifically designed for a budget form, you can still collect budget information from the calculation worksheet on Budget Worksheet, CH1001. Once all the various budget amounts have been entered into the appropriate rows and the worksheet totals them for you, you can transpose the totals onto the budget form. A completed budget form is illustrated in Exhibit 10.10.

Exhibit 10.10

Example Completed Summary Budget Form

	Project Budget Summary		
A. Direct Costs	**Requested**	**Support from Other Sources**	**Total**
1. Salaries	$155,200.00	$223,245.00	$ 378,445.00
2. Employee Benefits	29,488.00	42,416.55	71,904.55
3. Employee Travel	15,590.00	8,500.00	24,090.00
4. Equipment	85,000.00	95,500.00	180,500.00
5. Materials and Supplies	58,760.00	102,000.00	160,760.00
6. Consultants and Contracts	83,250.00	15,600.00	98,850.00
7. Other	0.00	0.00	0.00
8. Total Direct Costs	427,288.00	487,261.55	914,549.55
B. Indirect Costs	74,775.40	85,270.77	160,046.17
C. TOTALS	$502,063.40	$572,532.32	$1,074,595.72

Wise Guy and Wise Lady

Wise Guy

You put it all together and it's quite a deal, isn't it? I can see how it takes shape. That Activity Analysis Worksheet is key but it is SO MUCH WORK. I don't know if I have the time! Seriously.

Wise Lady

It should not be up to you alone to complete these Activity Analysis Worksheets. Delegate. There are others who will be overseeing parts of the project. You have other partners. Explain the sheet to them—give them a copy of this book and then have them fill out some of them. There's no reason you have to do it all. It gets them involved from the outset, and it provides valuable information for you and saves you time. After all, partners and staff have to buy into the project for it to be successful, and what better way than to get them to help work through the activity detail?

Conclusion

All the definitions, all the concepts, all the forms, all the checklists and worksheets have resulted in placing numbers into a little 10-by-3 matrix (Exhibit 10.10). We could have used a larger budget form, but the number of active cells would not change very much. The big forms that take up entire pages do not require any more work than our example. They require almost exactly the same number of totals, many have less if they do not require the contributions of an applicant and the partners. All this work for such a small outcome. It seems such a waste. Not if you are serious about winning grants. Literally hundreds of millions of dollars are up for grabs every year. The organizations that get their share are those that cross every "t" and dot every "i" regardless of work involved.

The budget is the means by which you communicate to a grant maker your knowledge and competence to handle the finances of the project. If an applicant will not take the time to get the budget right when asking for the money, what will the applicant do once it has the money? From the viewpoint of the grant maker everything we do, or fail to do, in an application sends a message. The message we want to send is one of financial acumen, experience, and competence. Our only opportunity is with a well-crafted budget that matches exactly the needs of the project explained elsewhere in the proposal.

Key Concepts

- Identify all the activities necessary for successful accomplishment of goals and objectives.
- Analyze activities carefully to identify all possible expenses.
- Estimate a cost for all aspects of each activity.
- When necessary, use calculation worksheets to compute costs.
- Collect and total costs from Activity Analysis Worksheets.
- Enter collected totals into the budget form.
- Pick and choose the parts of the overall budget development system that best serve your purpose.
- Learning a spreadsheet program is worthwhile for a person who will do any amount of budget work.

The complete example budget illustrated in Exhibit 10.10 shows $8,500 as support from other sources for Employee Travel (line item 3). What does this mean? What partner is providing this support, and how? Is this cash, or is it airline tickets, or is it a rental vehicle? Just how is a partner, or the applicant, providing support for employee travel? Answering these questions and others is the purpose of the budget narrative, sometimes called budget justification. A completed budget form is not the end of the budget process. Too much is left unsaid and too many questions are unanswered by the bare facts shown by a completed budget form. A budget narrative explains what the figures mean, where they came from, how they were calculated, and other information of use to a reader. The budget narrative is the topic of the next and final chapter.

Chapter 11

The Budget Narrative

If you can't explain it, how can you take credit for it?
Harold "Red" Grange, Chicago Bears halfback,
Associated Press, news summaries, December 31, 1951

What is a Budget Narrative? Simply, it's an explanation of your budget. Unlike a picture, budget figures are not "worth a thousand words." It is required that you write the "thousand words" so that readers fully understand where you got the summarized numbers in the budget you have submitted. The Budget Narrative is also sometimes called the Budget Justification or Budget Explanation. In many ways, the Budget Narrative is more important to the proposal than the Budget itself for without the Budget Narrative, the figures do not mean a lot.

Your Budget Narrative should be set up exactly as the potential funder required that the Budget be set up. If the potential funder required that the line item for personnel was first in the Budget Summary, then discuss personnel first in the Budget Narrative. If the line item for equipment was first in the proposal Budget, then discuss equipment first in the Budget Narrative.

Use the exact headings the funder required in the Budget Summary for the headings in the Budget Narrative. If the funder called a line item in the Budget Summary, "personnel," then you should call it "personnel," not "people" or "staff" or something else. Always remember that you are explaining and describing how you got the numbers in the Budget Summary. The Budget Narrative should follow the Budget Summary precisely in both headings and organization.

As noted earlier, the Budget submitted with a proposal should be accurate and realistic. It should match your project needs exactly. You should not be making up numbers just to arrive at some theoretical figures, but should be providing the funder actual figures from your research. In Chapter 7, we discussed resources for research and ways of getting the information for the budget.

Personnel and Fringe

Personnel involves a number of calculations depending on the personnel or job functions required by your project. We have thoroughly discussed these calculations and the definitions of the various aspects of personnel costing in previous chapters. What must be done in the Budget Narrative is to explain to the reader just why you need the personnel you listed and how you got the numbers.

The Why

From the rest of your proposal, it should be clear why you need the people you listed in the Budget. To underscore this, in writing objectives, we asked you to list "the Who"—who would be doing the various activities. This was not just an aimless exercise; it was for a purpose. It was to alert the reviewer that each person has a function and that if the reviewer disallows a personnel position, the goals and objectives of the project will suffer. The more you indicate in your proposal what person will be performing what function, the more solid your case for your personnel decisions. In the Budget Narrative, it is a good idea to indicate to which goal and/or objective the person/position relates. This can be easily done:

> Project Coordinator—salary at Grade 4, State of Ohio Personnel Wage and Salary Scale with a 32.75% benefit package as standard with the Weebene Fitu Agency. Base salary is $52,000. With benefits, the total salary comes to $69,030. Fringe benefits consist of 8% health insurance, 2.8% life insurance, 10% retirement, 2% Worker's Compensation Insurance, 0.3% FUTA, 2% SUTA, and 7.65% FICA. The Project Coordinator is required to accomplish Goals 2, 3, 4, and 5.

The How

As illustrated in the preceding example, the "how I came up with the numbers" is straightforward for personnel. State the way you came up with the base salary level and the makeup of the benefits package and how it was derived. You had to have these figures to list your personnel costs. Just explain succinctly how you developed the final number. An example of an explanation for an hourly wage person follows:

> Maintenance Superintendent—salary derived from average wages for similar positions listed with the Wyoming Employment Security Commission plus a 32.75% benefit package. Base salary is $12 an hour at an average of 12 hours a week for 48 weeks a year requested from grant funds. The balance of hours and benefits, 18 hours per week for 48 weeks, will be funded by Neighborhood Development Corporation. At the rates listed, the annual wages requested are $6,912 for a total of $9,175.68 including benefits. Fringe benefits consist of 8% health

insurance, 2.8% life insurance, 10% retirement, 2% Worker's Compensation Insurance, 0.3% FUTA, 2% SUTA, and 7.65% FICA. The Maintenance Superintendent is required to accomplish Goal 1, Objectives 3, 4, and 5; Goal 2, Objective 1; and Goal 4, Objectives 3, 5, and 6.

In the preceding example, only part of the wages are being requested of the grantor. If this is the case, then state how much is being requested and what group or partner will cover the balance of wages required. You would only elucidate the portion of the wages that you are requesting of the grantor in the budget request.

Travel

Again, you are simply explaining where you got the numbers for your budget request. Following are examples of a Budget Narrative for each category of travel.

Air Travel

Two trips to regional conferences are required. Regional conferences are usually held in large cities within 300 miles of our city. Average airline tickets to cities at the furthest distance from our city are $456 round trip Coach Class including tax and insurance. There will be three people traveling to each conference. Goal 1, Objective 2.

3 travelers × $456 × 2 conference trips = $2,736

Ground Travel

Train

New Jersey Transit Authority operates local train service between Maplewood and Jersey City. For quarterly district meetings, five staff members must travel from Maplewood to Jersey City. Round trip train fares are $12.50 per person. Goal 2, Objective 5.

5 travelers × 4 meetings × $12.50 round trip fare = $250

Car Rental

Four staff must travel to two regional planning meetings as required by the funder. The most cost-effective way to accomplish this is to lease a van. Meetings are three days in duration with added days for travel the day before and the day after the meetings. The most cost-effective leasing rates were for a one-week lease as compared to the daily rate. Leasing with unlimited miles was the option chosen because of the distance to and from the required meetings. Three bids were sought and the lowest bid chosen. Gasoline purchases will be paid according to receipts submitted and are based on average cost per tank of gas and average mileage per gallon for the van to be leased. Goal 1, Objective 3.

2 meetings × 1 van at a weekly rate of $356.75 including tax and insurance = $713.50

2 round trips for regional planning meetings × 3 tanks of gas at $45 per tank = $270.00 for gasoline

Bus Leasing

Thirty-five students will be transported to the state aquarium for a field trip. The distance is 78 miles and the most efficient transportation was to lease a bus and driver from Big Yellow Bus Limited. The cost of a bus, driver, and additional liability insurance totals $1,890 for the trip. Goal 3, Objective 5. This breaks down as follows:

Leasing of one bus for one day including gasoline = $1,360

Hiring one bus driver for one day = $180

Additional Insurance = $350

Taxi (Limousine or Hired Car) and Shuttle

Four staff members will travel to the Regional Training Conference by plane. They will each be traveling from different locations. They will each need a taxi to the hotel on arrival and back to the airport on departure. Taxi service is $25 plus $3.75 tip each trip. Goal 4, Objective 2.

4 travelers × 2 trips each × $28.75 = $230

Rapid Transit

Eight staff members travel by subway once weekly for 48 weeks to the Main Street facility for staff meetings. Each staff member takes the subway from the Oak Street facility. Round trip, the subway toll is $2.70 per trip. Goal 2, Objective 3.

8 travelers × 48 weeks × $2.70 = $1,036.80

Mileage

Five Social Workers must make home visits using their own vehicles monthly. Workers have an average caseload of 42 clients. Average round-trip distance from the main office to a household is 8.2 miles. Mileage charges are allowed at 35 cents per mile according to Improvement Now Agency Policy 3.5. Goal 4, Objectives 3 and 4.

5 Workers × 42 Clients × 12 Months (at one visit a month) × 8.2 miles × $0.35 per mile = $7,232.40

Meals

Staff members will travel a combined total of 27 days meeting the District per diem requirements at $39.75 per day. Goals 1, 3, and 5.

27 combined days × 39.75 per day = $1,073.25

or

Eight staff members will travel to the Regional Conference that lasts three full days with half-day travel days both before and after the conference. They will provide receipts of meals for reimbursement. Maximum allowed amounts, including gratuities, for breakfast is $8.50, for lunch is $12.50, and for dinner is $25.50. On the travel days, they are eligible for dinner only. Goal 5, Objective 2. At maximum, the cost is as follows.

Breakfasts $8 \times \$8.50 \times 3 = \$68$
Lunches $8 \times \$12.50 \times 3 = \$300$
Dinners $8 \times \$25.50 \times 5 = \$1,020$

Total for Meals = $1,388

Lodging

Four staff members travel to two area conferences, each of three days' duration plus a travel night before the conference. Lodging at midlevel facilities averages $93.87 including local and state taxes. Goal 3, Objective 2.

4 travelers × 2 conferences × 4 nights per conference × $93.87 per night = $3,003.84

Gratuities

As discussed in Chapter 7, this is a problem area. It is likely that unless a receipt can be presented, gratuities are not recoverable. Please refer to Taxi and Shuttle example for one way to handle gratuities. Also refer to Meals for another way to handle gratuities. Valet parking and ground travel drivers are handled in the same manner as taxi service.

The problem occurs primarily with baggage handling since the number of bags is dependent largely on the packing habits of the persons involved. Some people are good at compacting necessities into a small number of bags and some have little bundles of items stashed in every corner. One way to handle this is to set a fixed amount of gratuity according to the travel planned and then require receipts. If a receipt is not presented then there is no refund. It's then up to the traveler to get receipts or decide to handle gratuities out of personal funds. We will use the previous example under Lodging:

Four staff members travel to two area conferences, each of three days' duration plus a travel night before the conference. Travel is accomplished by airplane. Gratuity is set at $1 per bag for two bags for each staff member. Five gratuities in addition to those for meals and taxis are allowed as follows: for curb baggage handling at the airport each way;

for curb service at the hotel on arrival, and for bell service at the hotel on arrival and departure. Goals 1 and 3.

4 travelers × 2 Conferences × $2 total for bags × 5 gratuities = $80, receipts required

Tolls

As discussed in Chapter 7, information about tolls charged is readily available from a number of sources. One has to just figure the route and then add in the tolls:

Staff must travel to two District meetings in Overtown. Travel is by automobile via the Neway Freeway, which has a total toll fee of $10.50, one way between Middle Town and Overtown. Goal 3, Objective 1.

2 trips by 1 staff member with a total round trip toll of $10.50 = $21

Parking

Parking usually involves airport parking during a trip, Valet parking at a hotel if travel is by automobile, or city parking in a parking building or by meter. Following are examples of each:

Three staff members travel to two conferences each by plane. Each conference is three days in duration with one travel day. Daily parking at the airport is $10. Goal 1, Objective 2, and Goal 4, Objective 1.

3 travelers × 2 × 4 × $10 = $240

or

Three staff members travel individually to two conferences each by automobile. Each conference is three days in duration with one travel day (four total nights). Valet parking at the hotel is $7.50 per night plus $4 gratuity on leaving and recovering cars. Goal 1, Objective 2, and Goal 4, Objective 1.

3 travelers × 2 conferences × 4 nights × $7.50 per night = $180

Gratuity consists of 3 travelers × 2 conferences × $4 gratuity = $24

Total for Parking = $204

or

Three staff members travel individually to two conferences each by automobile. Each conference is three days in duration with one travel day (four parking days). City parking is $5 per day. Goal 1, Objective 2, and Goal 4, Objective 1.

3 travelers × 2 conferences × 4 parking days × $5 per day = $120

Courtesy Expenses

This is a tough one to figure but can cost a significant amount of money as mentioned in Chapter 7. If you want to allow for these expenses because of high costs through hotel services or other carriers, then here is an example of how to word the Budget Narrative:

> Three staff members travel to two conferences and stay for three days for each conference at a hotel that charges $1 per local call. Staff is required to check in to the main office via e-mail four times per day. This is a local call. Goal 1, Objective 2, and Goal 4, Objective 1.
>
> 3 travelers × 2 conferences × 3 days × 4 times a day × $1 = $72

Equipment

As noted in Chapter 7, the "trick" with equipment is knowing exactly what you want and spelling it out. Following are three examples of how to write a Budget Narrative for Equipment:

> To provide adequate lighting for computer repair classes, new light fixtures are necessary for the three workrooms. This entails rewiring, which is covered under Contractual Services. Five new lights for each of the three workrooms are required. Each fixture meets state standard codes for light output and safety. Each fixture is 6 feet long with two fluorescent bulbs. Goals 2, 3, and 4.
>
> 3 workrooms × 5 light fixtures each × $178.56 per fixture = $2,678.40

or

> Provide one computer, 15-inch color monitor, keyboard, and 600 dpi quality black-and-white laser printer for each of nine field offices, with high speed capability, internal modem, and printer cable. Each computer will have a three-year warranty and free setup service. Computers with monitors at the agency discount cost an average of $1,850 with high-speed processor and internal modem. Keyboards cost $15 each. Printer cables are $15 each. Laser printers cost $300 each on average. Three bids were taken on printers since no printer suppliers were on the agency bid list. All Goals and Objectives.
>
> 9 field offices × 1 computer with modem and monitor @ $1,850 = $16,650
>
> 9 field offices × 1 printer plus cable each @ $315 = $2,835
>
> 9 field offices × 1 keyboard each @ $15 = $135
>
> Total cost = $19,620

or

> Equip three examining rooms each with examining table, side table, movable light fixture, sink, and cabinet. Seven-foot standard clinic examining tables average $3,400 each. Rolling aluminum adjustable height side tables with 36" × 24" tray average $325 each. Movable overhead fluorescent hospital quality light fixture not including installation costs $760 each. Deep single sinks with high arched faucets cost $92 each not including installation and standard 6-foot wood cabinets with Formica tops cost $235 each, not including installation. The total price for equipping each examining room is $4,812 not including installation, which is covered under Contractual Services. Prices are based on average prices as listed in clinic and hospital supply catalogs. Goals 1, 3, and 5.

> 3 examining rooms × $4,812 each = $14,436

Capital

Building and Land Purchase

If the grant maker is being asked to cover all or a portion of the cost of purchasing a building for the project, many documents must be included in an Appendix including but not exclusive of the appraisal on the property, the inspection report, comparable costs of similar buildings, lot and building layout drawings, property survey, evidence of title insurance, property insurance, projected closing cost itemization, payment of all applicable taxes, and evidence of easements or access agreements. The Narrative explains why the building is needed and justifies the choice of the particular building in question as well as listing purchase price, but the real information will appear in carefully labeled appendixes:

> To accomplish Goals 2, 3, and 4, space must be available for project activities as described in the Proposal Narrative. Space requirements are for an outdoor recreation area to accommodate up to 125 children and adults, one large meeting room to accommodate 200 individuals at any given time, four smaller rooms each accommodating up to 35 children or adults for scheduled activities, 2 offices for staff, a kitchen meeting commercial codes, four bathrooms, and adequate storage. The building should be in easy walking distance of all town social service and healthcare facilities. Only three buildings were available that could adequately meet these requirements. One was overpriced for the appraised value. One did not have adequate adjacent recreation area—adults and children would have to cross a busy street to access the recreation area. That left the building described in Appendixes B, C, and D, which include appraisals, surveys, layouts and lot drawings, inspection reports, and cost

comparisons. Closing costs, taxes, and other costs are covered in Appendix E. Funding is requested for 25% of the cost of the building and property. Partners are covering 50% of the cost, and donations have been received to cover the remaining 25%.

Total cost including all fees, insurance costs, and taxes = $787,556. We are requesting $196,889 in grant funding.

Building and Land Improvement

Much of the same information must be exhibited if you are requesting grant funding for Building and Land Improvement that is required for Purchase. If Improvements are significant, blueprints, drawings, designs or plans must be included in the Appendixes. You must let the funder know your plans in as complete a manner as possible. Your grant funder is a key partner and will not fund items that its reviewers do not fully understand. Neither would you if the money being requested came from your own pocket. If you think about the evidence you would want if you were funding each item, it will be easier to come up with the documents and rationale needed. Following are two examples:

> Our building space is adequate to serve the proposed additional 150 persons due to four previously unused rooms, but the rooms must be renovated to accommodate planned activity as described in the Proposal Narrative. Two rooms have to be painted and carpets purchased and installed. One room has to have three additional 6-foot fluorescent lighting fixtures, and a work counter and sink installed. One room must be tiled and painted. Following are the costs for these renovations, all of which are requested for funding by the grant. All Goals and Objectives.
>
> Painting of three rooms on contract (see also Contractual Services) at $450 per room including labor and provision of top grade paint = $1,350
>
> Carpet of two rooms of approximately 700 square feet each with heavy traffic indoor-outdoor carpet costing $12.50 per square foot including installation = $17,500
>
> Three light fixtures installed @ $200 each = $600
>
> Work counter and sink installed = $1,245
>
> Tiling installed for one 15 × 30 room @ $7 per square foot = $3,150
>
> Total for building improvement = $23,845

or

> The agency is donating two acres of undeveloped land for the project recreation area. Currently, no water pipes run to the area for water fountains and restrooms. Also there is no electricity for lighting. Partners are

funding grading, trees, and shrubs. Donations are adequate to cover building picnic tables, grills, and shelters. The City is funding building and equipping men's and women's restrooms. We are requesting funding for running water pipes and electrical lines. In Appendix B, please find an approved schematic for the water piping to be installed by licensed and approved contractors to maximum state and local code. In Appendix C, please find an approved schematic for electrical lines and lighting outlets, also to be installed by licensed and approved contractors to maximum state and local codes. Goals 1, 2, and 4.

Cost for running all piping including grading, trenching, equipment, and materials, and installation = $24,560; itemization and cost comparisons appear in Appendix B.

Cost for running all electrical lines including poles, trenching, equipment, materials, and installation = $56,890; itemization and cost comparisons appear in Appendix C.

Supplies

Supplies are fairly easy to justify once you've worked out the project details and budget itemization. Following are three examples:

Four mailings of informational flyers will be made to approximately 1,500 individual households. Flyers will be printed in black and white on three $8\frac{1}{2}'' \times 11''$ sheets of colored paper. Printing will be done in-house on high-speed copiers, use of which is donated by the Agency. A ream of good-quality colored paper costs $19.26. Eleven reams are needed to complete each mailing including one ream for errors and reprints. Two toner cartridges will be used for printing at a cost of $120 each. Goal 3.

Cost of supplies for mailings: 13 reams × 19.26 + 2 toner cartridges @ $120 = $490.38

or

Postage will be necessary for monthly mailings to 1,500 individual households, quarterly flyers, and general office business mailings as follows. Goals 1, 3, and 5.

1,500 households × 12 months × 34 cents each = $6,120

1,500 households × 4 quarters × $1.10 each = $6,600

200 pieces × 34 cents each × 12 months = $816

50 pieces × 55 cents each × 12 months = $330

Total for postage = $13,866

or

> We expect to test an average of 150 patients a month each for Tuberculosis, AIDS, Thyroid Disease, and Cholesterol. TB kits cost $1.45 per person, AIDS test is $5 per person, TSH test kits are $5 per person, and Cholesterol kits are $3 per person. Total cost per screening for supplies is $14.45, not including labor and blood processing (covered under Contractual Services). Goal 2.
>
> 150 patients × 12 months × $14.45 each screening = $26,010

Contractual Services

Contractual Services often require detailed quotes, and if so, quotations should appear in an Appendix. Summaries belong in the Budget Narrative. Following are three examples of different types of contracting:

> Installation of cabling for computers for five workrooms is necessary for the 10 workstations needed as described in the Proposal Narrative. According to schematics provided in Appendix E, 1,550 feet of twisted pair, class 5 cable must be pulled through wall conduits and above drop ceiling tiles. It is estimated that 56 man-hours will be needed to pull the cable. Contractors charge $22.50 per hour to install cable.
>
> 36 man-hours × $22.50 = $1,260

or

> Internet access on-site license to serve two libraries costs $420 per site per month with access provided through Uconnect Incorporated. This fee compares favorably to Flibyenite.Com at $860 per site per month or EzgoEZ.com at $745 per site per month.
>
> 2 sites × 12 months × $420 per month = $10,080 annually

or

> Drawing blood, storage, and delivery for AIDS, Thyroid, Cholesterol, and TB tests for 150 patients per month by Vampira Laboratory, Inc. is $10 per patient per test series.
>
> 150 patients × 12 months × $10 per patient = $18,000

Endowment

This Budget Narrative is vastly different from the other categories. As discussed earlier, only certain grant funders contribute to an Endowment.

Fund-raising is more likely the avenue for increase of Endowment funds, and Budget Narratives are not applicable except as they apply to Annual Reports. If you are requesting contributions to an Endowment in your grant proposal, include a brief synopsis of what the funds are used for and perhaps the percentage of investment in various funds and the annual percentage of interest earned.

> Endowment funds are invested in T-bills and government bonds to draw interest. Interest is used to support our scholarship program as described in the Proposal Narrative. To review our Annual Report from our Foundation, please see Appendix F.

Wise Guy and Wise Lady

Wise Guy

Blast it! Just when I was with you on this! You mean I have to go back and explain all this? Good grief, Charlie Brown! Can't they just accept my numbers?!

Wise Lady

If I handed you sheets of budget numbers, would you automatically know what the numbers meant? Careful here. What if I list $4,500 for Materials and Supplies? Even if I've done a good job on the Proposal Narrative, as a reader, are you going to waste your mental energy reading back through all those words to figure out on what that $4,500 is likely to be spent? Not hardly. Your readers have very little time to grasp your concept. The budget is an important piece of the puzzle because what you're asking for is money to fund it. They are is not going to spend a lot of brainpower trying to figure out what you're doing. They're not mind readers either. You have to explain where you got the numbers. If you don't do a good job of explaining, even if you *do* get the award, watch for those fuzzy numbers to be cut out. If readers don't see what you need the funds for, then you're not going to get them.

Conclusion

Budget Narrative, or justification or explanation, need not be a feared section of any grant proposal. For some reason, it is—we suspect this is because the details of the Budget have not been worked out carefully. If you have guessed at the Budget, then it certainly will be hard to justify your guesses. If you have done your homework, as described in other sections of this book, the Budget Narrative is time consuming but it is not hard work. In fact, the hardest part may be laying out the information in a readable format. It is helpful to use tables and bulleted lists wherever possible. In reality, "narrative" may be a misnomer because most of the information is in numbers, calculations, and phrases rather than paragraphs. Spend your time wisely on the Project Development and the Budget and the Budget Narrative writes itself.

Key Definition

Of Course

The key to a good Budget Narrative is for the Reviewer to be able to easily find the information needed to understand your Budget request. Nothing in the Budget or the Budget Narrative should come as a surprise to the Reviewer. Your whole proposal should be set up so that the Reviewer, when reading the Narrative says, "*of course,* they need that item. Without it, they obviously cannot accomplish the overall Mission."

Key Concepts

- Set up your Budget Narrative in the same order and with the same headings as the Budget.
- The Budget Narrative is more important, in many ways, than the Budget. Without it, the Budget is just a collection of numbers.
- It is a good idea to tie Budget Items in the Narrative to Goals and Objectives so that the Reviewer clearly sees the necessity of each item.
- If you have a well-thought-out Project and Budget, then the Budget Narrative writes itself.
- If you guess at the Budget, you are reduced to trying to explain your guesses when writing the Budget Narrative.
- Use less narrative and more clearly stated numbers and lists.

- Back up your large expenditures with appropriate bids and descriptions in Appendixes, but do not overdo it. Appendixes are only for items that are absolutely necessary to prove your case on very large or complicated expenditures.

- Think of what information you would require to be provided if every dollar was coming out of your own pocket.

- You do not have to automatically take the low bid if you can justify the higher.

- Check your numbers several times to be sure they "add up."

What you have been reading about and hopefully doing as well, is a process. Each component builds on the next one. If you skip steps, then you have difficulty with the next component you tackle. If you build the solid foundation, step-by-step, however, no single component is a "stumper." No one component defeats you. People are defeated by the Budget and Budget Narrative usually because of one of two things. Some are just simply daunted by numbers. They think of themselves as non-number people. If you have no "number" person to help you with the Budget and Budget Narrative, then look at it as a puzzle to solve—a research project—a detective activity. It really is. The second factor that defeats people is that when they get to the Budget and in particular, the Budget Narrative, they don't have the information to write about. It is hard to admit to a potential funder that you want them to invest money in your project based on guesses and by-gollys. You would not invest your money that way, and you should not expect the funder to either.

If you follow the steps outlined in this book and further dissected and described *in Grant Seeker's Toolkit: A Comprehensive Guide to Finding Funding,* then when you get to the Budget, it will be the proverbial piece of cake. You will have the information you need to guide you in finding prices, getting quotes, and making selections and judgments. The Budget will no longer be a thing to be feared, but just another piece of the puzzle.

Index

Accountants, 1, 5–6
Activity Analysis Checklist, 218, 219–220, 227
Activity Checklist, 226, 227
Air travel, 112–114, 179–184, 200–202, 239
    air taxi, 112–113
    budget narrative, 239
    chartered flights, 112
    completed worksheet example, 183–184
    cost calculations, 179–181
    cost determination principle, 113–114
    finding prices of, 200–202
    scheduled airlines, 112
    segment flow, 180
    segment worksheet checklist, 181–183
Alignment (organization/problem), 32
Applicant (definition), 108
Asset (accountant's definition), 76. *See also* Capital asset (long-term or fixed asset)

Budget, project, 1–14, 24, 73–104, 129, 169, 217–236, 237–250
    accountants and, 5–6
    activities/tasks and, 24
    categories in (descriptive/generic *vs.* functional), 104
    characteristics of, 3, 4
    costs (two types: direct/indirect), 74–82
        (*see also* Direct cost(s); Indirect cost(s))
    data development, 217–230
    defined, 1–5, 11

effort involved in creating, 228–229
finalizing, 217–236
form completion, 231–234
fundamentals (concepts/terms), 73–104
vs. grant request, 1, 8–9, 222
master development checklist, 229–230
narrative, 237–250
partners, 88–90
project development and, 129
project revenue and, 88
source/origin of, 12
as summary, 6–8, 11, 79, 89, 224, 232, 234, 235
total (defined), 11
Budget forms:
    Department of Education:
        Form 424 (partial view of cover sheet), 108
        Form 524, 90–91, 92
        Technology Challenge Grant Program, 93, 94
    Disney Learning Partnership, Creative Learning Communities Grant Program, 100
    example, summary form, 7
    Illinois State Board of Education, Goals 2000 Professional Development Grant, 99
    Illinois State Library, Library Services and Technology Act (LSTA), 97, 98
    National Science Foundation: Summary Proposal Budget (Form 1030), 75

Budget forms *(Continued)*
    Public Health Service Grant Budget Form
        PHS-398, 83, 85
    South Carolina Governor's Youth
        Councils Grant Incentive Program,
        94
    U.S. Office of Management and Budget,
        Standard Form 424A (SF-424),
        86–87
Building(s), 198, 207–209, 244–246
    budget narrative, 244–246
    finding prices of, 208, 209
    improvements, 209, 245–246
    professionals recommended, 198
    purchase, 208, 244–245
Bus travel, 114–115
    budget narrative, 240
    cost calculations, 176–179
    finding prices of, 204, 205

Calculation worksheets. *See* Direct cost(s)
Capital asset (long-term or fixed asset),
    120–121
    budget narrative, 244–246
    cost calculations, 198
    vs. equipment, 121
    finding prices of, 207–209
Car rental, 114. *See also* Hired car
    budget narrative, 239–240
    cost calculations, 172–175
    finding prices of, 202–203
    vs. hired car, 176
Charity *vs.* investment (grant makers),
    34–35
Circular logic, 35–36
Competitive nature of grant programs, 11
Consultants, 125
Contractual services, 123–127
    budget narrative, 247
    cost calculations, 192, 194
    employee *vs.* contractor, 125–126
    finding prices of, 210–211
    shopping for, 211
    statement of work, 210–211, 212
Contributions: cash/in-kind, 95. *See also*
    In-kind
Corporate grants, 74
Cost(s). *See* Direct cost(s); Indirect cost(s)
Cost allocation (accountant's definition),
    76

Costing objects, 76, 97
Courtesy expenses, 118, 206

Department of Education, 90–94, 108
    Form 424 (partial view of cover sheet),
        108
    Form 524, 90–91, 92
    Technology Challenge Grant Program
        (budget form), 93, 94
Direct cost(s), 82–86, 105–133
    accountant's definition, 74
    in activity analysis, 67, 228
    calculations, 134–163, 164–186,
        187–198
    categories of (definitions/explanations),
        105–133
    definitions, 74–77
    finding prices, 198–211
    formula (method of calculation),
        188–189, 212
    unit of purchase, 188–189
Direct cost categories:
    capital, 120–121, 198, 207–209, 244–246
    contractual services, 123–127, 192, 194,
        210–211, 247
    endowment, 127, 193–198, 247–248
    equipment, 118–120, 121, 129, 190–191,
        206–207, 243–244
    fringe, 109–110, 145–152, 199–200,
        238–239
    materials, 122–123, 128–129, 191, 193,
        210
    "other/miscellaneous," 127–128, 192,
        195, 196
    personnel, 106–109, 134–163, 199,
        238–239
    supplies, 121–122, 128–129, 191, 193,
        210, 246–247
    travel, 110–118, 164–186, 200–206,
        239–243
Disallowed expenses, 118
Disney Learning Partnership, Creative
    Learning Communities Grant Program,
    100

Employees. *See also* Personnel
    vs. contractors, 125–126
    exempt/nonexempt employees,
        135–136
    two ways to pay (salaried/hourly), 162

Endowment:
    budget narrative, 247–248
    cost calculations, 193–198
    defined, 127
Equipment, 118–120, 129
    budget narrative, 243–244
    cost calculations, 190–191
    finding prices of, 206–207
    list of examples, 120
Exempt/nonexempt employees,
        135–136
Expenses. *See also* Direct cost(s)
    accountant's definition, 74
    disallowed, 118
    operating funds, 129–131

Facilities, 67
Federal Fair Labor Standards Act (FLSA)
        standards, 135–136
Federal government definition of indirect
        costs, 77
Federal grants, 74
Federal Insurance Contributions Act
        (FICA), 110
Federal Unemployment Insurance (FUTA),
        110, 125
Foundation grants, 74
Fringe, 109–110
    budget narrative, 238–239
    combination worksheet (spreadsheet
        style), 152–160
    finding prices of, 199–200
    more than one rate, 148–152
    one rate, 145–148
    worksheets available (list), 160
Functional budget categories, 104
Fund-raising *vs.* grant seeking, 34–35

Goals/objectives, 54–67, 217, 223–227
    activities and, 62–67, 226–227
    characteristics of (clear/measurable/
        realistic), 55, 61
    definitions, 55, 61
    general discussion of objectives, 59–61
    goals *vs.* objectives, 225
    project outline and, 54–59
    source of project goals, 56–59
    worksheets, 55–56, 57–59, 61, 225
        Goal Creation Worksheet, 55, 56,
            57–59

Objective Creation Worksheet, 61
    partial modified worksheet, 225
Grant(s):
    defined, 10
    purpose of (supplementing *vs.*
        supplanting), 138, 161, 162
Grant maker(s):
    categorized into four groups, 73–74
    corporate, 74
    defined, 10
    defining project budget, 2–3
    federal, 74
    foundation, 74
    state/local, 74
Grant program (defined), 11
Grant project budget (defined), 1–5, 13. *See
    also* Budget, project
Grant request:
    defined, 11
    vs. project budget, 1, 8–9
Grant seeking:
    vs. fund-raising, 34–35
    problems as core of, 28
    rules of, 80, 103
Gratuities, 117
Ground travel, 114–116, 168–179, 202–205,
        239–240
    animal, 116
    budget narrative, 239–242
    bus travel, 114–115, 176–179, 204, 205,
        240
    car rental, 114, 172–175, 239–240
    cost calculations, 168–179
    defined/explained, 114–116
    finding prices of, 202–206
    hired car, 116, 176–179, 240
    limousine, 116, 176–179, 240
    mileage, 114, 240
    rapid transit, 116, 176–179, 205,
        240
    rental car, 172–175, 202–203
    shuttle, 115, 176–179, 204–205, 240
    taxi, 115, 176–179, 240
    train, 114, 203–204, 205, 239
    watercraft, 116

Health insurance, 110. *See also* Fringe
Hired car, 116. *See also* Car rental
    budget narrative, 240
    cost calculations, 176–179

Hired car *(Continued)*
    finding prices of, 204–205
    vs. taxi, 116
Hit list, 44–45
Hourly position, 106–107. *See also* Personnel
    formula for cost of, 162–163
    funded from grant request, 141–144
    funded from other sources, 144–145, 146

Illinois State Board of Education, Goals 2000
    Professional Development Grant, 99
Illinois State Library, Library Services and
    Technology Act (LSTA), 97, 98
Indirect cost(s), 77–82
    accountant's definition, 77
    base, 80
    calculation of, 79–82
    defining, 77–78
    example calculation, 81
    federal government's definition, 77
    rate, 79–80
In-kind, 95, 96, 103, 108, 126–127, 139
    defined, 96, 103, 108
    employee or contractor, 126–127
    fair market value (accountant's definition), 96
Investment, grants as, 34

Jargon, 10–11, 19

Land:
    budget narrative, 244–246
    finding prices of, 207–209
    improvement, 208–209, 245–246
    professionals recommended, 198
    purchase, 207–208, 244–245
Life insurance, 110. *See also* Fringe
Limousine, 116
    budget narrative, 240
    cost calculations, 176–179
    finding prices of, 204–205
Lodging, 117
    budget narrative, 241
    cost calculations, 184–185
    finding prices of, 205
Logistics, project, 49

Mass transit, 116
    budget narrative, 240
    cost calculations, 176–179
    finding prices for, 205

Master checklist, 169, 229–230
Materials, 122–123, 128–129
    cost calculations, 191, 193
    finding prices of, 210
Meal expense, 117
    budget narrative, 240–241
    calculations, 181–184
    finding prices of, 205
Measurability, 55, 68, 69, 225–226
Medicare, 88, 110, 125, 145
Mileage, 114
    budget narrative, 240
    finding prices for, 172–175, 202–203
    ground travel by private vehicle, 168–172,
        202–203
    ground travel by rental vehicle, 172–175,
        202–203
Monitoring/management of project, 49–50

National Science Foundation, 74
    Form 1030 (Summary Proposal Budget),
        75
    Form 1030 modified, 89

Objectives. *See* Goals/objectives
"Of Course" (key definition), 249
Operating funds, 129–131
Organization/problem alignment, 32
Organization of project, 20–24, 54, 60
"Other/miscellaneous" (category of direct
    costs), 127–128, 192, 195, 196

Parking, 118
    budget narrative, 242
    finding prices of, 206
    valet, 242
Partners, project, 44, 49, 88–90, 109
People services, 124
Personnel, 67, 106–109, 134–163, 199,
    238–239. *See also* Fringe
    budget narrative, 238–239
    calculation worksheet, 153
    checklist, 155–156
    combination worksheet (spreadsheet
        style), 152–160
    cost calculations, 134–163
    definitions/explanations, 106–109
    exempt/nonexempt employees, 135–136
    finding prices of, 199
    fringe when more than one rate, 148–152

fringe when only one rate, 145–148
funding from grant request, 136–138, 141–144
funding from other sources, 138–141, 144–145, 146
hourly wage personnel funded from grant request, 141–144
hourly wage personnel funded from other sources, 144–145, 146
matrix (two-by-two; four categories), 134, 135
organization employees, 108
partner organizations: in-kind contribution, 109
project personnel: grant request, 107–108
salaried personnel funded from grant request, 136–138
salaried personnel funded from other sources, 138–141
TLSA "short test for high salaried employees," 135–136
volunteers: in-kind contribution, 109
wages/salary, 106–107
worksheets available (complete list), 160
Prices, finding, 198–211
air travel, 200–202
building improvement, 209
building purchase, 208
bus, 204, 205
capital, 207–209
contractual services, 210–211
courtesy expenses, 206
equipment, 206–207
fringe, 199–200
gratuities, 205–206
ground travel, 202–205
hired car, 204–205
land improvement, 208–209
land purchase, 207–208
limousine, 204–205
lodging, 205
mass transit, 205
materials, 210
meals, 205
parking, 206
personnel, 199
private vehicle or car rental, 202–203
shuttle, 204–205
subway, 205
supplies, 210

taxi, 204–205
tolls, 206
train, 203–204, 205
travel, 200–206
Private vehicle, 168–172, 202–203
Problem(s), 28–47
absence of solution becoming, 35–36
alignment of organization and, 32
causes of, 38–41, 43
characteristics of, 30–31
circular logic in stating, 35–36
defined, 29–30
examples of, 29, 39, 40, 41
in project profile, 43
resource identification, 42–43
solution identification, 41
solution masquerading as, 36
statement of, 31, 37, 38, 46
target populations, 32–34, 36, 37, 38, 42
Program, grant (defined), 11
Program *vs.* project, 18–20
Project(s), 17–27
budget (*see* Budget, project)
costs (*see* Direct cost(s); Indirect cost(s))
definitions, 25, 26
example, with three approaches, 130–131
grants for (*see* Grant(s))
hit list, 44–46
implementation with target population, 49
logistics/preparation, 49
mission/goals/objectives, 22
monitoring/management, 49–50
organization, 20–24, 54, 60
outline, 50–54
partnerships, 44, 49, 88–90, 109
preparation/logistics, 49
problem as core of (*see* Problem(s))
profile, 43–44, 45, 48
vs. program, 18–20
purpose, 22, 23
real aspect definition, 25
revenue, 88
as set of activities, 18, 20, 21, 24
similarities among all, 48–50
source/origin of, 24–25
synopsis, 43
terminology, 10–11, 23, 24
theoretical aspect definition, 25

Project budget. *See* Budget, project
Project design, 38–43, 48
  step 1: stating large problem, 38
  step 2: listing causes of problem, 38–39
  step 3: eliminating/recasting/
    grouping/choosing causes, 39–41
  step 4: identifying solution, 41–43
  step 5: identifying resources needed,
    42–43, 44
Project development, 48–69, 73, 129
  activity analysis, 62–67
  budget and, 129
  creating project outline, 50–54
  four components common to all projects,
    49
  goals/objectives, 54–61
  grant project budget and, 73
Public Health Service Grant Budget Form
  PHS-398, 83, 85

Rapid transit, 116
  budget narrative, 240
  cost calculations, 176–179
  finding prices for, 205
Resources needed, 42–43, 44, 67
Revenue, project, 88

Salaried position, 106–107. *See also*
  Personnel
  calculation worksheets, 136–138
  cost of (formula for), 162
  FLSA "short test for high salaried
    employees," 135–136
  funded from grant request, 136–138
  funded from other sources, 138–141
  vs. wages (hourly employees),
    106–107
Services, 123–127
  consultants, 125
  contractors, 124
    vs. employee, 125–127
  in-kind contributions, 126–127
  people, 124
  professions, 124
  technical, 124
Shuttle, 115
  budget narrative, 240
  cost calculations, 176–179
  finding prices of, 204–205

South Carolina Governor's Youth Councils
  Grant Incentive Program, 94
State/local, 74
State Unemployment Insurance (SUTA), 110
Strategy, 225
Summary budget, 6–8, 11, 79, 89, 224, 232,
  234, 235
Supplies (category of direct costs), 121–122,
  128–129
  budget narrative, 246–247
  cost calculations, 191, 193
  finding prices of, 210
Synopsis, project, 43

Target populations, 32–34, 36, 37, 38, 42,
  49
Taxes, 125–126
Taxi, 115
  budget narrative, 240
  cost calculations, 176–179
  finding prices of, 204–205
  vs. hired car, 116
Technical services, 124
Technology Innovation Challenge Grant
  program, 223
Terminology, 10–11, 23, 24
Time line, 43, 67
Tolls, 117–118
  budget narrative, 242
  finding prices of, 206
Train, 114, 203–204, 205, 239
  budget narrative, 239
  finding prices of, 203–204
Travel (category of direct costs), 7, 8,
  110–118, 164–186, 200–206, 239–243
  budget narrative, 239–243
  cost calculations, 164–186
    air travel, 179–184
    compiling/summing, 164, 185
    example trip, 167–168
    ground travel, 168–179
    initial planning, 164, 165–168
    lodging, 184–185
    master checklist, 169
    meal expense, 181–184
  definitions/explanations, 110–118
  finding prices of, 200–206
  planning questionnaire, 166
  sample itemizations, 7, 8

Unemployment insurance, 110. *See also*
    Fringe
Unit of purchase (cost calculations),
    188–189

Valet parking, 242
Vision purpose mission, 32
Volunteers: in-kind contribution, 109

Wages *vs.* salary, 106–107. *See also* Hourly
    position; Salaried position
Watercraft, 116
Worker's Compensation Insurance, 110

About the CD-ROM

Contents

Title	File Name
Exhibit 4.4 Goal Creation Worksheet	CH0401.DOC
Exhibit 4.7 Objective Creation Worksheet	CH0402.DOC
Exhibit 4.9 Activity Analysis Worksheet	CH0403.DOC
Exhibit 5.3 Indirect Cost Calculator	CH0501.XLS
Exhibit 7.2 Calculation Worksheet: Salaried Positions Funded from Grant Request	CH0701A.XLS CH0701B.XLS CH0701C.XLS
Exhibit 7.5 Calculation Worksheet: Salaried Positions Funded from Other Sources	CH0702A.XLS CH0702B.XLS
Exhibit 7.8 Calculation Worksheet: Hourly Wage Personnel Funded from Grant Request	CH0703A.XLS CH0703B.XLS
Exhibit 7.11 Calculation Worksheet: Hourly Wage Personnel Funded from Other Sources	CH0704A.XLS CH0704B.XLS
Exhibit 7.14 Calculation Worksheet: Personnel Fringe (One Rate)	CH0705.XLS
Exhibit 7.17 Calculation Worksheet: Personnel Fringe (More Than One Rate)	CH0706.XLS
Exhibit 7.20 Personnel and Fringe Expense Calculation Worksheet	CH0707.XLS
Exhibit 8.2 The Travel Planning Worksheet (Short)	CH0801.XLS
Exhibit 8.3 The Travel Planning Worksheet (Long)	CH0802.XLS
Exhibit 8.5 Calculation Worksheet: Ground Travel by Private Vehicle	CH0803.XLS
Exhibit 8.8 Calculation Worksheet: Ground Travel by Rental Vehicle	CH0804.XLS
Exhibit 8.9 Completed Example of Calculation Worksheet: Fuel Expense from Miles Driven	CH0805.XLS
Exhibit 8.12 Calculation Worksheet: Ground Travel by Hired Vehicle	CH0806.XLS
Exhibit 8.16 Calculation Worksheet: Air Travel	CH0807A.XLS CH0807B.XLS CH0807C.XLS CH0807D.XLS CH0807E.XLS

Title	File Name
Exhibit 8.19 Calculation Worksheet: Meals (Per Meal)	CH0808.XLS
Exhibit 8.20 Calculation Worksheet: Meals (Per Day)	CH0808.XLS
Exhibit 8.21 Calculation Worksheet: Lodging	CH0809.XLS
Exhibit 8.22 Calculation Worksheet: Compile and Total Travel Expenses	CH0810.XLS
Exhibit 9.2 Calculation Worksheet: Equipment	CH0901.XLS
Exhibit 9.3 Calculation Worksheet: Materials and Supplies	CH0902.XLS
Exhibit 9.4 Calculation Worksheet: Contractual Services	CH0903.XLS
Exhibit 9.5 Calculation Worksheet: Miscellaneous Cost	CH0904.XLS
Exhibit 9.7 Calculation Worksheet: Endowment	CH0905.XLS
Exhibit 10.1 Activity Analysis Checklist	CH1001.DOC
Exhibit 10.5 Activity Checklist	CH1002.DOC
Exhibit 10.6 Master Budget Development Checklist	CH1003.DOC

Introduction

The forms on the enclosed CD-ROM are saved in Microsoft Word for Windows version 7.0. To use the forms, you will need to have word processing software capable of reading Microsoft Word for Windows version 7.0 files.

System Requirements

- IBM PC or compatible computer
- CD-ROM drive
- Windows 95 or later
- Microsoft Word for Windows version 7.0 (including the Microsoft converter)* or later or other word processing software capable of reading Microsoft Word for Windows 7.0 files.

NOTE: Many popular word processing programs are capable of reading Microsoft Word for Windows 7.0 files. However, users should be aware

---

*Word 7.0 needs the Microsoft converter file installed in order to view and edit all enclosed files. If you have trouble viewing the files, download the free converter from the Microsoft Web site. The URL for the converter is: http://officeupdate.microsoft.com/downloadDetails/wd97cnv.htm

Microsoft also has a viewer that can be downloaded, which allows you to view, but not edit documents. This viewer can be downloaded at: http://officeupdate.microsoft.com/downloadDetails/wd97vwr32.htm

that a slight amount of formatting might be lost when using a program other than Microsoft Word. If your word processor cannot read Microsoft Word for Windows 7.0 files, unformatted text files have been provided in the TXT directory on the CD-ROM.

How to Install the Files onto Your Computer

To install the files follow these instructions:

1. Insert the enclosed CD-ROM into the CD-ROM drive of your computer.
2. From the Start Menu, choose **Run.**
3. Type **D:\SETUP** and press **OK.**
4. The opening screen of the installation program will appear. Press **OK** to continue.
5. The default destination directory is C:\QUICK. If you wish to change the default destination, you may do so now.
6. Press **OK** to continue. The installation program will copy all files to your hard drive in the C:\QUICK or user-designated directory.

Using the Files

Loading Files

To use the word processing files, launch your word processing program. Select **File, Open** from the pull-down menu. Select the appropriate drive and directory. If you installed the files to the default directory, the files will be located in the C:\QUICK directory. A list of files should appear. If you do not see a list of files in the directory, you need to select **WORD DOCUMENT (*.DOC)** under **Files of Type.** Double click on the file you want to open. Edit the file according to your needs.

Printing Files

If you want to print the files, select **File, Print** from the pull-down menu.

Saving Files

When you have finished editing a file, you should save it under a new file name by selecting **File, Save As** from the pull-down menu.

User Assistance

If you need assistance with installation or if you have a damaged CD-ROM, please contact Wiley Technical Support at:

Phone: (212) 850-6753
Fax: (212) 850-6800 (Attention: Wiley Technical Support)
E-mail: techhelp@wiley.com

To place additional orders or to request information about other Wiley products, please call (800) 225-5945.

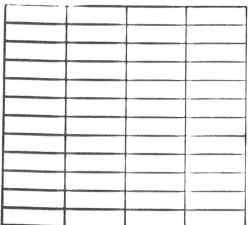

For information about the disk, see the **About the CD-ROM** section on page 259